Books by Kenneth Lamott

$$$$$ THE $$$$$ MONEYMAKERS

The Great Big New Rich in America

by KENNETH LAMOTT

BOSTON   LITTLE, BROWN AND COMPANY   TORONTO

The poem on page 54 is reprinted from *Cannibals and Christians* by
Norman Mailer. Copyright 1966 by Norman Mailer. Reprinted by
permission of the author and his agents, Scott Meredith Literary
Agency, Inc., New York, N.Y. 10036.

*Published simultaneously in Canada
by Little, Brown & Company (Canada) Limited*

PRINTED IN THE UNITED STATES OF AMERICA

Contents

CONTENTS

Illustrations

THE
MONEYMAKERS

ONE

The Condition of the Rich

Barring accidents, the *nouveaux arrivés* are a picked body.
> — *Thorstein Veblen*

The very rich in America are culturally among the very poor, and are probably growing even more so. The only dimension of experience for which they have been models to which serious conservatives might point is the material one of money-making and money-keeping.
> — *C. Wright Mills*

It has been remarked many times by observers both foreign and domestic that the American is a mercenary animal who lusts after money as the hart panteth after the water brooks. For myself, I do not think that Americans are on the whole any greedier than, say, Japanese peasants or Brussels slumlords. Yet we have produced through the course of the past century and a half a remarkable number of men who acquired wealth that was literally beyond the dreams of avarice. My concern in this book is less with the Mellons, Rockefellers, and Fords and their compeers than with the Great Big New Rich of our own time and the peculiar phenomenon they represent in a society that seems to be growing increasingly indifferent to the overriding attractions of great personal wealth.

Although there are still among us some spiritual descendants of the grandees and merchant princes of the Gilded Age, there are hardly enough of them to occupy the cabins of a respectable steam yacht. Few of the Great Big New Rich of today are distinguished by the lordly scales of their lives; many are distinguished by twin passions — the first for money and the second for anonymity. As an object lesson, let me record the names of some of the richest men in the United States today: Allen, Corrigan, Crown, Hirshhorn, Jonsson, Land, Ling, Ludwig, MacArthur, Simon, Smith, Stone, Taper, Thornton. Some of these men control more wealth than the original Vanderbilt and Astor fortunes put together. Their obscurity is a matter of record: When I searched the *New York Times Index* for 1964 and 1965, three of the biggest of the Great Big New Rich — Charles Allen, Jr., Leo Francis Corrigan, and Robert E. Smith — were not mentioned even once.

We have evidently come a long way from the days when the first- and second-generation Astors and Harrimans and Morgans regularly entertained the ungodly and outraged the pious with

4

the extravagance of their yachts and private railroad cars, with their French mistresses and their Italian counts, with their Fifth Avenue mansions and their fifty-room Newport cottages, with their squadrons of thoroughbreds and battalions of servants.

> The condition of the rich, though it inspires the passionate curiosity of millions of men and women, is on the whole a question serious writers and sociologists have chosen to ignore . . .
>
> — Goronwy Rees

This book has been impelled by two principal motives. The first is a curiosity regarding the conditions of existence of the new rich of our time. The second is an interest in the rise and fall of the institution of the tycoon, of the great entrepreneur who put together a personal empire, whether in industry or finance, and who lived largely in the public eye.

For a theory of tycoonery, I am in the debt of Bart Lytton, the flamboyant and compulsively articulate former president of Lytton Financial Corporation, which looms large in the booming savings-and-loan business of Southern California. Over lunch in a private club with the improbable name of the Caves des Roys, Mr. Lytton expounded on this matter approximately as follows: "In any given industry there is a time of the tycoon that lasts for fifteen or twenty years, rarely longer. Afterward, in unconscious concert with the government, industry tends to close the door to others. In automobiles, for example, all the tycoons appeared between 1905 and 1927. Walter P. Chrysler was the last one.

"Every industry has its own tycoons. Giannini was the last in banking, and Douglas and Lockheed were the last in aircraft. After the initial thrust there are no more tycoons. In my business the time of the tycoons was 1945 to 1960. You had to be a tycoon by 1961. I was the last.

"Tycoons are dominant forces, not just rich men. They have a certain charisma. The tycoon should not be confused with the mogul or shogun. The mogul or shogun is the hired commander of an area. Moguls get rich raiding and raping in their territory. The tycoon is a conqueror who both owns and commands."

This book is about tycoons, although, as will become evident, few of them share Bart Lytton's romantic *Weltansicht*.

I have chosen to organize my material in a rather idiosyncratic fashion, alternating chapters of straightforward exposition with pictures from a portrait gallery of the Great Big New Rich. Some of these are portraits of men I have interviewed; others are collages assembled from the results of researches.

By way of forewarning the reader, let me set forth some of my own bias in approaching this theme: In general, I am inclined to think that great personal wealth is an anachronism today and that the Great Big New Rich represent perhaps the last of their breed. In general, I am inclined to the view that in our time, as in earlier times, large numbers of the very rich have been the principal beneficiaries of the wars and economic catastrophes that have brought disaster to less canny and fortunate men. In general, I am inclined to think that if anybody

6

comes across this book a hundred years from now, he will regard it as describing the gross anatomy of an exceedingly curious animal.*

* Ferdinand Lundberg's *The Rich and the Super-Rich* appeared after this book was in manuscript. I have no quarrel with Professor Lundberg (whose *America's 60 Families* has for thirty years been required reading for students of the rich) except in one important matter. He is, I think, seriously mistaken and quite wrongheaded in denying that there are any Great Big New Rich. The evidence of this book as well as the sources on which it is based will, I hope, make the truth of the matter plain to the reader.

There are, furthermore, some curious lacunae in *The Rich and the Super-Rich*, which I am inclined to think are the result of the author's headlong rush to establish his thesis that the only really Big Rich in the United States are the Old Rich. The absence, for instance, of the name of Howard Hughes from a book on the Super-Rich surely calls for some explanation, but no explanation is forthcoming. Hughes is not merely richer than any of the Old Rich, but he is also very likely the richest man in the country today. (Hughes' name does appear in the index, but the single reference to him is in a list of the rich taken from *Fortune*, a list whose validity Professor Lundberg undertakes to demolish.)

TWO

The Great Big New Rich

The Truth is that though there are in that country few People so miserable as the Poor of Europe, there are also very few that in Europe would be called Rich; it is rather a general happy Mediocrity that prevails.

— *Benjamin Franklin*

The virgin land was possessed by its invaders in a feudal style more typical of the Old Continent than the New, and the fortunes that were made were reckoned in land rather than money. The first rich Americans were created by the Dutch West India Company, which turned any plump burgher or lean adventurer who could gather fifty adult followers into a landed gentleman, offering him the options of sixteen miles along the shores of a river, or alternatively of only eight miles, but with his ownership going as far back into the interior as the new

8

owner could make his way. And so some of the Dutch adventurers became great lords of the land, patroons as they called themselves, princes of great principalities over which, in theory at least, they and their descendants would exercise sole and absolute rule forever.

The most powerful of the patroons was Kiliaen van Rensselaer, an Amsterdam pearl merchant and a director of the West India Company who acquired in 1630 some 700,000 acres, comprising the present counties of Albany and Rensselaer, part of Columbia County, and part of Massachusetts. Although van Rensselaer appears never to have personally visited his estate, his American descendants were frugal and tenacious and survived as the owners of remarkable holdings until almost the time of the Civil War, when they were destroyed by the march of events. Yet while they reigned they possessed riches that were great and awesome by the standards of their times, with the last of the great van Rensselaers, Stephen, enjoying an annual income from his harvests and rents that was in the neighborhood of a million dollars.

Despite the popular folklore that has grown up to celebrate the simple democracy of the English settlers, the sizes of the estates that were obtained in New England and the South by grateful royal grant or by seizure or bribery vastly exceeded in scale the feudal domains of even the van Rensselaers. In 1692, the land that now makes up the entire state of New Hampshire was claimed as the private estate of one man, Samuel Allen. Maine became the fiefdom of Sir Ferdinando Gorges, who had betrayed Essex to Queen Elizabeth. It remained in the Gorges family until Ferdinando's grandson sold it to a Boston merchant who, under pressure, deeded it to the governor and company of Massachusetts.

Among the other Englishmen who held vast tracts of wood- and grasslands were Captain John R. N. Evans of the Royal Navy, who was granted 1200 square miles on the west bank of the Hudson, and Nicholas Bayard, who owned another 1200 square miles on both sides of Schoharie Creek. In the South the greatest grandees were of the order of Robert "King" Carter, who is reported to have owned 300,000 acres in Virginia on which he worked more than a thousand slaves. His style of life was expansive.

It is virtually impossible to translate these great holdings of land into their contemporary equivalents in dollars. Not only has the value of money changed beyond all reasonable calculation, but also the economic behavior of the colonists has little in common with ours, based as it is on the idea of credit and the manipulation of collections of digits that we understand to represent wealth. We think in terms of money, they thought in terms of property. Although "King" Carter was among the wealthiest of the colonials, during a year his business affairs might require the exchange of no more than £1000 gold. (We have surely come full circle, for even the richest American now handles little cash except his pocket money.) Another standard of comparison is provided by the Knox family of New York who were regarded as lavish spenders on account of their annual outlay of £365 for food, £180 for wine, and £120 for enter- tainment.

The colonial landowners were rich men in the European style. The first of the New Rich on a distinctively American model emerged quietly while the princes of the land were at the height of their affluence and power. The vast majority of immigrants to the New World had of course arrived without land grants and, in fact, without any capital at all except the hope of doing better in their new home than they had in their old. The yearly wages for a laborer in revolutionary New England amounted to about £18. Those who did better than this all became, in a sense, *nouveau riche*, and from these modest fortunes came the classic New Rich in the American style.

The new-model rich were the city merchants, particularly the frugal merchants of Boston, who cultivated a sharper eye for the value of cash than was usual on the great estates. Unimpressive as the figures are by present standards, by 1687 ten or fifteen Boston merchants had acquired £5000 each, making them capitalists of a not contemptible order. Five hundred other Bostonians were said to be worth £3000 each.

The generality of Boston fortunes was built on the shipping industry, which was based solidly on privateering and the traffic in rum and slaves. In a lyric passage, Charles and Mary Beard have described how "New England boys in their early years fled from the stony fields, picked up the art of navigation, saved a little money, and at the age of nineteen or twenty commanded brigs of their own. The sea permitted them to escape from the terrible sermons of the Mathers, to make a fortune, to rise to a social position, and to wear with dignity the title of gentleman. Sea breezes carried them into distant lands where they saw strange peoples and stranger customs which slowly dissolved in skepticism the faith and usages of their fathers."

By the late 1700's shipping had made many fortunes and the Continental Congress was to a considerable extent the creation of men who had made their piles in privateering and piracy, in the China trade, in the cod and whale fisheries, in rum and Negroes — or whose fathers and grandfathers had.

The rise of the eighteenth century shipping master foreshadowed the emergence in the next century of men who counted their wealth in the control of enormous holdings of money rather than of land. It was not until the Industrial Revolution that it was either possible or necessary to put away large amounts of cash. The rich man as we know him was, consequently, an invention of the nineteenth century. The mechanism by which he accumulated his wealth, often through the shrewd manipulation of wars, panics, and other general disasters, will concern us at some length in a later chapter. Our business here is to organize a scale of wealth in the light of which we can better observe the Great Big New Rich of our own time.

A man who has a million dollars is as well off as if he were rich.
— *John Jacob Astor*

The word *millionaire* first appeared in print in *Vivian Grey*, Disraeli's novel of 1826, giving us a clue to the time when private fortunes visibly crossed the formidable threshold of a million pounds. There is no record of the word's crossing the Atlantic until the 1840's, yet when, in 1847 and again in 1852, Moses Yale Beach of the New York *Sun* published pamphlets identifying the richest men in New York, there were twenty-five millionaires among them. Preeminent among these were Peter Cooper (of Cooper Union), the Goelets (who

owned large tracts of prime New York real estate), Moses
Taylor, A. T. Stewart, Cornelius Vanderbilt, and William T.
Crosby. Each of these men was worth at that time between $1
million and $2 million, although some (notably Vanderbilt)
were to multiply their fortunes many times in the future.

The richest man in New York, however, was John Jacob
Astor, fur trader, real-estate shark, debaucher of Indians, and
general skinflint. Astor already had $20 million standing in his
account, which was equivalent to one-fifteenth of the money
invested in manufacturing in the entire United States. But even
Astor's fortune was to become unimpressive before long; Vanderbilt was soon to amass five times as much during fifteen
years of prowling the jungle of railroad financing. When he
died, Vanderbilt left $105 million, which was reckoned the first
industrial fortune of the world, and which his late-blooming
heir, William Henry Vanderbilt, was to double, making him in
his own estimation (and probably in fact) the richest man in
the world.

How much was the Vanderbilt fortune at its prime worth in
present-day dollars? In the years after the Civil War, a skilled
worker made a little more than $1000 a year. We must,
accordingly, apply a factor of 8 or 10, which raises Billy Vanderbilt's $200 million to the equivalent of about $2 billion current
dollars. As it happens, $2 billion, plus or minus, is the magni-
tude of the fortunes popularly ascribed to Haroldson Lafayette
Hunt and Jean Paul Getty, who are commonly regarded as the
richest living Americans. (In fact, however, each is probably
worth a little more than $1 billion.) Whether or not we may
establish as a general proposition that the richest American of

any era will control an amount equivalent to the yearly wages of 100,000 skilled workmen is a question I must leave for a more scholarly investigator. Nevertheless, it is a statistic that stimulates thought.

> In their absorbing passion for the accumulation of wealth, men were plundering the resources of the country like burglars looting a palace.
>
> — *David Saville Muzzey*

> These men and women have become wealthy because they have been thrifty.
>
> — *Daniel Guggenheim*

Five years after Appomattox, according to Lucius Beebe's account, "San Francisco was so well supplied with millionaires that the popular relaxation of estimating fortunes on the comparative basis was in full swing." Among those whose names are still venerated along the Coast were Leland Stanford of the Central Pacific, with (then) $10 million; Darius Ogden Mills of the Bank of California, with $3.5 million; and James Ben Ali Haggin of Wells Fargo, with $2 million. As prosperous and as colorful as these Western nabobs were, they lagged somewhat behind their compeers of the East, where old Vanderbilt was soon to pass on his $100-million-plus, and where Rockefeller was to become our first billionaire.

> A man is lucky to have five dollars; if it is ten, it is his jooty to keep it if he can; if it's a hundherd, his right to it is th' right iv silf-dayfinse; if it's a millyun, it's a divine right; if it's more thin that, it becomes ridickilous.
>
> — *Finley Peter Dunne*
> (*"Mr. Dooley"*)

14

In pursuing the changing scale of great riches into the new century, we are in the debt of Ferdinand Lundberg, who in *America's 60 Families* (1937) produced the first systematic examination of modern American wealth. Extracting the first ten family groups from Lundberg's list (which is based on 1924 tax data), we can draw up the following table, which is full of suggestive leads:

Family and Number of Members	Source of Wealth	Gross Adjusted Fortune
1. Rockefeller (21)	Oil	$1,077,300,000
2. Morgan (34)*	Finance	728,000,000
3. Ford (2)	Automobiles	660,000,000
4. Harkness (5)	Oil	450,600,000
5. Mellon (3)	Mining, Oil	450,000,000
6. Vanderbilt (22)	Railroads	360,300,000
7. Whitney (4)	Oil	322,000,000
8. Du Pont (20)	Munitions	238,500,000
9. McCormick (8)	Manufacturing, Newspapers	211,200,000
10. Baker (2)	Banking	210,000,000

Three facts make themselves immediately apparent:

First is the dominant position enjoyed by the production of oil as the source of great new wealth. If we throw in the Mellons — whose fortune was founded on aluminum, iron, and coal as well as oil — we may then conclude that almost half of the greatest American fortunes were founded on the extraction of minerals. (Of the entire Sixty Families, only ten, however,

* Lundberg includes Morgan partners and executives.

became rich from oil, coal, and metals.) Of the non-mineral fortunes, there is a considerable variety. One family grew rich by building motorcars in the midst of the greatest revolution in transportation that the world has seen. Another rode the crest of the industrialization of agriculture. One manufactured chemicals, notably the explosives with which the country destroyed its enemies and blasted loose its mineral wealth. Another had been for three-quarters of a century the country's premier banking house. Still another's holdings included control of aluminum, a metal transformed from a curiosity to an everyday necessity by the discovery of a practical refining process. But if the role of the Industrial Revolution in producing great private wealth is clear, the overwhelming importance of the oil that fueled that revolution remains even clearer.

Second is the size of the fortunes. With five families having fortunes of about half a billion or more, the scale of wealth on exhibit here far overshadows the family fortunes of the nineteenth century and has no understandable relation at all to the mercantile fortunes of the eighteenth century.

Third, it is plain that these are our classic rich, the families whose names come immediately to mind as paradigms of wealth — rich as Rockefeller, rich as a Du Pont, rich as a Vanderbilt.

The latter point needs to be followed a little farther, for the classic rich no longer follow the same line of march and, in fact, some have quietly dropped out of the parade entirely. An instructive comparison can be made between Lundberg's list and a similar list compiled by *Fortune* in 1968. If we abstract · from this list the inheritors of old wealth, we have:

$500 Million to $1 Billion

Ailsa Mellon Bruce
Paul Mellon
Richard King Mellon

$200 Million to $300 Million

Mrs. Alfred I. Du Pont
Marjorie Merriweather Post
Mrs. Jean Mauze (Abby Rockefeller)
David Rockefeller
John D. Rockefeller III
Laurance Rockefeller
Nelson Rockefeller
Winthrop Rockefeller
Cordelia Scaife May (Mellon family)
Richard Mellon Scaife
Mrs. Charles Payson (Joan Whitney)
John Hay Whitney

$150 Million to $200 Million

Doris Duke
Lammot Du Pont Copeland
Henry B. Du Pont
Benson Ford
Mrs. W. Buhl Ford II (Josephine Ford)
William C. Ford
Helen Clay Frick
Allan P. Kirby
Mrs. Lester J. Norris
Mrs. Arthur Hays Sulzberger (Iphigene Ochs)

Of those on the earlier list, the Mellons, Rockefellers, Du Ponts and Whitneys are still represented in full measure, with the extraordinary prominence of the Mellons being the only real surprise. The Morgans, Harknesses, and Vanderbilts, however, have disappeared entirely, with not even a token member of these families qualifying.

Where has the money gone? One immediate answer is furnished by the arithmetic of *thirty-four* Morgans and *twenty-two* Vanderbilts, which, even with a billion dollars, more or less, for each family to split, allows an average of less than $50 million a head. A more penetrating explanation has been provided by John Tebbel, who, in his excellent and diverting book *The Inheritors*, has made himself the historian of this decay. It is Mr. Tebbel's thesis that the fortunes such as belonged to the Astors and Vanderbilts were dispersed not only by the multiplication of heirs but also by the tendency of the inheritors to leave great chunks of their riches in the grateful hands of their multiple ex-spouses.*

> Any businessman can tell you that two and two make four, but even though he knows equally well that two million and two million make four million, the mere magnificence of the figures deters him from looking at them squarely. Instead, he trembles with fright.
>
> — William Zeckendorf

In trying to come to grips with the ideas represented by really large sums of money, we are all the victims of the simple

---

* Probably the classic example of the dissipation of an inheritance is the case of John Jacob ("Jackaster") Astor VI. In applying to the courts for a share of the fortune left by his brother Vincent, who died in 1959, Astor revealed that his inheritance of $75 million had wasted away to a mere $5 million. His financial difficulties included expensive divorces from three wives.

inability of most people to function normally in the presence of large numbers. Most of us are quite capable of recognizing a substantive difference between $200,000 and $2,000,000. I can, for instance, readily imagine what $200,000 represents. It represents about four times the value the tax appraiser has put upon my house, a sum of money of which I am regularly and painfully reminded. I can't, however, conceive of $2 million as easily. It represents the equivalent of forty of my houses, and at this point my mind begins to boggle, although I am still perfectly capable of mentally calculating the annual taxes on these houses. But when I try to imagine the difference between $2 million and $2 billion, my standards of comparison dissolve and my thinking melts like warm gelatin as it enters that steamy region in which exceedingly large sums of money are found. Two billion dollars could buy 40,000 of my houses, and at this point my conceptual machinery grinds to an ignoble halt.

Great wealth is a metaphysical rather than an economic concept. With thanks to Mr. Dooley, it can be identified by its ridickilousness. The threshold above which riches become ridickilous is, of course, subject to the general progress of infla tion. For the past century, a million dollars has been the traditional measure of extraordinary success with money. It has been a long time since a million dollars meant really great wealth, however, and today there are about 100,000 families in the United States who have amassed a million dollars in property. Pleasant as it is to contemplate a net worth of this magnitude, a cool million no longer holds any arcane mysteries. To paraphrase John Jacob Astor, a man who earns $50,000 a year is as well off as if he owned a million. Millionaires — and non-

millionaires whose income equals the interest on a million —
have become so commonplace that we are obliged to disregard
them.

Let us adopt as our working hypothesis the proposition that
in the United States today, to belong to the Great Big New
Rich a man must be able to exercise personal control over a
substantial fraction of a billion dollars. The lower limit is $100
million. Below $100 million a man belongs merely to the Lesser
Rich.

> Today, after a four-month study that entailed analysis of
> public records (e.g., proxy statements) and hundreds of inter-
> views, we believe we can identify 153 individuals whose net
> worth, including wealth held by their spouses, minor children,
> trusts and foundations, makes them centimillionaires.
> — *Fortune*

For various reasons the identification of Americans controlling $100 million or more in personally acquired and personally
controlled wealth is bound to be defective. For reasons that
range from a retiring temperament to a highly practical regard
for modesty, many very wealthy men are happy to be spared the
light of publicity. Ostentation is out of fashion. The student of
the new rich cannot, for instance, get very far by noting in
Lloyd's Register the owners of yachts longer than 200 feet
length overall. (There were only six in a recent edition. One
belongs to an automobile scion, one is registered in the name of
a lady, and two are registered to corporations.)

Furthermore, the nature of great wealth makes it hard to
appraise. Oil fortunes, for instance, include the presumed value

of untapped underground reserves whose values vary with the market and whose exact size is a matter of wild estimate. This matter was neatly demonstrated by J. P. Getty's biographer, Ralph Hewins, who after arriving at the precise figure of $1,441,253,578 in oil company holdings, tankers, real estate, and aircraft, then threw in the towel abjectly with the remark that if Getty's oil holdings in the Neutral Zone of Kuwait proved to be workable, "such an enormous figure is attained for his wealth that it becomes meaningless." After trying to decide whether Getty or Howard Hughes was the richest American, *Fortune* gave up and announced a photo finish.

Our attention in this book will be focused on the careers and personalities of thirteen of the Great Big New Rich. All are reputed to be worth more than $100 million. All but four have made the bulk of their fortunes since World War II. Only one began his career with a substantial inheritance. As I write, all are alive except one, who died while this book was in progress.

D. K. Ludwig, born in 1897, is principally the builder and operator of the world's greatest fleet of tankers. His office is in New York. Ludwig is worth in the neighborhood of a billion dollars.

Henry Crown, born in 1896, is a Chicago entrepreneur who once owned the Empire State Building. He is probably worth a half-billion dollars.

W. Clement Stone, born in 1902, also of Chicago, is an insurance man who is a leading apostle of the gospel of self-help in the style of Horatio Alger. Stone is worth about a third of a billion.

Joseph P. Kennedy, born in 1888, has made his present

fortune largely in real estate. He is, of course, from Boston. Kennedy's fortune is somewhere between $200 million and $300 million.

Charles B. Thornton, born in 1913, is founder and chairman of the board of Litton Industries of Beverly Hills. A specialist in the metaphysics of modern management techniques, his net worth is probably around $100 million.

James J. Ling, born in 1924, is the youngest of the Great Big New Rich. Like Litton Industries, Ling's Ling-Temco-Vought (LTV) engages in an astonishing variety of enterprises. Ling is a leading citizen of Dallas and controls something better than $100 million of personal wealth.

John W. Mecom, born in 1911, is an oilman and entre-preneur-at-large who works out of Houston. His wealth has been estimated at a half billion.

Howard Ahmanson, born in 1906, was the richest of the savings-and-loan moguls of Los Angeles. Worth about a half-billion, Ahmanson died in June 1968.

S. Mark Taper, born in 1901, is now the richest savings-and-loan man. His personal wealth is on the order of $150 million.

Howard R. Hughes, born in 1905, is the Great Nonesuch of American enterprise. He is worth about a billion, or perhaps more. Hughes' present residence is Las Vegas.

Norton Simon, born in 1907, has made his fortune — something better than $100 million — acquiring and reorganizing ailing corporations. Western-born, Simon operates out of Los Angeles.

Joseph H. Hirshhorn, born in 1900, is a speculator who made his greatest pile in Canadian uranium. Like Simon he is a noted collector of art. Hirshhorn, who lives in Greenwich, Connecticut, is worth, probably, $150 million.

H. L. Hunt, born in 1890, is the oilman and right-wing propagandist of Dallas. His fortune approaches one billion.

Occasional references will be made to other men who hold equal qualifications as Great Big New Rich. These include J. Paul Getty (oil, presently living in England), Charles Allen, Jr. (investment banking, New York), Edwin H. Land (Polaroid, Cambridge, Massachusetts), John D. MacArthur (insurance, Chicago and Florida), R. E. (Bob) Smith (oil and real estate, Houston), J. Erik Jonsson (Texas Instruments, Dallas).*

In addition to these very rich men, we shall consider the careers of four other men of lesser wealth. One of these — John H. Johnson of Chicago — is a Negro. One — Chinn Ho of Honolulu — is a Chinese-American. The third — Bart Lytton of Los Angeles — is a high-flying entrepreneur of money who was shot down in flames in the spring of 1968. The fourth — Patrick J. Frawley, Jr. — is a patron of politicians of the right wing.

---

* A candidate who emerged too late for this book is H. Ross Perot, whom *Fortune* billed in its November 1968 issue as "the fastest richest Texan ever." Six years ago, the thirty-eight-year-old Perot was an IBM salesman. He is now the proprietor of a computer software company, Electronic Data Systems Corporation of Dallas, in which his personal holdings are estimated at $300 million.

THREE

Gallery One: Tanker Man

He is a brilliant man; it gets you all upset sometimes, the way his mind runs.

— Morris Shapiro

The greatest of the Great Big New Rich of the postwar era is Daniel Keith Ludwig, who since the beginning of World War II has amassed a personal fortune that has propelled him to the dizzy heights of around a billion dollars where the world's handful of truly rich men live. He is not the richest man in the United States, but his only rivals are H. L. Hunt, the oracle of the crackpot Right; J. Paul Getty, the columnist for *Playboy*; and Howard Hughes, the landlord of Las Vegas. Unlike the others, Ludwig did not become rich until after the war, and unlike Hunt and Getty, he has a passion for keeping his mouth shut.

A commuter from Darien, Connecticut, Ludwig conducts an astonishing variety of business from the office of National Bulk Carriers at 360 Lexington Avenue. Although his basic fortune was made while he was putting together the world's largest tanker fleet (which is also the largest individually owned fleet of vessels of any kind in the world), he also owns (or has owned) a salt mine in Baja California, a 10,000-acre orange grove and a 55,000-barrels-a-day refinery in Panama, a monster river dredge at the mouth of the Orinoco, and (also in Venezuela) a 15,000-head cattle ranch so vast it has never been surveyed, and a site in Southern California on which he was planning to build a community for 100,000 people, coal mines in West Virginia, oil wells in Canada, a marine insurance company and two hotels in Bermuda, a 30,000-barrels-a-day refinery in West Germany, a potash mine in Ethiopia, iron mines, shipping and river-dredging operations in India, and a $20-million cargo transfer complex in Japan. In order to build his supertankers with the greatest of speed and economy, he also leased the former Japanese naval shipyard at Kure (pronounced Koo-reh), where the world's greatest battleship, Yamato, was built.*

In spite of his great wealth and his multifarious business activities, Ludwig's name is hardly a household word in the United States; it is even to be doubted that many citizens of Darien are aware that their quiet neighbor commands wealth greater than the combined fortunes of the original Vanderbilts, Morgans, and Du Ponts. In a profile in Fortune, Dero A.

---

* Ludwig entered another field in the fall of 1968, when he was found to have been buying up California savings-and-loan associations. The five he had acquired as of that date had combined assets of about $200 million.

Saunders attributed Ludwig's characteristic half-smile to his private amusement at the knowledge that he is "one of the outstanding business figures of the age and almost nobody knows it." *Business Week* once called him "one of the most mysterious figures in American business today" and then went on to demonstrate neatly how Ludwig had acquired this reputation. In June 1963, Ludwig bought 15 percent of the outstanding stock of the Union Oil Company. The editors of *Business Week* worked themselves into a state of nervous concern over this purchase and cluck-clucked audibly about the conflict of interest between Ludwig's roles as a producer of oil and as a carrier. Some time later, Ludwig sold his Union Oil stock, not by any means out of distress over a conflict of interest but simply because the transaction brought him a profit of $46 million, thereby demonstrating again why he wears a shy half-smile.

I'm in this business because I like it. I have no hobbies.
— D. K. Ludwig

For an essentially quiet man, Ludwig has enjoyed some curious publicity. An Italian paper once spread the news that Ludwig was in the habit of shooting seagulls from his yacht and eating them raw. On another occasion, Reuters reported from Cannes that it was believed locally that Ludwig had Hitler aboard the yacht.

In person, Ludwig is a rather retiring and even diffident fellow. A very rich man who knows and likes him told me that he was, nevertheless, the "most uncouth man I know." (He

D. K. Ludwig, builder and operator of the world's greatest fleet of tankers. WIDE WORLD PHOTOS.

was, I think, commenting less on Ludwig's manners than on his total lack of interest in anything except business.) Ludwig is most evidently a man of great talent and complexity, a classic example of the very rich man who (despite the evidence of his yacht) takes his primary pleasure in the making of money rather than in the amenities that his money might provide.

The anecdotes told about Ludwig are mostly concerned with his compulsive regard for the value of a penny. A typical story concerns the time he flew on an urgent mission from New York to Panama. Arriving at Tocumen airport without any baggage, wearing seersucker slacks and an old sports shirt, he was driven by a waiting car to Las Minas Bay, on the Atlantic coast. There he stopped at the village store to buy a twenty-cent roll of string and a five-cent bolt. After knotting the string every six feet, he tied the bolt to the end and set off in a rented motorboat to check personally every sounding on the navigation chart of the bay.

Ludwig is a not unhandsome man in his early seventies, trimly built, who often works in his shirt-sleeves and often wears suspenders. His office is furnished with a small desk, a single telephone, a leather sofa, and five brass-studded leather chairs. A nautical touch is added by barometers, ship models, and a ship's clock.

He lives with his wife, a widow whom he married in 1935, in a house in Darien that has been described as unostentatious. He has no children of his own. A magazine writer once observed him poking around his lawn, looking irritably at his crabgrass. His only known dissipation is his yacht. At 257 feet 5 inches length overall, *Danginn* (a combination of his own first name and his wife's nickname, Ginger) is one of the few great American yachts still in commission. A steel-hulled three-decker, *Danginn* was designed in Ludwig's own shop, built in his yard at Kure, and outfitted in Hong Kong in 1960. She is registered in Monrovia, Liberia, as are the great majority of Ludwig's working vessels.

A semibillionaire friend of Ludwig's told me not long ago that he had heard that D.K. had ordered a new and larger yacht in order to keep up with a new vessel belonging to Getty. If this is so, the new yacht will surely contain one of the features of *Danginn*, a floating office which ensures that Ludwig will never have to get too far away from his work.

> Nearly everyone has these antennae. Most people just don't use them.
>
> — *D. K. Ludwig*

From his boyhood, Ludwig displayed a sensitivity to the profitable deal that is not vouchsafed to many of the rest of us. The story is told that at the age of nine young Ludwig bought a sunken 26-foot boat for $75, repaired it, and chartered it for over a hundred dollars. Even if the story is apocryphal, it *should* have happened.

The original Ludwig was a Hessian soldier who stayed behind after the Revolution and whose descendants moved westward. Daniel Keith was born in South Haven, Michigan, in 1897, the only child of parents who separated when he was fifteen. Ludwig accompanied his father to Port Arthur, Texas, where he quit school after the eighth grade. In Port Arthur he worked for a ship chandler while studying marine engineering at night. Then he went back to Michigan and took a job in the Fairbanks, Morse marine engine plant in Three Rivers. He was apparently an apt student and a capable practical engineer, for Fairbanks, Morse sent him to the Pacific Northwest and Alaska to install their engines. At the age of nineteen he quit and went into business for himself.

Ludwig's first ship was an ancient side-wheel excursion steamer called *Idlewylde,* which he bought from a Detroit bank on his father's signature. Selling off the boilers and machinery, Ludwig converted her into a barge and chartered her to a blackstrap molasses tycoon from whom he received some painful lessons in shrewd trading. After his education with the molasses man, Ludwig recalls, "For a couple of years I was barely one jump ahead of the creditors. In fact, I was broke all the time, but I didn't know enough to lie down. . . . I had to hit on something or I was busted. It was just a step from molasses to oil, and the profits looked good."

In 1921 he acquired control of his first oil tanker, the *Anahuac,* which he chartered from the War Shipping Board. He didn't know how to pronounce the name, but he decided to keep it anyway — "It would have cost $50 to paint out the name, so we just kept the old one." In 1923, he bought his first tanker, *Wico,* giving a Baltimore scrap outfit $5000 down on a purchase price of $25,000.

Something went wrong with the *Wico* partnership, and then, with the backing of Boston gas-station money, Ludwig bought the tanker *Phoenix* from the War Shipping Board. Although the *Phoenix* almost cost him his life, he operated it for seventeen years, until in 1942 he sold it to a Greek named Stavros Niarchos, who was looking for his first tanker.*

In the 1920's and early 1930's, Ludwig was the classic small-time operator who lives just one jump ahead of disaster. "In those days he didn't even have a desk," an old friend of Ludwig's once said. "He was working from the windowsill."

> I spend my time putting projects together and then I let Mr. Wagner find the money. That's his job.
>
> — *D. K. Ludwig*

Although he has received some competition in recent years, Ludwig's tankers have often been described accurately as the world's largest. (The attraction of the very large tanker is that as ships grow in size, their capacity increases at a much faster rate than their operating costs, which means that oil can be delivered at a lower cost per barrel.) The first of Ludwig's "world's largest" tankers was a ship named *Ulysses*, a 14,000-ton collier which he converted to carry oil. He lost his first charter when the conversion missed its deadline, and he was subsequently obliged to operate *Ulysses* on such a slim margin that he sometimes lost money on every barrel he carried. Salvation came in 1933, when a whaling syndicate bought the ship for $800,000 and allowed Ludwig to get out of debt.

With money in the bank, Ludwig expanded his horizons and began to build a staff. His most notable acquisition was William W. Wagner, the former auditor of the Shipping Board,

---

* A gas explosion once blew Ludwig through the deck of the *Phoenix*. Twenty-eight years later he spent nine months in a shoulder-to-knees cast as a final consequence of the accident.

who has been his right arm ever since. Wagner's skill in the financial end has been a critical factor in making it possible for Ludwig to exploit those favorable constellations of circumstances that have revealed themselves to him but not to less gifted entrepreneurs.

Ludwig has said that the turning point in his career was a 1936 loan from the Chemical Bank & Trust Company which allowed him to buy some surplus World War I dry-cargo ships, convert them into tankers, and operate them on charters. Chartering turned out to be the magic ingredient that, added to Ludwig's sense for a deal and Wagner's sense for dollars, not only made it possible for Ludwig to get off the windowsill, but created his present vast fleet of ships.

In 1938, after more than a year of discussion, Ludwig and Wagner prevailed on the Bank of Manhattan Company (now the Chase Manhattan Bank) to lend them $200,000 for expansion and conversions, assigning to the bank the charter of the *Phoenix*. As it happened, the 1938 hurricane blew over the horizon almost simultaneously with the signing of the charter. Charles Fagg, the Bank of Manhattan official who authorized the loan, has recalled that "I couldn't sleep that night, because the ship was in northeastern waters. The next day I called and said 'How's my collateral?' Ludwig answered, 'When we find the goddamn thing I'll let you know,' and slammed down the phone."

The *Phoenix* was found on a street in Fall River, Massachusetts, and a canal had to be dug to get her back into the water.

Although loans against future income are common banking practice, they had never been tried before in financing tankers.

In essence the technique that Ludwig worked out calls for the shipowner to go to the banker with a charter to an oil company for, say, five years in his hand. The bank then makes a loan, the maximum amount occurring at the point where the monthly amortization and interest equals the monthly charter income. The oil company then makes its charter payments direct to the bank, which deducts the loan payment due and credits the rest to the owner's account. It is a preferred loan, a "two-name paper" that is backed both by the charterer and the shipowner. The shipowner, for his part, takes his loan and plows it into the construction or conversion of ships whose charters will in turn serve to raise money to build still more ships. (It should be noted that although American writers have given Ludwig-Wagner the credit for this innovation, Goronwy Rees, a British writer, has given the credit to the Greek tanker man Onassis.)

You can't carry oil in grand pianos

— D. K. Ludwig

Besides the charter-loan technique and his predilection for ever-larger tankers, there is a third element in Ludwig's modus operandi that has enabled him to stay ahead of the competition. This is a systematic and sometimes hardly believable dedication to cheese-paring that puts any of the proverbial Scotsmen to shame. When one of Ludwig's employees was asked to suggest a design for a fleet flag, he recommended two hands stretching a rubber dollar bill.

When I asked a friend of mine who used to sail on tankers what he thought of Ludwig he almost dropped his drink with the violence of his reaction. Respectable tanker men, I gathered, looked on Ludwig ships as hardly more humane than the ships of the African slave trade. In fact, except for the officers, American seamen are never tempted to sign on any of Ludwig's ships, and his crews are made up of Cayman Islanders, dark-skinned men from the British West Indies, and Okinawans. Hiring American officers is justified not on policy grounds, but rather because sharp officers can save the owner $5,000 to $10,000 a day by cutting down the turnaround time in port.

Ludwig's ships are built to carry oil, nothing else. The captain sleeps in a bunk, not a bed. The deck coverings are about half the normal thickness. Ludwig once asked his designers to see if there wasn't some way to carry oil in a tanker's hollow masts. When the designers reported that there wasn't any way to do it, Ludwig got rid of the masts. The navigation lights on his ships are now mounted on steel pipes.

Somebody once reported to Ludwig that Onassis had acquired a grand piano for the officers' quarters in each of his supertankers. Ludwig's answer was direct and characteristic: "You can't carry oil in grand pianos."

It is hard to imagine that the profits gained by sacrificing grand pianos, masts, and normal deck-plates have added much to the net income of National Bulk Carriers. The point to be observed, however, is that the mind that worries about such matters is a mind to which the making of money is an exceedingly serious business.

He might not be able to discuss academic economics on a university level, but he has an uncanny ability to detect the basic economics underlying any really big deal.

— A competitor

Ludwig's breakthrough into the world of the Great Big New Rich was propelled not only by his understanding of the economic necessity of building tankers ever larger, but also by his understanding of the opportunities offered by World War II. The conversions financed by Ludwig's charter-loans were being carried out at a Pennsylvania Railroad dock in Virginia when the German Army marched into Poland in the fall of 1939. When the Navy took over this dock, Ludwig was obliged to finish these conversions at a former Army pier near Norfolk. Here he also built tankers of 12,000 and 19,000 deadweight tons. After Pearl Harbor the Navy evicted him. He responded by building Welding Shipyard, still near Norfolk.

At Welding, where a peak labor force of 1200 turned out large all-welded tankers that were launched sideways, Ludwig in a literal sense laid the keels of his postwar fleet. As soon as a ship was finished it would be requisitioned by the government, to be returned to him after the war. Ludwig came out of the war with what *Fortune* has described as an "exceptionally up-to-date fleet of tankers whose average age was less than five years." His fleet had at the same time become the fifth largest tanker fleet under the U.S. flag.

After experimenting with the conversion of wartime T-2 tankers (16,300 dwt), Ludwig went for increasingly large ships, and in the face of a good deal of skepticism from his competitors, built what were then considered to be monsters of 30,000 tons, the largest ships that Welding Shipyard could handle. Going beyond this figure forced Ludwig to make two decisions that were critical in his drive to the very top. The first of these decisions was to lease the former Japanese naval yard at Kure.

The second was to meet the competition abroad by getting out from under the U.S. flag and hiring foreign crews.

Kure had the demonstrated capacity to turn out large ships; its greatest was the battleship *Yamato*, the largest and most heavily gunned battleship afloat during World War II, and consequently the largest of all time. (Wardroom wits in the Japanese fleet used to describe *Yamato* as having the largest 16-inch guns in the world.) Furthermore, Kure was manned by a trained labor force accustomed to working for considerably less than their American counterparts, and was owned by a government that, in the period before the peace treaty, was made nervous by the possibility of reparations. Early in 1951, Ludwig leased Kure for ten years.

Six years later, Ludwig placed the biggest shipbuilding order ever placed until then by a private firm. The order was for five supertankers of 104,500 dwt each, at a cost estimated from $75 million to $125 million. These ships were 131 feet shorter but 16 feet wider than the *Queen Mary*, too beamy to go through the Suez or Panama canals. Characteristically, Ludwig neglected to make any public announcement of this order, even though it increased the size of his fleet to more than 3 million deadweight tons, causing him to overtake and pass Niarchos as the world's greatest independent shipowner.

The operation of the Kure yard gave Ludwig a number of advantages over his competitors, among which speed and flexibility were not the least important. His construction boss, Elmer Hann, once said, "We'll be laying the keel of one ship, and he'll cable, 'The pressure is on — I need that one.' I'll wire back, 'But we have an ore boat scheduled.' He'll say, 'No, no, not that one; hold everything; I need this one instead.' He might change his mind four times a week. With an ordinary shipbuilder you couldn't do that: it would cost too much."

The speed of the Kure operation, which owed much to prefabrication and sectional building, was phenomenal. The keel for the *Universe Leader*, a supertanker, was laid at the end of January 1956; the ship finished her trial runs eight months later. Ludwig's ships are built to highly standardized patterns, which not only simplifies and speeds construction but has an additional bonus in that crews can be moved efficiently from ship to ship. Not only is the cost of everything except steel much lower than it would be in the United States, but also, as *Fortune* has put it delicately, the taxes are not crushing, the Kure yard being "deemed by the Japanese government to make little profit."*

It is not unusual for a shipowner to operate each of his ships under a different company in order to limit possible liabilities. This has not been Ludwig's practice. Nine out of ten of Ludwig's fleet sail under the flags of the Republic of Liberia and Universe Tankships, Inc., of Monrovia. The corporate structure Ludwig has built to support this deceptively straightforward statement resists analysis by anybody but an expert. Ludwig owns outright Oceanic Tankships, SA, of Panama. Oceanic Tankships controls the Liberian company Universe Tankships. Universe Tankships owns the Gem Navigation

---

* Ludwig's previous "world's largest" tankers were eclipsed in the fall of 1968, when the 312,000-ton *Universe Ireland*, built for Ludwig in Japan for charter to Gulf Oil, made her maiden voyage from Kuwait to Bantry Bay, Ireland.

Company; the Ulysses Shipping Co., Inc.; 15 percent of Erdoel-werke Frisia, AG; Central Industries, Inc.; and Seatankers, Inc. Central Industries in turn owns 50 percent of Refineria Panama, SA. Seatankers owns Eastend Properties, Ltd.; West-end Properties, Ltd.; Hato La Vergarena, CA; Citricos de Chiriqui, SA; Exportado de Sal, SA; Emder Tankschiffahrt–GmbH; and Argyll Shipping Co., Ltd.

And so it goes, a complex network that literally covers the world and at the center of which is found D. K. Ludwig himself, smiling diffidently.

We never play politics but we always make a point of getting acquainted with the premier and the finance minister.

— *Allen Cameron,*
vice-president of National Bulk Carriers

Besides his shipyard in Japan and his holding companies in Panama and Liberia, Ludwig has also made investments in West Germany, India, Australia, Ethiopia, Venezuela, Bermuda, Canada, and Mexico. The motives which have impelled him to invest tens of millions of dollars sometimes appear to be misleadingly casual. When, seven or eight years ago, friends sent him some oranges from Panama that he liked, Ludwig sent soil experts into the interior of Panama, and on their advice developed 10,000 acres of land and planted on it 800,000 Valencia orange trees.

To what extent a compulsion to conceive enterprises that are the largest of their kind in the world is the propelling force behind D. K. Ludwig is a matter that is not easily settled; the evidence, however, would seem to support a prima facie argument of this sort. Even as he was thinking of a 200,000-dwt supertanker — the largest, of course, in the world — Ludwig was also developing his salt-processing plant at Guerrero Negro in Baja California. Producing a million tons of crude salt annually for the chemical industry by the natural evaporation process, it was predicted that it would become the largest in the world. His ventures at home are on the same grand scale: About five years ago he bought for $32 million the 11,500 Albertson Ranch at the western edge of Los Angeles County. Strategically located, Ludwig's property is twenty minutes from the Rocketdyne plant of North American Aviation and ten minutes from the Concjo industrial park. When a 20 year development plan to convert the ranch into a vast housing complex has at last been realized, it is estimated that its value will be a billion dollars.

> The raw materials of a deal before it is assembled look very different from the final arrangement.
>
> — *D. K. Ludwig*

In the spectrum of divergent interests and personalities presented by the Great Big New Rich, D. K. Ludwig, more than any other man, represents the classic entrepreneur, the man who understands deals and understands money and whose antennae are tuned eighteen hours a day to detecting the presence of precisely the right raw materials for a successful enterprise. Unlike the Texas oil rich, his genius lies in the mechanics of enterprises. Unlike the savings-and-loan and insurance rich, he is interested in manipulating things rather than money. Unlike the rich men of the new technology, his style is that of the slightly eccentric genius rather than that of the skilled and polished manager.

It is also not unlikely that D. K. Ludwig is the last of the great entrepreneurs.

FOUR

Vital Statistics

It may be worthwhile to point out that the dolicho-blond type of European man seems to owe much of its dominating influence and its masterful position in the recent culture to its possessing the characteristics of predatory man in an exceptional degree.

— *Thorstein Veblen*

Ludwig, Crown, Stone, Kennedy, Thornton, Ling, Mecom, Ahmanson, Taper, Hughes, Simon, Hirshhorn, Hunt, Getty, Land, MacArthur, Smith, Jonsson. The Northern European names fall on our ears like the strokes of a tribal drum. The great majority of the Great Big New Rich are native-born Americans whose ancestors came from the British Isles, Germany, and Scandinavia. There is a scattering of Jews, but, curiously, their names are not conspicuously "Jewish." There are no names that reveal a family origin in France, Italy, or elsewhere along the Mediterranean littoral. Only two men were born abroad.

We can make some other generalizations about the Great Big New Rich. The future great tycoon is likely to have been born to parents of the lower middle class in the Northeast, the Middle West, or the Southwest. Only one was born on the Pacific Coast, and none at all south of the Mason-Dixon line. The tycoon is more likely to have come from the city than the countryside.

About the same number graduated from college as dropped out of school before the twelfth grade. (The tycoon with the greatest number of academic honors is a college dropout, although from Harvard rather than some humbler institution.) With a few exceptions, the tycoons have sustained marriages of respectable duration that have generated an average of three offspring each.

The Great Big New Rich are not on the whole politically active, although the group includes a former member of the Republican National Finance Committee as well as the father of a former president. The most conservative, a man so far out in right field that he is virtually invisible in the game of practical politics, counts himself a Democrat. The rich do not on the whole appear to be devout and enthusiastic churchmen, although those who have made their affiliations public are overwhelmingly of the Protestant denominations.

Although women have begun to appear in the ranks of simple millionaires, no woman has yet by her own efforts qualified as a member of the Great Big New Rich.

Vital Statistics

The Great Big New Rich are also, to a man, white.

The black bourgeoisie . . . has created a world of make-
believe to shield itself from the harsh economic and social
realities of American life. This world of make-believe is created
out of the myth of Negro business, the reports of the Negro
press on the achievement and wealth of Negroes, the recognition accorded them by whites, and the fabulous life of Negro
"society."

— *E. Franklin Frazier*

There are no Great Big New Black Rich.

In his absorbing study of the black bourgeoisie, the Negro
sociologist E. Franklin Frazier has written corrosively of the
economic and social goals of the American Negro: Cadillacs,
mink coats, Greek letter societies, suburban houses, debutante
cotillions and the other ephemerae which also drive their
brothers and sisters of the white middle class. Unlike the
whites, however, among the Negro population the incidence of
an overwhelming drive to accumulate a very large amount of
money for its own sake (or for the sake of the game) appears to
be statistically insignificant.

The decreased opportunity available to the Negro is surely
one reason for this phenomenon. The social matrix in which
the Negro is reared and in which he forms his attitudes is
certainly another factor that discourages ambitions of acquiring
great wealth. It may even be true that, as Veblen suggests, there
is a genetic factor át work, and that the innate predatoriness of
the dolicho-blond Northern European type of man makes it
difficult for other racial types to compete successfully for the
senseless accumulation of wealth.

43

There are, to be sure, rich black men — several years ago *Ebony* magazine estimated there were thirty-five Negro millionaires — but the magnitude of their wealth leaves them well below the $100-million threshold of great wealth. Virtually no Negroes have made notable successes in businesses other than insurance, banking, funeral parlors, and the Negro press. These businesses have catered almost exclusively to Negro customers.

John H. Johnson of Chicago is the Henry Luce of the Negro world. His Johnson Publishing Company publishes the million-circulation magazine *Ebony* as well as *Jet*, *Tan*, and *Negro Digest*. In addition, he owns a cosmetics company and is the largest stockholder and chairman of the board of the Supreme Life Insurance Company, where he had his start as an office boy thirty years ago. Johnson and his family live in an apartment with paintings by Chagall on the wall.

Johnson, who was born in 1918, was brought up in Arkansas. His father died when he was six. In 1933, his mother brought young Johnson to Chicago to see the World's Fair; they stayed, though on relief. His start in life came when the president of Supreme, having admired an address the young man had made at a high school honors convocation, suggested that he go to the University of Chicago part-time while working as an office boy in his firm.

While helping publish Supreme's house organ, Johnson was seized with the idea of publishing a Negro magazine resembling the *Reader's Digest*. He pawned his mother's furniture to raise funds to send twenty thousand letters to Supreme's customers. This bread cast on the waters brought back three thousand subscriptions at two dollars each, which, in November 1942,

John H. Johnson, the Henry Luce of the Negro world.

bankrolled the publication of the first issue of five thousand copies. When Johnson induced Eleanor Roosevelt to contribute to *Negro Digest* an article in a series, "If I Were a Negro," the circulation jumped from 50,000 to 150,000. (Mrs. Roosevelt said, "I would not do too much demanding.")

Johnson's greatest success came with the launching of the *Life*-style *Ebony* in 1945. *Ebony's* prosperity has been credited to Johnson's ability to attract advertising from white-owned businesses, to whom the Negro market is a *terra incognita*. (In 1967, *Ebony's* advertising revenues were $7 million.)

In spite of his position as a standard-bearer in the Negro's march up the economic ladder, Johnson is not universally beloved in the Negro community. When he emerged as a power in Supreme, there were some who commented on his arrogance and ruthlessness. Others have been critical of his, and *Ebony's*, slowness to join the civil rights crusade. Although *Ebony* is now forthright in its advocacy of Negro rights, its main editorial stock-in-trade is the celebration of that same Negro middle-classness that Franklin Frazier found so offensive in *The Black Bourgeoisie*.

Another of the most successful of Negro businessmen is S. B. Fuller, also of Chicago, who owns the Fuller Products Company (cosmetics) and controls eight other corporations. Among these are a Chicago department store, a real estate trust in New York, and the *Courier* newspapers in Chicago, New York, Detroit, and Pittsburgh. Born in Louisiana, Mr. Fuller, like many of his white counterparts among the rich, dropped out of school early — in his case the sixth grade. In 1935, he started the Fuller Products Company on $25 capital. In 1963, Fuller Products had gross sales of something more than $10 million. Fuller himself is a member of the National Association of Manufacturers and a member of the board of the Chicago Association of Commerce and Industry.

The concentration of Negro business effort in insurance and banking has the sanction of history, going back to the Civil War and the establishment by Congress of the Freedmen's Savings Bank to receive deposits "by or in behalf of persons heretofore held in slavery in the United States or their descendants." (In fact, there were many prosperous free Negroes in the United States before Emancipation. *Gens de couleur* held real estate worth $800,000 in Philadelphia, over a million in New York, $630,000 in the District of Columbia, and about a half-million in Baltimore. In all, it has been estimated, free Negroes accumulated $50 million in real and personal wealth before the Civil War.)

The Freedmen's Bank was managed badly and foundered as a consequence of the Panic of 1873, with the unfortunate abolitionist and Negro leader Frederick Douglass, who had been installed as a figurehead at the last minute, sitting at the helm as the ship went down. But the Freedmen's Bank had pointed the direction, and, between 1888 and 1934, Negroes organized at least 134 banks, mostly in the South. Founded to furnish credit and capital to the small Negro businessman, they have largely retained this character to the present day.

The most successful Negro enterprises have not been banking but insurance companies, again catering mainly to a Negro clientele. The leading Negro insurance man is Asa T. Spaulding, president of North Carolina Mutual Life of Durham, the largest Negro-owned and -operated business in the country. In 1966 North Carolina Mutual dedicated its new office building, the tallest in Durham, a city which has traditionally been a citadel of the black bourgeoisie. Next in order come Atlanta Life (Jesse Hill, Jr.) and the Supreme Life Insurance Company of Chicago. Moving with the times, the Negro insurance companies are extending their sales efforts to whites — and, also, complaining that white-owned companies have begun pirating their more capable employees.

Time has nominated Jackie Robinson, who first broke the race barrier in organized baseball, as the "fastest rising Negro businessman in the United States today." In 1966, at the age of 47, Robinson held executive positions with a bank and a professional football team and was co-chairman of the Hamilton Life Insurance Company. He was described as living in a $75,000 house in Stamford with his wife, who is an assistant professor of nursing at Yale, and their three children. He was driving a dark greenish-gray Lincoln. (A Cadillac, Robinson told the reporter, was "too ostentatious.") According to *Time*, Robinson's net worth was $200,000.

There is clearly a difference of considerable magnitude between the richest black men and the richest white men. It does not necessarily follow that the closing of this gap is a worthy goal, although, sadly, it is no doubt true that the emergence of a Negro of vast wealth who was known to be just as predatory on the grand scale as his white compeers would be greeted with the ringing of church bells and orgiastic editorials in *Ebony* and the *Courier* papers.

Vital Statistics

Of great wealth among the other darker races, there is little to report. Depressed even below the Negroes in California, the Mexican-Americans strive toward more modest goals. The Japanese-Americans, for all their industriousness and all their cultural drive toward success, have produced battalions of doctors, dentists, teachers, civil servants, and successful small businessmen, but no great tycoons.

Only the Chinese-Americans remain in the running.

What makes Ho hum?

— *Paradise of the Pacific,* 1965

In size of personal fortune, probably the most successful American whose ancestors came from elsewhere than Europe and whose skin is other than pinko-gray is a Honolulu financier and real-estate operator named Chinn Ho, who is generally conceded to be the richest man in the Hawaiian Islands.[*]

Ho's grandfather, a rice farmer, migrated from Canton. His grandson's emergence at the top of the heap in Hawaii is not an isolated phenomenon; it has now been several years since the per capita personal incomes of the Chinese-Americans of Hawaii overtook and surpassed that of the *haoles*, or whites. Chinn Ho's career is only a single prominent chapter in the story of the social and economic revolution that is now taking place in Hawaii.

---

[*] Probably not as rich as Chinn Ho, but equally colorful, is Hung Wo Ching, a Cornell Ph.D. whose father was a cook on an inter-island steamer. The success of Aloha Airlines under Hung Wo Ching's direction was a major blow to the economic domination of Hawaii by the white businessmen.

Chinn Ho's father was a clerk at the Pacific Club, which for generations has been a bastion of the Honolulu *haoles*. The elder Ho went to night school, opened a business importing Chinese foodstuffs, and sent nine children to school. Chinn graduated from McKinley High, a remarkable institution which has served as a staircase upward for almost sixty graduating classes made up largely of the bright and ambitious children of Chinese and Japanese families not long out of the cane and pineapple fields. Among his other activities at McKinley, Ho organized a *hui*, or Chinese-style mutual fund for small investors among his schoolmates, and thereby set the course for his future career.

After graduating from McKinley, Ho went to work as an office boy at the Bishop Bank for $75 a month and then moved to a firm of stockbrokers who were the predecessors of the Honolulu branch of the Dean Witter firm. He became a first-rate stock salesman, but his salary remained notably less than his *haole* equivalents were earning.

In 1944, Chinn Ho forsook his paycheck and formed the Capital Investment Company, which remains his principal medium of business. He was, at last count, president of five companies, vice-president of four, and director of three. His interests include the 1014-unit Ilikai Hotel on the western edge of Waikiki; a hotel in Hong Kong; a tourist development at Makaha, in a fold of the Waianae mountains on the relatively unsettled shoreline beyond Pearl Harbor; the Honolulu minor-league ball team; the Honolulu stadium; the Honolulu *Star-Bulletin*, of which he is publisher; and assorted real estate. Chinn Ho's net worth was calculated several years ago at $25 million.

Vital Statistics

Three years ago Chinn Ho invited me to lunch in his suite on the second floor of his thirty-story Ilikai Hotel. He turned out to be a short, solidly built man with a broad fleshy face, wavy graying hair, and a bluff, no-nonsense manner. He looks like exactly what he is, a man who finds keen pleasure both in business affairs and in the amenities — such as golf and foreign travel — which his money has made possible.

The other guests at lunch turned out to be members of the state legislature, Chinese-American, Japanese-American, and Filipino-American. Around a table spread with "thousand-year-old" eggs, pond-raised mullet, chicken and shrimp, Ho and his guests rang the changes on that most fascinating of all topics, local politics. As a confessed writer working for a Mainland magazine, I was rather surprised to find myself in this company, but so far as I could tell nobody was actually being corrupted by the succulent food. After lunch, Chinn Ho pressed on me one of the fat and aromatic cigars that are his trademark and we walked out on the veranda that overlooks his corner of Waikiki.

I didn't find him particularly easy to talk to, although he maintained an air of cordiality. Casting about for a congenial topic, I inquired about the probable future economic development of the Islands, which is closely tied to the entertainment of tourists, in which Ho has a substantial interest.

Taking his cigar from his mouth, Ho said briskly, "You're going to see change, change, and then more change." Then the cigar went back in.

Anyone who so desires can easily become a member of the poor group. Most of those who want to be rich cannot fulfill their wish.

— *Pitirim Sorokin*

Our folklore insists that millionaires must start their careers in humble circumstances. By and large, our folklore is right.

Cornelius Vanderbilt began his life as the son of poor farmers on Staten Island, and could hardly write his name at the age of twelve. He escaped from the island by becoming a ferry boy, taking passengers to and from Manhattan. In the early days of his career, his wife ran a tavern in New Brunswick.

Daniel Drew, who in later years, aided and abetted by Jay Gould and Jim Fisk, was to diddle Vanderbilt out of $7 million in an afternoon, started life in Carmel, Putnam County, and grew up a cattle drover herding rustic beasts to the great city. (Drew is said to have invented the device of watered stock — not giving his cattle anything to drink until they were at their destination, where they were at last permitted to fill themselves up.)

Jay Gould, the son of poor Yankee farmers, managed to attend Hobart Academy in upstate New York by living with the village blacksmith and keeping his books for him. He left home at sixteen. (There is a persistent belief that Gould was Jewish, perhaps due to his dark and contemplative aspect and the closeness of his family name to "Gold." Matthew Josephson identifies the originator of this mistake as Henry Adams, who once called Gould a "complex Jew" — whether metaphorically or in error it is not clear.) *

---

* As Stephen Birmingham reports in "Our Crowd," Gould's putative Jewishness "was supported by the discovery that Gould was descended from one Nathan Gold, who had settled in Fairfield, Connecticut, in 1646, and that the 'u' had been added to the family name as late as 1806." Birmingham goes on to comment that the best reason for believing that the obnoxious Gould was gentile is that, given Gould's temperament, if he had been Jewish, he would not have troubled to deny it.

Jay Cooke was said to be the first (or almost the first) white male infant to be born in Sandusky, Ohio, which was in those days a boom town on the frontier soon to be served by Erie and Mad River Railroad. Although Cooke's father, Eleutheros, was later to become a congressman, Cooke's own education was received largely in practical trading rather than the academy.

John D. Rockefeller's father was an itinerant peddler of patent medicines who generally left his wife and five children in some degree of want. Moving from western New York to Cleveland, young Rockefeller studied bookkeeping for a year in high school, was dazzled by the insights this dark art gave him into the management of money, and promptly went to work keeping books.

Andrew Carnegie was the offspring of poor Scottish weavers of radical political bent who came to western Pennsylvania in the great migration of Scots and Scotch-Irish fleeing the chaos the Industrial Revolution had wrought along the Firth of Forth and in northern Ireland. Carnegie went to work at fourteen as bobbin boy in a cotton mill.

Jim Fisk, born in Bennington, Vermont, became a Vermont peddler, hawking silks, silverware, and Yankee notions door to door. He also worked in a traveling menagerie, and during the Civil War ran contraband cotton and sold Army blankets at great profit.

Of the Robber Barons, only J. Pierpont Morgan came of a prosperous family, his father, Junius S. Morgan (who had himself begun life as a farm boy and dry goods clerk), being a millionaire engaged in the banking business. The only one of the great nineteenth century tycoons whose education went beyond high-school bookkeeping, Pierpont Morgan was sent to study at the University of Göttingen and then went to work in London at the banking house of George Peabody & Co., of which his father was a partner.

> Money
> is a
> river
> flowing
> downhill
> over
> hills
> of
> character
> in the
> rich
> — *Norman Mailer*

Making due allowances for changing times and changing circumstances, the origins of our own Great Big New Rich are not remarkably different from those of the last century.

H. L. Hunt, who owns more oil than anybody else in the world with the possible exception of J. Paul Getty, was born in Vandalia, Illinois, and went only as far as fifth grade — although it is reported that by the time he left school he could memorize a page of type in two readings. (Later he spent some time at Valparaiso University.) His career immediately subsequent to dropping out of grade school is obscure, although the legends have it that at various times he worked as a cowhand in the Dakotas and Canada, and as a lumberjack in Arizona, finally making his first pile growing cotton in Arkansas. He was wiped out, temporarily, when the bottom fell out of the cotton market in 1921.

James J. Ling, the youngest of the Great Big New Rich and the organizer of the sprawling conglomerate corporation Ling-Temco-Vought, was born in Hugo, Oklahoma, and was orphaned at twelve. While living with an aunt in Louisiana, he grew bored with high school and after four footloose years joined the Navy. His first, modest success came in the electrical contracting business.

Joseph H. Hirshhorn, a self-described speculator who recently gave his $50 million collection of paintings and sculpture to the public, to be installed in a gallery on the Washington mall, was born in Latvia, the twelfth of thirteen children. His widowed mother brought Hirshhorn and nine siblings to Brooklyn, where she worked in a sweatshop. Hirshhorn's first job was as a Wall Street office boy.

Charles Allen, Jr., reputedly the richest man on Wall Street, was born in the Bronx, the son of an inventor. He left high school before graduation and went to work on the street as a runner for the firm of Sartorius and Smith. At the age of nineteen, he invested a thousand dollars of savings in his own bond-trading business, in which he was joined by two younger brothers. Allen made his first million by 1929, when he was twenty-six, lost it in the Crash, and made it back again during the next three years.

As we have already noted, the tanker man D. K. Ludwig was born in Michigan of parents who separated when he was fifteen. He quit school after the eighth grade.

The insurance man John D. MacArthur was born in Pittston, Pennsylvania. He never graduated from high school.

Clement Stone, the Chicago insurance man, is Chicago-born. Stone sold papers on downtown streetcorners while his widowed mother sewed. He dropped out of high school when he found he was making more money selling insurance than his teachers were teaching.

Charles B. (Tex) Thornton, the managerial whiz who heads the multicircuited Litton Industries in Beverly Hills, was brought up largely by his mother, while his father, having departed the family circle, tried to make his fortune blowing out oil-well fires with nitroglycerine. Thornton finished college while working as a government clerk in Washington.

Mark Taper, who is a power in the savings-and-loan industry in Southern California, was born of Jewish parents in Poland and was reared in England, where he became prosperous before moving to Los Angeles, ostensibly to retire. His biographical literature casts no light on his education.

Although our sense of the dramatic possibilities of life is fulfilled in the most satisfying way when a great tycoon can point back to the ragged urchin he once was, selling papers in a snowstorm or walking behind the plow at the age of four, a substantial number of the Great Big New Rich started life in agreeable circumstances.

The most notable of these are Howard Hughes and J. Paul Getty, both of whose fathers enjoyed more than ordinary affluence. The elder Hughes ("Big Howard") was a Harvard man whose contribution to the world of commerce and industry was the invention of a drill bit that would cut through the

Charles Allen, Jr., said to be the richest man on Wall Street.

hardest oil shale. Hughes senior left an estate of about $600,000 after the adjustment of his considerable debts, which included an unpaid bill at Brooks Brothers for six suits, three overcoats, and fifty shirts. Young Howard, who was to inherit the Hughes Tool Company, was sent to the Thacher School in California and the Fessenden School in Massachusetts, and attended Rice Institute and Cal Tech without taking a degree.

Getty's father was a Minneapolis lawyer who became infected with the oil fever while doing business in the Indian Territory. He did exceedingly well, but puritanically left his son only $500,000 of his estate of $15 million. (By this time, however, Getty *fils* was already wealthy through his holdings in the Getty Oil Company.) Getty attended the University of Southern California, the University of California at Berkeley, and took a degree in economics and political science at Oxford.

Of the other comfortably born, Howard Ahmanson, the recently deceased Los Angeles savings-and-loan king, was the son of a prosperous insurance man in Omaha, and by his own account spent an idyllic Middle Western boyhood, untroubled by want. He studied at the University of Nebraska, but took his bachelor of science degree at the University of Southern California.

J. Erik Jonsson, mayor of Dallas and chairman of the board of Texas Instruments, was born in New York City and took a degree in mechanical engineering at Rensselaer Polytechnic Institute.

Joseph P. Kennedy went to Harvard.

Edwin H. Land, the inventor of Polaroid, was born in Bridgeport, Connecticut, attended Norwich Academy, and took a leave of absence from Harvard after his freshman year to do

Edwin H. Land, the intellectual of the Great Big New Rich.
WIDE WORLD PHOTOS.

some inventing. He returned with a patent, but never took his bachelor's degree. Land holds an honorary Sc.D. from Harvard, however; his other honorary degrees are from Tufts, Polytechnic Institute of Brooklyn, Colby College, Bates College, and Northeastern University. Doctor Land is or has been a member of the Royal Photographic Society, the Royal Microscopic Society, the American Philosophic Society, the Optical Society of America, the National Academy of Sciences, and has been president of the American Academy of Arts and Sciences. He is surely the intellectual of the Great Big New Rich.

(It is worth pausing a moment to comment on the frequency with which Harvard crops up in the biographies of the educated Great Big New Rich. Yale surely deserves its reputation as a trade school for the upper reaches of finance and industry, but in the process of performing this honorable function, it apparently discourages the entrepreneurial spirit.)

Norton Simon, the Los Angeles-based financier and art collector, was born the son of a department-store owner in Portland, Oregon, thereby making him the only native Westerner among the Great Big New Rich. He graduated from high school in San Francisco and was admitted to the university at Berkeley, but stayed for only six weeks. He is now a regent of the university, an honor that in California is approximately equal to having been created a baronet in the old country.

> The possession of wealth also allows the purchase of an environment which in time often leads to the development of those "intrinsic" qualities of individuals and families that are required for higher prestige.
>
> — C. Wright Mills

In the end, to judge by their personal styles, there is little to choose between the poor-born rich and the comfortably born rich. The mellowing effects that can be exerted by large sums of money is probably exemplified nowhere quite so forcefully as in the career of Colonel Henry Crown, the man who once owned the Empire State Building. (His rank is for World War II service in the Corps of Engineers.) The son of Jewish immigrants from Lithuania, Crown's formal education stopped in the Chicago public schools and his practical education was in the rough-and-tumble of the building materials industry. Yet Crown was once described by that acute observer Stewart Alsop as the "very archetype of the great industrialist and entrepreneur — urbane, articulate, well dressed, and remarkably well preserved. . . ."

Although he was fired from a four-dollar-a-week job for not knowing the difference between sand and gravel, Crown's quarries, gravel pits, cement mixers, and barges have for many years played an essential part in the erection of new buildings in Chicago. Crown owns substantial parts of General Dynamics, the Rock Island Railroad, and the Hilton Hotel chain. His coalfields make him the second biggest producer in Illinois. Although he lives in middle-class Evanston, he rides in a chauffeur-driven Rolls Royce. The estimates of his wealth run up to half a billion dollars.

Today's successful industrialist [Crown] has never conceded any umbilical connection with the free-wheeling operator of the Twenties.

— Editors of *Fortune, The Art of Success*

Starting his career as a fourteen-year-old clerk with a company that manufactured fire brick, Crown went on to become the youthful traffic manager of the Union Drop Forge Company, and then a partner in S. R. Crown & Company. At twenty-three he was treasurer of the Material Service Corporation and at twenty-five its president. Material Service supplied building materials to the Chicago market.

Building materials is a tough business and Chicago is a tough city. A pair of anecdotes will give the flavor of the times and of our subject.

In the 1920's, Crown was already being hard-pressed when one of his competitors induced the teamsters to strike Material Service. Crown wangled an introduction to State Senator John Dailey, whom he persuaded to take on his case. The senator accompanied Crown to the competitor's office where, without taking off his hat, he announced, "I'm representing Henry Crown as an attorney. I understand his materials are tied up by a strike of the teamsters. Unless those teamsters go back to work, I am going to call my committee together and investigate you and this whole affair." The teamsters went back to work that afternoon. In 1924 Dailey acquired ten percent of the stock of Material Service and went on the board of directors.

(In the later Twenties, presumably with Dailey's help, Crown broke into the exclusive club of contractors, who until then had followed the pleasant custom of submitting identical bids and rotating the award, rather than going through the arduous and expensive discipline of competing for a low bid. There were rumors of an understanding between Crown and Anton Cermak, the soon-to-be-martyred mayor, with Cermak

Henry Crown, who once owned the Empire State Building, helped to build modern Chicago. WIDE WORLD PHOTOS.

thought to own a piece of Material Service, but Crown has denied this and the evidence seems to uphold his version.)

The other anecdote has a style that is not unfamiliar in the life stories of successful entrepreneurs. In 1931, when Crown owed a million on notes alone, the bank with which he was doing business was absorbed by a bank to whom Crown was a stranger. The new banker called Crown in and asked for collateral. Ignoring the advice of his friends and associates that the bank intended to sell him out, Crown offered the new bank his accounts receivable, his life insurance, and the deed to his house. Instead of selling him out, the bank lent him, successively, $750,000 and $900,000, with which he went on to buy quarries, mines, the Rock Island and the Empire State Building.

> Owing money has never concerned me so long as I know where it could be repaid from.
>
> — Henry Crown

When, in December 1964, Crown sold the Empire State Building to a syndicate of New Yorkers, the price of $65 million included a personal profit of $50 million, which Crown made on an investment of about $6 million.

Crown and several associates had bought the Empire State in 1951. The announced price was $51 million but the land was immediately resold to the Prudential Insurance Company for $17 million. The remaining $34 million included some $20 million in mortgages. Crown's 24 percent interest in the building therefore called for an investment of only about $3.4 million. Instead of taking out profits, Crown plowed his share back into the building, steadily increasing his equity. Three years after the purchase, Crown bought out all his associates.

A diverting story is told about Crown's techniques in one of these cases, that of Robert Young, who owned 19 percent of the building. Crown suggested to Young that it might be better if one of them owned both shares, and proposed that one man fix a price and the other man have the option of buying or selling. Young said he'd take the option. Crown came up with a price of $45 a share on stock that had cost him $30 six months earlier. According to Crown's son Lester, Young was "the most amazed individual I have ever seen." Young, of course, sold at Crown's price, and Crown put an additional $2.5 million of Empire State Building securities into his pocket.

When the sale to the New Yorkers was concluded, Crown's investment was $6 million and the mortgages were down to $8 million, leaving Crown about $50 million before the capital-gains tax.

Virtually the last that was seen of the old Henry Crown who had hustled his way through the Twenties and Thirties occurred with the publication of a story in the Chicago *Sun-Times* in 1946, alleging that Crown and Jacob Arvey, the political boss of Cook County, and others had been buying up buildings along the route of the proposed Congress Street Expressway. (They were eventually exonerated by the Chicago Bar Association.)

Since then, the man in view has been Colonel Crown, quiet, modest, polished, the industrialist, financier, and public figure, the man who presented Nikita Khrushchev with a model of the

Empire State Building, saying, "Now Mr. Khrushchev is a capitalist too — he owns a building without a mortgage."

> Only one of them, Fisk, was given to free living, drinking, and fleshpots in youth; in private life they were generally discreet, sober, well-controlled, their strongest lust being the pecuniary appetite.
>
> — Matthew Josephson

By and large there is little scandal to be found in the lives of the Great Big New Rich, either of our own time or of the Gilded Age. The descendants of the Vanderbilts and Astors and such have been much given to multiple marriages and other expensive carryings-on and have in the process managed to dissipate their inheritances to remarkable degrees. The first-generation rich, by contrast, tend to be settled family men whose private lives, though they lack high colors, could be set up as salutary models for the ambitious youths of the middle classes.

Henry Crown, as an example, became a widower after twenty-three years of a marriage that produced three sons. Three years after the death of his first wife he married again. Two of his sons, who are now in their middle forties, went to Northwestern. One went on to the Harvard Business School; the other took a law degree. One is a vice-president of General Dynamics. The other is on the board of so many corporations and civic organizations that his biography in *Who's Who in America* is three times as long as his father's.

Charles Allen's first wife was Rita Friedman, the theatrical producer (*The Grass Harp, My Three Angels*). Their marriage ended in divorce in 1951 after twenty-three years. Allen has now been married to his second wife for sixteen years. Ahmanson, MacArthur, and Hunt have also been married twice.

The only cases that relieve this chronicle of domesticity are those of J. Paul Getty and Mark Taper. Getty has been married five times. His own account of his life at home is the dismal record of a man whose mind is so thoroughly focused on a single topic — money — that his bewilderment at the souring of his attempts at marriage appears genuine and even touching. The world was reminded of the enduring place that money holds in the Getty family when in 1966 Getty's son Gordon sued his father and the rest of his family (including his own young son) for his share of a $300-million trust fund. Gordon Getty explained that it was merely a friendly suit designed to straighten out a matter of business. "I and all my brothers have the utmost respect and affection for our father," he said.*

Mark Taper's domestic life has also been somewhat out of the general pattern. In 1958, Taper's wife Amelia died. In 1962, like other rich and elderly men before him, Taper married a former actress, twenty-eight-year-old Roberta Gale. They were

---

* The private life of one of these brothers, Paul Getty, Jr., deserves at least this footnote. In 1967 young Getty was reported to have bought a forty-room Moorish palace inside the walled city of Marrakesh, Morocco. A year and a half-later he was living in a Rome apartment, a Renaissance villa twenty miles north of Rome, and the Aga Khan's Costa Smeralda in Sardinia. A member of this well-housed household was Getty's two-month-old son, who bore the euphonious name of Tara Gabriel Galaxy Gramophone Getty. His mother explained, "Every name has a precise significance and my son will be very proud of them when he grows up. Tara is an Irish aristocratic name. Galaxy means galaxy, and he was born under the stars. He will undoubtedly be fond of music so we named him Gramophone." She neglected to explain Gabriel.

67

separated less than a year later, the separation being followed by an annulment after Taper charged his wife with adultery.

Otherwise, little evidence appears in the lives of the very rich to suggest that they are moved in domestic matters by any motives more exciting than the conventional ones of a quiet life at home and a decent education for the kids. D. K. Ludwig married in 1935. W. Clement Stone's marriage has produced three grown children. Charles B. Thornton married in 1937; one of his sons went to Harvard and the Harvard Business School, and the other to Stanford and the Harvard Business School. In 1933 Norton Simon married a Wellesley-educated social worker. They have two sons. Even Howard Hughes, whose life fits nobody's pattern except his own, has not been excessive in the matter of marriages, his sole ventures being his marriage to Ella Rice in 1925, and to the actress Jean Peters in 1957.

In summing up, one can do worse than return to Josephson's characterization of the Robber Barons — generally discreet, sober, well controlled, their strongest lust being the pecuniary appetite.

> The industrial revolution had turned numbers of greedy dullards into monstrously rich men. . . . Nothing could be more flattering and fortifying to them than the assumption that they were rich because they were virtuous.
>
> — *George Bernard Shaw*

> God gave me my money.
>
> — *John D. Rockefeller*

When, early on the morning of January 4, 1877, old Cornelius Vanderbilt was dying, he rose in his death bed and called, "Frank! Sing me my hymns!" Those around him responded with "Come All Ye Sinners, Poor and Needy," a selection which was followed by "Nearer, My God, to Thee," and "Show Ye Pity, Lord."

When he had experienced a particularly unrewarding day, Daniel Drew was in the habit of climbing under the covers of his bed and relieving himself of his spiritual burdens in solitary prayer. When his affairs went particularly well, he would demonstrate his gratitude (or, more likely, relieve his conscience) by contributing to the erection of a religious edifice.

The president of the Philadelphia and Reading Railroad, George F. Baer, made his unforgettable contribution to the cause of religion in the United States when in the midst of a bitter strike he declared, "The rights and interests of the laboring man will be protected and cared for by the Christian men to whom God has given control of the property rights of the country."

John D. Rockefeller, who never felt himself on distant terms with his God, once explained to a Sunday School class that "The growth of a large business is merely the survival of the fittest. . . . This is not an evil tendency in business. It is merely the working-out of a law of nature and a law of God."

The Robber Barons were of such dogged and gloomy piety that one searches almost vainly for some saving irreverence or humor. Not entirely in vain, however, and for this we are in the debt of that old atheist Andrew Carnegie, whose poor but radical parents brought him not up in the fear of the Lord. The story has been told that when an early partner of Carnegie's, a true Christian named E. M. Ferguson, arrived at their office on a Monday morning, Carnegie innocently inquired, "Well,

Fergy, how was your friend Jesus Christ yesterday?" Ferguson quit the partnership.

The classic description of the mutual dependence of Protestant Christianity and the capitalist economy was formulated by the great German sociologist Max Weber in *The Protestant Ethic* and further explored by R. H. Tawney in *Religion and the Rise of Capitalism*. The main point of these two books is that the rise of private capitalism in the form that is familiar to us was encouraged by the metaphysical notions that triumphed in northern Europe with the Protestant Reformation. In point of theology, the central doctrine was that of Predestination, which, according to the illumination granted John Calvin, meant that at the moment of Creation God decided upon the future fate of all the souls who were to pass this way, determining before their birth whether they would be counted among the Elect or the Damned. A man cannot change his preordained fate, but he *can* test the Almighty's inscrutable purpose by applying himself wholeheartedly to his business. Success is a plain indication that God has smiled upon one; failure is equally plain evidence that one has been marked for damnation. As Tawney put it caustically, "A society which reverences the attainment of riches as the supreme felicity will naturally be disposed to regard the poor as damned in the next world, if only to justify itself for making their life a hell in this."

Although the Weber-Tawney propositions have been challenged forcefully, most recently by Lewis Mumford, who, in *The Myth of the Machine*, has pointed out that the origins of the capitalist spirit can be found in medieval times well before the Reformation, it is surely still true that the constellation of the traditional Protestant virtues — thrift, sexual puritanism, punctuality, and diligence in one's calling — are more congenial to an industrial society than is the remission of sin that is offered by Catholic doctrine. It is also true that the Robber Barons were Protestant Christians who had no reason to quarrel with the proposition that great worldly success is a sure sign of the Lord's benevolent intentions. When Rockefeller declared that God gave him his money or George Baer asserted the divine right of Christian gentlemen to make their livings swindling other Christian gentlemen, they were not necessarily being pious hypocrites. Even worse, they probably believed what they were saying.

The Protestant Ethic, so far as it applies to success in one's occupation is also still with us. During the course of an interview with Wallace Johnson, one of the founders of the Holiday Inns, Charles Sopkin had the good fortune to be offered the text of a prayer that Mr. Johnson declared he used to pray in 1948. The prayer went:

"O Lord, make us one of the greatest leaders of the nation in the building of men and homes, and help the city officials of Memphis to understand that this is our goal, so they will help us instead of hinder us. Make me, O Lord, one of the leading Baptists and teach me how to win souls. O Lord, help me to be one of the biggest businessmen in the United States, and if it be Thy will, let me be a vice-president of the National Home Builders' Association.

"God, please, oh, please let us build two thousand units this year, and if it be in accordance with Thy divine purpose, let us accumulate two hundred and fifty thousand dollars in cash during that time. O Lord, help us to build a good house cheaper than anyone else in the United States. Help us to get lumber, or sawmills, or whatever else we need. May we be able to house the Negro citizens of our community as they have never been housed before. And God, please, oh, please help us to make connection with the right kind of banks, that understand that mortgages on Negro property are as safe an investment as any other kind, so that we can go on and on and on. Amen."

Except for his refreshing directness, Mr. Johnson is not alone among successful Christian businessmen in assuming that the Lord God Jehovah watches with a warm and friendly eye over his dealings with city officials, sawmills, Negro citizens, and banks. Sopkin reported a similar, though somewhat more sophisticated response from Philip J. Sagona, owner of Lancôme Perfumes (U.S.A.), who told him: "I am sure that I am not unlike other executives in that the first thing I do when I get to my desk in the morning is to say a prayer. I say a prayer that everything I do and all the decisions that I make will be correct for this day. I don't think that is being sacrilegious at all. All I am asking is that He guide me to make the right decisions. When one goes into battle he says a prayer asking that he come out alive. This is the same thing. I am going to battle."

Texas millionaires appear to be on particularly cordial terms with their God and his representatives on this earth. Howard Butt, Jr., a Corpus Christi millionaire and the executive vice-president of a chain of supermarkets, has substituted in the pulpit for the Reverend Doctor Billy Graham himself. Toddy Lee Wynne of Dallas sold his American Liberty Oil Company in 1957 for a net profit of $20 million; of this, he gave the Texas Presbyterian Foundation a $2 million tithe. Wynne also donated Wynne Hall to the Presbyterian Theological Seminary in Austin, and a chapel to the First Presbyterian Church in Dallas. The spirit that lies behind these donations was put into words by Michel Halbouty of Houston, who once said, "If I made a *billion* dollars, I wouldn't quit work. . . . Whatever the good Lord has done for me, I figure I should try to do something in return."

The sentiment is beyond exception, except perhaps to observers soured by too much philosophy, who find something degrading or even blasphemous in the notion that the Creator amuses himself by causing large amounts of money to descend on one man while he visits poverty and privation upon his brother. And it is also true that not all of our preachers have made a profession of preaching the pious duty of becoming rich.

As the late Ernest Henderson, founder of the Sheraton chain of hotels, wrote several years ago, "I certainly wish our churches and other uplift institutions would raise a great outcry against the wickedness of earning less than one's maximum capacity. Exhortations to avoid the evils of riches . . . constitute a dangerous poison coursing in our national veins."

There, in our own time, speaks the pure and undiluted voice of the Protestant Ethic.

God has need of rich Christians and He makes them, and He assigns particular duties to them.

— *The Congregationalist*, 1869

The rich man's view of God's intentions has not changed appreciably during the last hundred years, although the level of personal piety does not appear to be quite as elevated now as it was during the high days of the Great Barbecue. The Great Big New Rich are not particularly distinguished by their devoutness; at the same time there is no unbeliever as outspoken as Carnegie among them.

Two of the Great Big New Rich who are conspicuous for their churchmanship are both from Texas. In the late 1950's, H. L. Hunt, who had previously been noted for his skill at the poker table, brought his second wife and four children to the First Baptist Church of Dallas (the largest Baptist church in the world), where they were baptized en masse by the Reverend Doctor Wallie Amos Criswell, who is known for the hardness of his shell even in the heartland of the hard-shell Baptist.

R. E. (Bob) Smith was led to the First Methodist Church of Houston by his wife and children. In his characteristic way, he has since played an enthusiastic part in the affairs of that church. In commenting on his dedicated Methodism, a friend of Smith's once said, "Bob could never have been a Roman Catholic. He couldn't be Pope."

W. Clement Stone is a trustee of the First Presbyterian Church of Evanston, and a director both of the McCormick Theological Seminary (Chicago) and of Religious Heritage of America, Inc., an organization with its headquarters in Washington, D.C. Religious Heritage of America, Inc., named him as Layman·of the Year in 1962.

Of the others, most do not reveal their religious affiliations in their public biographies. Ahmanson was Presbyterian, Mecom is Episcopalian, and Joseph Kennedy is Catholic. Mark Taper has been active in Jewish causes. That is about the extent of the known religious commitments of the Great Big New Rich.

> We are experiencing the collapse of the economic and political pillars of the ideology which has dominated Western thought for several hundred years.
>
> — *David T. Bazelon*

A final word remains to be said about the real religion of the rich.

The growth of the business phenomenon that John Kenneth Galbraith identified (in *The New Industrial State*) as the Technostructure is at the center of a movement that is very close to a theological crisis. "In the past," Galbraith wrote, "leadership in business organization was identified with the entrepreneur — the individual who united ownership or control of capital with a capacity for organizing the other factors of production and, in most contexts, with a further capacity for innovation. With the rise of the modern corporation, the emergence of the organization required by modern technology and planning and the divorce of the owner of the capital from control of the enterprise, the entrepreneur no longer exists as an individual person in the mature business enterprise. . . . There is no name for all who participate in group decision-making or the organization which they form. I propose to call this organization the Technostructure."

The prosperity of the Great Big New Rich — who are, to a man, entrepreneurs in the pre-Technostructure sense — does not refute Galbraith's main argument. Some of them, in fact, have accommodated themselves without strain to the changing order. Charles B. Thornton and James J. Ling, for example, are chief executive officers of the giant corporations that each has been personally instrumental in organizing. Thornton and Ling are among our most formidable entrepreneurs, and yet their dominant style is that of the management team of the Techno-structure.

When I wrote to the insurance man John D. MacArthur — a maverick entrepreneur by any definition — I received in return a pleasant and courteous letter in which MacArthur said modestly, "A number of newspapers and magazines have billed me as being a very rich man. Admittedly I own several insurance companies that I could sell and be rich. However, I have no intention of liquidating my assets or changing my status. As of now I am an employee of a company I happen to own."

The point here is not that our corporate styles are changing to the extent that the owner willingly becomes an employee of the corporation he has founded, but that this change in style has been accompanied by a crisis in thinking that is much more truly theological than it is economic. There is probably no better example of the doctrinal nature of this crisis than the reception of *The New Industrial State* by the guardians of our faith and morals. Although its interest to the general reader raised the book to the top of the best-seller list for a number of weeks, it occasioned among some true believers a scandal approximately equal to that precipitated by Martin Luther when he nailed his ninety-five theses to the door of the Wittenberg church and went on to marry a nun.

Vital Statistics

Fortune, Time, the *Wall Street Journal,* and *Nation's Business,* each in its own way, undertook to disparage Galbraith's scholarship, wit, or good faith. The shrillest reaction came from *Nation's Business,* which commissioned Al Capp, the cartoonist of "Li'l Abner," to destroy Galbraith with one mighty round-house swing. Capp portrayed the author both in text and cartoon not merely as a superannuated flower-child, the spiritual peer of Louis Abolafia (whom he identified as a hippie-nudist candidate for the Presidency), but also as a dangerous heretic whose views could lead the faithful into the wickedest of sins. After quoting Edna St. Vincent Millay on burning candles at both ends, Capp wound up pungently but obscurely with, "Galbraith says it better of course, and Abolafia says it even better than Galbraith. But it is the sort of thinking that made the Insull empire, Farouk, and Billie Sol Estes the household words they are today." (The editors at *Nation's Business* offered at a nominal price reprints in bulk quantities, apparently to be distributed as secular St. Christopher's medals.)

Like most talented heretics, Galbraith is less of an innovator than a gifted enunciator of ideas that have been percolating in many other heads. The central part of his heresy lies in his arguments that the market is really not free, that many great bureaucratic corporations are in league with both their competitors and the government to ensure their common survival, and that all men are not moved primarily by the profit motive. He further compounds his error and exacerbates his sin by suggesting that there are occasions when a regard for the quality of our lives is more important than a regard for the gross national product.

Of these heresies, the most purely theological one and the one that has most seriously upset the faithful, concerns the profit motive, and rightly so, for belief in the profit motive, like belief in original sin, is a belief in something that cannot be demonstrated. If we choose to believe in the primacy of the profit motive, we help to preserve many things that are unpleasant and sometimes disgusting; if we deny its universality we open up other alternatives. There is really nothing new in this proposition except the proof that it is still considered a dangerous doctrine.

To put the matter in another way, in the business community as a whole and among entrepreneurs in particular, the central religious myth is not that of the crucifixion and resurrection of Jesus Christ but of the lonely passion and eventual triumph of the Horatio Alger hero. It is not easy for the intellectually sophisticated to understand how the symbol of the young Horatian hero can compete against the other great symbols of our civilization for the devotion of men of demonstrated intelligence and capability. As W. Lloyd Warner explained this phenomenon in a sympathetic study of business leaders, "Each myth has its simple value that even children can understand. Horatio Alger, often mentioned by the business leaders as an important influence in their lives, embodies this myth of man's triumph and his progress from rags to riches." That this is surely the case, I discovered when two of the Great Big New Rich spontaneously raised in conversation the necessity of recalling today's youth to the true faith.

The central agency of the Horatian cult is the Horatio Alger Awards Committee of the American Schools and Colleges

Association, which, having become concerned "about the trend among young people towards the mind-poisoning belief that equal opportunity was a thing of the past," has for more than twenty years been giving annual awards to nine or ten Americans who have typified the traditional Horatian ideals. Dr. Norman Vincent Peale is, somewhat predictably, the national chairman; Colonel Henry Crown is a district chairman. Among those honored have been such professional receivers of awards as Herbert Hoover, Dwight Eisenhower, Eddie Rickenbacker, Alfred C. Fuller, the original Fuller Brush man, and John H. Johnson, the Negro publisher. The Great Big New Rich who have been beatified are Colonel Crown, John D. MacArthur, James J. Ling, Charles B. Thornton, and W. Clement Stone.

The most devout of all in the purity of his faith and the energy of his missionary efforts is W. Clement Stone.

FIVE

Gallery Two: Salesman

Regardless of who you are or what you have been, you can be
what you want to be.

— *W. Clement Stone*

My first impression of William Clement Stone was of a pudgy
man in shirt-sleeves — small features, an Adolph Menjou moustache, slicked-back hair — who was carrying a cardboard carton
from one office to another on the top floor of an undistinguished commercial building in a low-rent section of Chicago.

Our subsequent conversation confirmed my original impression
that Stone is in many ways the most unlikely of the Great Big
New Rich. He is not an oil man. He does not manipulate the
affairs of great corporations. He does not own great buildings.
He doesn't *look* like a rich man. He is, instead, the salesman
incarnate.

Stone is also an author, his best-known works being *The Success System That Never Fails*, *Success Through a Positive Mental Attitude* (with Napoleon Hill), and *The Other Side of the Mind* (with Norma Lee Browning). Furthermore, he is a publisher, owning Hawthorn Books,* a house whose list consists largely of inspirational works; he also edits and publishes a magazine called *Success Unlimited*.

When I asked him why the individual entrepreneur like himself seemed to be vanishing in favor of the company man, Stone assured me that there was still ample scope for the individual, provided he understood the immutable rules that regulate the path to success. A college degree, it quickly appeared, is not among the desiderata.

"The entrepreneur who is not college-educated has the jump," he assured me, in a firm, quiet, earnest voice, and lighted one of the cigars that appear to be his only dissipation. "Take myself, for instance. I worked eighteen hours a day, plus. The high-school kid will take a job — any job. He'll start at the bottom and work his way up, and perhaps he'll go from office boy to president. The college student who can get a salary of six, eight, or ten thousand a year is too proud to do menial tasks. It takes guts to keep going. You can't expect to start out with a home and a Lincoln."

It is not surprising that Stone himself exemplifies the virtues he preaches in his books, his record album (*The System That*

* Hawthorn Books' contribution to the political literature of 1968 was a 116-page, $1.50 paperback with the title *Where He Stands — The Life and Convictions of Spiro T. Agnew*. Clement Stone himself was an alternate delegate from Illinois to the Republican convention.

Never Fails), and in his daily contacts with other people, whether they be salesmen who stand in need of a shot of inspiration or visiting journalists. Stone is a true believer, and with good reason, for his steadfastness in the faith has made him one of the richest men in the United States.

Born in Chicago in 1902, the story of Stone's subsequent life has been Horatian in the purest ray serene. His father died when he was young. His mother became a seamstress. They lived with relatives. At the age of six Stone was selling newspapers in Chicago's tough South Side, an experience which first set him on the road to success. As he recalls the story, "Hoelle's Restaurant was near the corner where I tried to work, and it gave me an idea. It was a busy and prosperous place that presented a frightening aspect to a child of six. I was nervous, but I walked in hurriedly and made a lucky sale at the first table. Then diners at the second and third tables bought papers. When I started for the fourth, however, Mr. Hoelle pushed me out the front door.

"But I had sold three papers. So when Mr. Hoelle wasn't looking, I walked back in and called at the fourth table. Apparently the jovial customer liked my gumption; he paid for the paper and gave me an extra dime before Mr. Hoelle pushed me out once again. But I had already sold four papers and got a 'bonus' dime besides. I walked into the restaurant and started selling again. There was a lot of laughter. The customers were enjoying the show. One whispered loudly, 'Let him be,' as Mr. Hoelle came toward me. About five minutes later, I had sold all my papers."

In Stone's accounts of his life, the essentials of this story are

W. Clement Stone, leading apostle of the Horatio Alger gospel.

repeated again and again, for contained in it are the three keys to the Success System That Never Fails: inspiration to action, know-how, and activity knowledge. He is also firm in his belief that anything is possible for the person with PMA — a Positive Mental Attitude.

As in any well-conceived morality play, young Stone's life was not without its shadows. Although he would rise from bed to kneel beside his mother while she prayed for guidance, his feet were not always on the paths of righteousness. He kept bad company. He played hooky. He smoked cigarettes. Mrs. Stone enrolled her wayward son in the Spaulding Institute, a parochial boarding school at Nauvoo, Illinois, and there young Stone was saved. As he has put it, "Where can one develop *inspiration to action* to search for self-improvement better than in a religious school? And who has greater *know-how* and necessary *knowledge* to teach character than those who are devoting their entire lives to the church, striving to purify their own souls while trying to save the souls of others?"

Money makes money.

— *W. Clement Stone*

While Stone was at Nauvoo, his mother left the women's clothing store, where she had been in charge of designing, fitting, and sewing, in order to set herself up in business as a dressmaker. Stone continued to sell newspapers and added the *Saturday Evening Post* to his sources of income. While his mother moved to Detroit, pawning her diamonds to raise the

84

cash to buy into an insurance agency, young Stone stayed behind in Chicago in order to avoid leaving his high school.

In Detroit, Mrs. Stone sold no policies at all during her first day on the job. In desperation, she called for divine help. As Stone reports his mother's account of what happened, "That night I prayed for guidance. And the next morning I prayed for guidance. When I left home, I went to the largest bank in the city of Detroit. There I sold a policy to the cashier and got permission to sell in the bank during working hours. It seemed that within me there was a driving force that was so sincere that all obstacles were removed. That day I made forty-four sales."

Stone's own career as an insurance salesman followed much the same pattern: initial failure, dissatisfaction, redetermination, success. He also acquired much in the way of practical wisdom. *Do it now. Know when to quit. Don't look a prospect in the eye — he might shake his head. Play to win.*

In 1922, having already dropped out of school when he found he could make more money selling than his teachers could teaching, Stone set himself up in the insurance business under the name of the Combined Registry Company. He had a hundred dollars working capital and rented a desk for twenty-five dollars a month. His landlord persuaded him not to list his name on the building directory as "C. Stone," but instead to adopt the style "W. Clement Stone." He married his high-school sweetheart.

In the forty-five years since then, Stone has prospered mightily. He owns the Combined Insurance Company of America (Chicago), which in turn owns the Combined American Insurance Company (Dallas), the Hearthstone Insurance Company of Massachusetts (Boston), and the First National Casualty Company (Fond du Lac, Wisconsin). Although these companies were formed to sell accident and health insurance, Stone branched into life insurance in 1966. He operates not only in the United States but also in Canada, New Zealand, Australia, and the Caribbean.

His own estimate of his fortune is a third of a billion dollars.

> *Thought is the most tremendous force in the universe.*
> Think kind thoughts . . . you become kind.
> Think happy thoughts . . . you become happy.
> Think success . . . you become successful.
> Think good thoughts . . . you become good.
> Think evil thoughts . . . you become evil.
> Think sickness . . . you become sick.
> Think health . . . you become healthy.
>
> YOU BECOME WHAT YOU THINK!
>
> — W. Clement Stone

Stone is the salesman's Mary Baker Eddy. At times the parallel becomes striking and close. Stone tells the story of how he inspired a district sales manager struck down by a heart attack not only to live and to go on selling but to raise his sights to include an early retirement, a doubling of his annual volume of business, the accumulation of a million dollars, the inspiration of his salesmen and sales managers, and, most importantly, "to share with others the inspiration and wisdom he had gained from the study of the Bible and the Science of Success course." It hardly needs to be added that the objectives were triumphantly achieved.

The power that can be exerted by self-inspiration has for a long time been a mainstay not only of the marginal religious movements but also of the apostles of the businessman's creed, particularly of those who belong to the selling fraternity. In accounting for the sources of his own faith in the power of thought, Stone credits his mother, his teachers at Nauvoo, his study of Dr. Emil Coué's formulas for conscious autosuggestion ("Every day in every way I am getting better and better"), and the Horatio Alger books, fifty of which he discovered in an attic during a summer vacation and promptly read. (He particularly recommends *Robert Coverdale's Struggle*.) He is also an admirer of Peter Hurkos, the "telepathic detective," and Dr. Joseph B. Rhine, the parapsychologist of Duke University.

To the unbeliever, the practical application of the power of faith and self-inspiration often seems somewhat unworthy of the spiritual afflatus that has been invoked. Stone recounts with admiration the story of how a meeting of salesmen was inspired by the reading of the following letter from one of their brotherhood:

> Six weeks ago, my six-year-old daughter Pamela came to me and said, "Daddy, when are you going to win your Ruby? . . . When are you going to write 100 policies in a week? Daddy, I have been asking God every night to help you make your Ruby. I have been asking Him for many nights and, Daddy, I don't think He is helping you." A child's faith in God, a child's faith in her father — so innocent, so honest, so sincere. I answered my daughter after long thought and consideration, for I realized that she was confused as to why God hadn't helped. My answer was, "Pam, God is helping Daddy, but I don't think Daddy is helping God."

Happily for the cynic, Stone's anecdotes that testify to the powers of his success system are not always so elevated. On a more profane level, he recalls a lunch he once had with Napoleon Hill and Dr. Norman Vincent Peale, both eminent keepers of the flame. Hill told his companions a pleasant story of how his book, *Think and Grow Rich*, happened to get its title. Unhappy with the working title, *The Thirteen Steps to Riches*, Hill's publisher had served him with an ultimatum: If the author failed to come up with a better title within twenty-four hours, he would christen the book with his own favorite, *Use Your Noodle and Get the Boodle*. Horrified, Hill held a conference with his subconscious mind that evening. "You and I have gone a long way together," he said to his subconscious in a loud voice. "You've done a lot of things for me — and some things to me. But I've got to have a million-dollar title, and I've got to have it tonight. Do you understand that?"

At two o'clock, Hill jumped out of bed, a new title glowing in his mind. He wrote it down on his typewriter and then phoned his publisher, crying, "We've got it, a million-dollar sales title." The title was *Think and Grow Rich*, which, Stone assures us, has sold millions of copies and become a classic self-help book.

As Dr. Peale pointed out over the lunch table, the real lesson was that Hill's subconscious had given the publisher precisely what he wanted, *Think and Grow Rich* being Standard English for *Use Your Noodle and Get the Boodle*.

As Stone has remarked in another context, "Thought is the most tremendous force in the universe."

As the shrewd practical psychologist that he is, Clement Stone does not depend on the power of thought alone. He offers as another of his cardinal principles, *To motivate . . . romance*, and tells how he helped the members of one of the boys' clubs he sponsors to raise their grades in school by *romancing* the thrill, the joy, and the need of each school subject. In addition, he encouraged them to open and close their meetings with the following ritual:

President: "How is your PMA?"

Group: "Terrific!"

President: "How do you feel?"

Group: "I feel *healthy!* I feel *happy!* I feel *terrific!*"

When I asked Stone whether his principles of self-inspiration and romance could be applied successfully to solving such major social problems as depressions and the blight that is threatening to destroy our great cities, he replied promptly that they could. "Even in a depression," he told me, "you can follow the universal laws of cycles. Things level off and die except when new life is created." Reminding me of his general principle that the seeds of success can be plucked from the weed of adversity, he went on to say that many men first learned to discipline themselves during the Depression. Many of those who started at the bottom during the Depression, he assured me, are now millionaires. (He does not, incidentally, forecast another depression in the foreseeable future.)

Stone's thoughts in regard to the problems faced by the Negroes of the city ghettos are, in fact, not far from those suggested by some more sophisticated observers, although the emphasis and the language is somewhat different. He told me, "There can't be a fear that we can't pull through any emergencies. We'll be reaching through schools and industry and boys' clubs. We show how a poverty-stricken individual can

89

become wealthy. We're doing something about it. Chicago didn't have a long, hot summer [in 1967].

"It's imperative we teach character in the schools. In the South Side of Chicago these people are without hope — we give them hope. The big thing is to give them PMA and hope."

Stone is confident that his success formula can be extended to assure national prosperity, although his point-by-point prescription contains some grave practical difficulties. His first recommendation is that all raw materials must come from within the borders of the nation, which would seem to raise some obnoxious questions in key industries as well as tending to sour our commercial relations abroad. After going confidently through the virtues of domestic labor, domestic currency, a strong credit system, the preservation of private enterprise and property rights, and the avoidance of war by a strong defense, Stone winds up with a vision of utopia in which the "attitude of the people is positive and develops pride in personal achievement, which engenders the joy of work, and the desire to make their nation and the rest of the world a better place to live in."

I have the experience, knowledge, and know-how to motivate persons in all walks of life.

— W. Clement Stone

Clement Stone is a good citizen.

He is president of the Chicago Boys Club and belongs to the national executive committee of the Boys Clubs of America. He is a trustee of the Interlochen Arts Academy and National Music Camp. He was a founder and is board chairman of the

Stone-Brandel Center, a mental health institute. He is chairman of the American Foundation of Religion and Psychiatry. He is also chairman of the Foundation for Research on the Nature of Man. In addition, he has been active in the John Howard Association, a prison reform group, and Teen Challenge, which works with adolescents. He is a director of George Williams College, which trains social workers.*

"Money is power," he told me. "Like all power it can be used for good or evil. I'm unable to perform miracles like healing the blind, or to be a missionary in Africa, or to work in a leprosarium in Taegu — but I can be there. If it weren't for money, the blind man wouldn't see, and they wouldn't have a leprosarium in Taegu.

"The government can't teach character. We cure the teenage narcotic addict and alcoholic. We take a strong religious approach. With money, we can do godly deeds."

It is entirely too easy to be amused at the expense of Clement Stone with his Paul Whiteman face, his paunch, his jade ring and floppy hat, his brown-and-white shoes and his talent for scattering platitudes as if he were engaged on a holy mission. One is tempted to set his earnest insurance-salesman's glibness alongside Henry Crown's urbanity, D. K. Ludwig's practiced reticence, John Mecom's ruddy Texas warmth,

---

* Not long after he became acting president of the embattled San Francisco State College in November 1968, the semanticist S. I. Hayakawa announced that Stone had pledged $100,000 to be used to prepare unqualified young adults to prepare themselves for the college. Stone, who is a personal friend of Hayakawa's, also put his own West Coast press agent, Mike Teilmann, at Hayakawa's disposal. One of Teilmann's first assignments was to help Hayakawa distribute baby orchids flown to San Francisco as a gift from a right-wing student group at the University of Hawaii.

Howard Ahmanson's upper-class men's-club good manners, or Norton Simon's intellectualized ambivalence. By contrast, Stone seems almost suspiciously simple, if not outright simpleminded.

The truth is, of course, that he is as complex as any of the other men who rank him in terms of their personal fortunes. To put the matter bluntly, Stone did not amass $300 million by being a fool. He is in fact an extraordinarily interesting personality, for even though he often sounds like Benjamin Franklin at his worst, the articles of his belief define a typically American creed — the all-conquering power of optimism, the practicality of divine guidance, and the holiness of money.

SIX

The Catastrophe Theory of Wealth

The most significant thing about the American frontier is that it lies at the hither edge of free land.

— *Frederick Jackson Turner*

As a hundred historians have already pointed out, our national ego has always been closely bound up with the idea of the frontier and the wilderness beyond. Just as it was once true that the geographic frontier was the skirmish line from which restless, bold, and acquisitive men sallied out to pillage the rich continent, so it has also been true that the economic frontier has existed at the "hither edge" of free land. War, depression, and catastrophe generally have always served to accelerate the exploitation of both the geographic and economic wildernesses.

I resolved to do my best to be worthy of Mama and to help my country crush its enemies to the last ounce of my strength.

— *J. Paul Getty*, December 31, 1941

Patriotism is always profitable.

— *Haroldson Lafayette Hunt*

One should approach the war records of wealthy men without prejudice. The young man who has acquired a chestful of merit badges by shooting Filipino rebels or German bicycle mechanics or Japanese factory hands or Vietnamese rice farmers is not necessarily a more virtuous and admirable fellow than his brother who stays home.

Yet a clear difference of sensibility is evident between the young man who answers the trumpet call of what he believes to be patriotism and the young man who understands instinctively that war is a mug's game. It is not at all a simple opposition of bravery and cowardice, but a gift for putting first things first. To the ambitious young banker Joseph P. Kennedy, as to most of the Great Big New Rich, it does not appear to have been a difficult decision. The difference in sensibility was underscored by Kennedy's classmates of Harvard '12, one of whom, Ralph Lowell, has been quoted as saying, "They took pride in not being drafted, and they didn't appreciate a man not going into the war, as, for instance, in the case of Joe."

There are, of course, honorable veterans among the Great Big New Rich. Howard Ahmanson, the savings-and-loan king, served as a Navy lieutenant in 1943–45. Henry Crown was a colonel in the Corps of Engineers, serving in the Chicago area. Charles B. (Tex) Thornton, chairman of Litton Industries, was also a colonel, serving in the Air Force and winning the Distinguished Service Medal for his innovations in the business management practices of that branch. Ernest Henderson, the

94

late landlord of the Sheraton hotel chain, ferried trimotored Capronis from the factory in Turin to northern France while he was a junior officer in the Navy during World War I. James J. Ling, of Ling-Temco-Vought, was a Navy electrician's mate in the South Pacific, stringing wire under fire. J. Paul Getty, who made his first fortune during World War I, tried to join the Navy during the Second World War. He was passed around from office to office of the Navy Department — gingerly, for he was an acquaintance of men in high places — until he allowed Colonel Frank Knox to persuade him that he could contribute most to his country by putting the Spartan aircraft factory into successful production.

Unless I am much mistaken, there is not an infantryman or artilleryman or Marine or gunner's mate in the lot, nor, so far as I can find out, did any of the future Great Big New Rich suffer themselves to be drafted in either war. Those who did serve are surely honorable men, but men whose careers point up the proposition that the genius that leads to military glory is clearly different from the genius that leads to the great tycoon's office. For the group as a whole, the archetypical case is that of the insurance man John D. MacArthur, whose career as a Navy seaman in World War I came to an inglorious end when he was discharged as being "unsuited to naval discipline."

Most of the Great Big New Rich, unsuited to any discipline except their own, stayed home and made money.

For good or ill, calamities are unquestionably the supreme disruptors and transformers of social organizations and institutions.

— *Pitirim Sorokin*

The yea-sayers and flute players of history reassure us that selflessness, self-sacrifice, and nobility in the common cause flourish in times of disaster. We are, for instance, urged to believe that whenever a hand grenade rolls into a crowded dugout, the bravest soldier present will throw himself upon it to save his comrades from the explosion. This happens so rarely, however, that we honor the dead hero with the highest of our medals for gallantry. If we turn our ears from the flutes and bend them toward the harsh voices of the veterans, we learn that for each occurrence of this classic act of self-sacrifice there are a hundred other cases in which soldiers crush each other in a wild scramble for the exit, and the explosion takes the hindmost.

To take a catastrophe that is neutral to our main argument but revealing of the historic truth involved, let us consider for a moment the sequelae of the great disaster in Halifax, Nova Scotia, where in 1917 a munitions ship was rammed in the harbor, causing an explosion that killed 1800 people, injured 20,000 more and destroyed a good part of the city. There were heroism and sacrifice to be sure, but there was also an epidemic of ruthless selfishness. Plumbers refused to work more than their accustomed eight hours without their accustomed overtime pay; truckers charged exorbitant prices for their services; shopkeepers squeezed the last farthing out of their helpless customers. It was a scandal of the human spirit; yet there is nothing essentially different about the population of Halifax, no mass taint of the blood that caused its citizens to act so meanly. Instead they were only behaving as human beings always have, furtively snatching pennies from the dead eyes of their neighbors. Seen from this point of vantage, history is a dismal document.

The history of the making of large sums of money in the United States can most usefully be interpreted in terms of a theory of catastrophes. Whenever a war, flood, earthquake, depression or other natural or man-made catastrophe has upset the established order, keen-witted and money-hungry men have become rich. Some of this activity has amounted to nothing more substantial than petty profiteering on the order of the plumbers of Halifax or of the camorra of politicians who plundered San Francisco after the great earthquake of 1906. Catastrophes have, in fact, been the midwives to our greatest fortunes, and the Great Big New Rich are, in the phrase Stewart Holbrook used so happily of Jay Gould, men of disaster.

I felt like an undertaker in a plague.

— *Howard Ahmanson*

For the Great Big New Rich of the immediate past, the most fruitful catastrophes have been the two world wars and the Great Depression. The most certain mechanism by which men can survive while other men are going under is to bet on the side of the disaster. In a plague, corner the market in coffins; in an earthquake, invest in concrete; in a war, sell guns or oil; in a depression, sell short.

It is remarkable how many men who were to become rich heard a different drummer even while the great bull market of 1928 and 1929 was thundering toward its glorious climax. Joseph P. Kennedy has told the story of how, while having his

97

shoes shined, he found out that the bootblack had been calling the turn on the market. He promptly and correctly concluded that a bootblack's market was not a safe market for him. In a similar vein, Howard Ahmanson has told how in September 1929, warned by the rise of a stock in which he had no faith, he ordered his broker to sell everything except his shares in an insurance company which his father had owned. Having survived the crash in good order, he went on to specialize in insuring foreclosed properties, of which there were a great many at that time. At the age of twenty-five Norton Simon hedged so cannily that, when the crash came, he survived with $35,000. With $7000 of this money he bought a bankrupt orange-juice plant and was on his tortuous way to becoming the most formidable corporate operator in the country.

Among the bears who cleaned up by selling short after the Crash were Tom Bragg, Percy Rockefeller, William C. Danforth, Joseph Kennedy, and Bernard E. ("Sell 'em" Ben) Smith. (Smith acquired his nickname when he pushed his way through a panic-stricken crowd in a broker's office on Black Tuesday, shouting, "Sell 'em all! They're not worth anything." He is said to have made $10 million in a month of short operations.) The morality of selling short, which is to bet that the market will get worse and worse, has always made sensitive types uncomfortable; a congressional investigation of market practices in 1930 was spurred on by both a presidential and popular feeling that selling short was somehow not in the national interest, but in the end the investigation didn't amount to much.

All of the Great Big New Rich were neither so foresighted nor so lucky as Kennedy, Ahmanson, and Simon. Prominent among the victims was Charles Allen, Jr., now the richest man on Wall Street, who had in 1929 just scratched his way to his first million. He lost it all in the crash. Yet, the real point of the story is that he had recovered it all within a couple of years during which the Depression had hit rock bottom. Even more significant is the Internal Revenue Service's report that the number of citizens reporting incomes over a million actually increased between 1932 and 1933.

Modern warfare has been the express and select handmaiden of the oil rich. Getty made his first million during World War I. H. L. Hunt prospered so well during World War II that, by the time it was over, his personal holdings of oil reserves were greater than all the Axis countries combined. As we have seen, D. K. Ludwig, the tanker king, went into the war as a relatively small operator whose principal asset was a process for welding the plates of ships; he came out as the owner of the world's fifth largest tanker fleet. As the smoke cleared away, Sid Richardson, Clint Murchison, Glenn McCarthy, John Mecom, Bob Smith and others of the Texas wildcatters emerged as the new lords and princes of the land.

Whether short-sellers or wildcatters, many of the Great Big New Rich represented both in their personal characteristics and their methods of operation a familiar American type, the hard-skinned, arrogant, and tough-minded lone wolf who opted out of polite society and headed for the frontier. Let us return to the beginnings of these things.

. . . the Revolution was largely an uprising of a class of newly enriched individuals who itched for honors and offices.

—*H. L. Mencken*

The destruction of the patroons was brought about by the establishment of a new nation whose founders did away with the ancient institutions of entail and primogeniture, which by limiting inheritance to the oldest son had ensured that large estates would be held intact instead of being dissipated among many heirs. The name of van Rensselaer, as we have noted, loomed large among the Hudson River landgraves. Yet, even the van Rensselaer estate was soon to disappear entirely under the new dispensation. In 1839, when the 75-year-old Stephen van Rensselaer, the last of the great patroons, passed on to his Calvinistic reward, his estate was divided among his ten children. Fifty years later the ancestral acres were in other hands.

The first of the Great Big New Rich to emerge from the ruins of the colonial system was Israel Thorndike. Beginning life as a cooper's apprentice, Thorndike was nineteen when independence was proclaimed. Seeing better things ahead for himself than slogging through the mud with a musket on his back, Thorndike turned away from Brooklyn Heights and the banks of the Brandywine and, instead, signed on a privateer in the Salem-Beverly fleet. Life aboard a privateer was a hard and hazardous one, but, unlike the hard and hazardous life of the soldier ashore, it promised rich profits. Thorndike emerged from the Revolution not only as the citizen of a newly independent country but also as a very rich young man. He became a very rich old man, the first American millionaire, by putting his privateering fortune to work in the fisheries, in foreign trade, in real estate and in manufacturing enterprises. He was looked on as an oracle in business matters, and apparently with good reason, for when he died at the age of seventy-five, Thorndike left legacies amounting to $1,800,000. It was said to be the greatest fortune that had ever been amassed in New England.

There were other great fortunes made from privateering, an activity that is hard to distinguish from piracy except that it has been formally legitimatized. With the war over, other rich privateers did as Thorndike did and turned to merchant shipping and trade, or, as a new technology emerged, invested their loot in factories, canals, and turnpikes. The scope of their enterprises was truly impressive — witness Colonel Thomas Handasyd Perkins, who turned down an invitation to become Washington's Secretary of the Navy with the explanation that since his own fleet was larger than that of the United States, it would require his undivided attention. The great landed estates disappeared in this new and unfriendly world, and the seat of power moved irreversibly from the manor house to the countinghouse.

> Property is not theft, but a good deal of theft becomes property.
>
> — R. H. Tawney

The catastrophes which have enriched men who have the golden touch are not by any means limited to wars and revolutions, but include those catastrophes generated by the economic system itself. As we have seen, the Great Depression of the 1930's created its millionaires, as has every panic and business collapse in our history. Among the first of the notable fortunes that grew even larger thanks to a general disaster was that of John Jacob Astor.

Astor, the German butcher's son who had landed in the promised land with, as the legend goes, one good suit, seven flutes, and five pounds sterling, was a pincher of pennies, a paranoid, and a man with a fine indifference to laws that threatened his profits. (We know the profits were outrageous, for in 1831 Astor's son and partner wrote the Secretary of War that the American Fur Company enjoyed a return of a half-million dollars annually on an investment of a million.)

The Panic of 1837 was precipitated when the New York banks, feeling nervous about the state of the economy, declined to pay out any deposits except in the form of those curious notes called shinplasters that they were privileged to manufacture. In May of that year, eight hundred banks throughout the country suspended payment and in some cases stationed in their lobbies goons with orders to shoot if the frustrated depositors became ugly. Gresham's Law took force, legitimate currency disappeared from circulation, and in its place were circulated only shinplasters and counterfeits of shinplasters. Businesses went bankrupt, one-third of the working men in New York lost their jobs, and the almshouses overflowed with the newly destitute who were fortunate enough to enjoy their sorry comforts.

Gustavus Myers has proposed as the "centripetal principle" of all business panics that they are the means by which the very rich make themselves even richer. The working man is laid off, the modest merchant or manufacturer loses his business, his home, and his station in life, but the very rich man only adds to his richness. So it was with Astor. As the holders of financial paper became desperate, Astor bought it up at his price. When mortgages were put on the market, Astor bought them at less than their face value. If his 7 percent interest was late, Astor foreclosed. The general ruin and despair thus served as the fertilizer for the Astor fortune, which during the next ten years grew to $20 million, making this obnoxious citizen by far the richest man in the country.

Astor was not the only ambitious young immigrant from Germany who heard the sirens singing above the general lamentations. August Belmont (née Schoenberg), who had been working without salary for the Rothschilds in Frankfurt-am-Main, was on his way to Havana on company business when he heard the good news of the business collapse. Finishing his assignment as quickly as he could, he sped to New York, where in a modest office on Wall Street he began his rise to becoming one of the country's most powerful bankers. It was not an accident that he planted the seeds of his fortune while other men were being buried in the wreckage of their careers.

> But besides the young men who marched to Bull Run, there were other young men of '61 whose instinctive sense of history proved to be unerring. Loving not the paths of glory they slunk away quickly, bent upon business of their own.
>
> *— Matthew Josephson*
>
> It is only greenhorns who enlist. You can learn nothing in the army.
>
> *— Judge Thomas Mellon, 1861*

The Civil War was the greatest disaster the United States has endured, and will remain so unless we manage to bring upon ourselves a racial or nuclear holocaust. Killing a half-million young men out of a total population of 35 million, it far exceeded even in absolute body-for-body terms the American dead in either of the two world wars. As an event in economic history, it destroyed forever the traditional Southern economy. In terms of the catastrophe theory of wealth, it provided an unparalleled opportunity for the making of money. The Great Big New Rich of the Civil War became the classic new rich in the American style. They introduced not only a totally new scale of great wealth but a style of life to go with it.

Wars — even the insane crusade in which we are now engaged — have always been feasts of fraud and corruption and it should surprise not even a high-school teacher of civics that the great American fortunes were founded in times of danger and confusion and nourished by the blood of young men. The corruptions of the Civil War became notable both because of their scale and because they became public scandals. In recent wars we have learned to become not less greedy but more circumspect.

In those more innocent days, it soon became evident that patriotism was the kept mistress of corruption. Christian gentlemen, both North and South, paid off their mortgages and provided for their children's education by furnishing the troops in the field with uniforms that fell to pieces in the rain, with boots that gave out under a day's march, with meat from diseased and dying cattle and hogs, with cavalry mounts that had been doctored by every means available in the armamentarium of the horse trader, and with rifles which either didn't fire at all or which blew up in their user's faces. As John Chamberlain, who is no enemy of laissez faire, has observed, the "incredible thing" was that even the luxury trades expanded during the Civil War.

The elder Vanderbilt bought up inland steamers stricken with dry rot and sold or chartered them to the Union as ocean-going transports. (Of Vanderbilt's *Niagara*, it was testified in Congress that "in perfectly smooth weather, with a calm sea, the planks were ripped out of her, and exhibited to the gaze of the indignant soldiers on board, showing that her timbers were rotten.") Jim Fisk, a fellow of such overwhelming obnoxiousness that his partners once paid him $60,000 just to leave them alone, sold bad blankets to the Army. Jay Cooke and Pierpont Morgan handled vast government loans and were made rich by the "drippings of the Treasury." Morgan, furthermore, was a party to the sale of five thousand defective Hall's carbines to Frémont's Western Army, a stroke of business which was accomplished by buying condemned carbines from the quartermaster in Washington for $3.50 apiece and delivering them to Frémont in St. Louis at a price just under $22. (This case has been argued vigorously both by muckrakers and by apologists; the upshot seems to be that Morgan indeed did make a fast buck, and the only question that still can be argued is whether his sin was venial or mortal.)

In the West, the demand for gold and silver to finance the war produced the first crop of millionaires from Nevada's Comstock Lode. Philip Armour butchered hogs and cattle wholesale in Chicago as Peter Widener did in Philadelphia. (Just as Grant began to fight his way through the Wilderness, Armour sold pork short. Within three months he had made a million dollars.) Four million pounds of Du Pont gunpowder went up in smoke. A great river of wheat flowed to the armies from the fields of the Middle West. As Judge Thomas Mellon's son reported from Wisconsin, "They continue growing richer and don't care when the war closes." The same song was sung by the owners of the New England woolen mills, which paid dividends of 10 to 40 percent during the war.

By 1865, the United States counted more millionaires than it had ever seen before, and the Great Barbecue had begun.

> No longer were the titans of industry portrayed as lean, grasping men clutching at the bowels of the poor. They were the colossi of the earth, supermen in a superman's world, titanic Americans appropriate to a titanic America; and if villains, titanic villains.
>
> — *Alfred Kazin*

In any rational society, one would expect to find that men who had grown prosperous while other men were dying in the hundreds of thousands, who had bought exceedingly cheap and sold very dear, who had given the word *shoddy* a permanent place in our language, who had scamped the workmanship of the guns they manufactured, and who had turned their eyes away from the tubercular and anthrax-smitten cattle in their stockyards, would be condemned after the debauch was over to a moral leprosarium and shunned by all virtuous citizens as if they were cannibals or grave robbers. Quite the opposite turned out to be the case. In Josephson's expressive words, in the twenty years after the Civil War the Great Big New Rich "literally sunned themselves in the affection of popular opinion."

Whether we follow Parrington in calling this period the

Great Barbecue or Mark Twain in calling it the Gilded Age, it was a time whose characteristic style was naïve and unbridled vulgarity. Ostentation, as Lucius Beebe once observed, arrived with the Civil War. A river of champagne flooded the land, cigarettes were wrapped in hundred-dollar bills, and dogs wore diamond-studded collars. Social life became public, and the ballrooms of the great hotels were turned into imitations of Versailles or, more in the American grain, into replicas of the interiors of gold mines. (At one of these affairs, waiters dressed in miners' clothes scurried from the kitchen to a dining hall where picks and shovels had been hung on the walls.)

Devout worshipers of the profit motive as well as more rational economists and historians have argued on behalf of the Robber Barons that despite the crudeness of their methods and the glorious vulgarity of their private lives, they were in fact great public benefactors, for they not only girdled the continent with railroads but were also responsible for developing such other necessities of our industrial civilization as the coal, steel, and oil industries.

The sufficient answer to this argument is that every one of these great endeavors could have been accomplished with immensely more benefit and immensely less harm if there had been more concern for public good rather than private gain. Not only did the recklessness and greed of the great entrepreneurs lay waste to vast areas of the continent, but a more subtle and more pernicious destruction was accomplished by the corruption of officials both public and private, which notoriously and ironically reached its height during the administration of the great generalissimo of the North. In public, huge grants of money and land were made to private corporations; in private, smaller but not contemptible sums of money passed from the officials of the corporations to the officials of the generous governments. The continent was raped while capitol buildings were turned into bawdyhouses of the spirit. Small investors were bankrupted by the thousands, and the robbing of widows and orphans became not merely a sentimental figure of speech.

Nor were the methods of the Robber Barons justified by the quality of their products. In time of war, as we have noted, the unfortunate infantryman risked grievous injury from his own rifle or mortal disease from his food; in time of peace, the unfortunate traveler was too often turned into a bagful of broken bones and spilled guts somewhere between his home and his destination. The most notorious of these passenger-killing roads was the Erie of Drew, Vanderbilt, Fisk, and Gould. The iron rails that had been laid down in place of steel were worn and broken; the roadbed was porous; and the rolling stock regularly became rolling coffins. A New York diarist has left us a splendidly indignant passage written in 1868: "Another accident on the Erie. Scores of people smashed, burned to death, or maimed for life. We shall never travel safely until some pious, wealthy and much beloved railroad director has been hanged for murder, with a conductor on each side of him. Drew or Vanderbilt would do to begin with."

It should not surprise us that fortunes that had been bred in catastrophe were now breeding catastrophes of their own.

From the personal standpoint of America's richest families the World War was the single most constructive event since the Civil War.

— *Ferdinand Lundberg*

The Catastrophe Theory of Wealth

Although the Spanish-American War produced its profits and its scandals (notably "embalmed beef"), it was by any standards a piddling affair, killing only 385 Americans. The Panic of 1907, too, was only a third-rate disaster, but still there were those who managed to turn it to profit. Eminent among them was Jesse L. Livermore of Boston, who sold short and emerged from the carnage with $3 million and the epithet of the "Boy Plunger." It was not until the great European war broke out in 1914 that American industrialists took up their arms in earnest again. (I speak, of course, metaphorically.)

The contrast between the First World War and the Civil War is striking. The Civil War was, above all, the war of the Great Big New Rich. The World War enriched many Americans, but these were by and large those who held stock in well-established corporations: Bethlehem Steel, Du Pont, and Standard Oil, for example. Men became rich, but few men who were not already rich became very rich. Lundberg believes that the only man to come out of the World War with a new and noteworthy fortune was the Morgan executive Floyd B. Odlum.

Among the corporations that did particularly well out of the war were the steel companies (U. S. Steel, Bethlehem, Midvale, and Carnegie), the arms manufacturers (Remington, Winchester, and Savage), Du Pont, the Electric Boat Company (submarines), and the infant aircraft industry (Packard and other firms that were primarily automobile manufacturers). Some of their profits are matters of record. While the young men of France, England, and Germany were destroying themselves in the trenches, the annual profits of Republic Iron and Steel rose from a prewar average of $2.5 million to $148 million in 1916. In the same two years, Anaconda Copper profits went from $12 million to $58 million and International Nickel from $4 million to $74 million.

The firm of E. I. Du Pont de Nemours & Company, which had been founded during the War of 1812 (during which it tripled its gross sales in a single year), was one of the great beneficiaries of World War I. Du Pont manufactured 40 percent of all the explosives used by the Allies, and, as Du Pont officials testified at a postwar Senate hearing, between 1915 and 1918 the company paid dividends equal to 458 percent of the original par value of the stock. During the same years, Bethlehem Steel sold Great Britain about $300 million in guns and shells as well as twenty submarines, making itself by the war's end not only larger than Krupp but larger in shipping tonnage under construction than all the German yards combined.

Although the profits of the First World War tended to enrich corporations before enriching individuals, and although few Great Big New Rich emerged in 1919, the war years were not unkind to the making of personal fortunes in the United States. The Internal Revenue Service reported that the 7,509 millionaires of 1914 had blossomed into 17,805 by 1916, while 174 multimillionaires had been transmogrified into 582. (We are speaking here of fortunes rather than of annual incomes.) Figures are lacking for the rest of the war years, but an economic historian of the period assures us that the 1916 fortunes were multiplied by two or three times before the war was over.

The bargain days of 1932 and 1933 were not exploited to the full.

— J. Paul Getty

The Catastrophe Theory of Wealth

If there is any substance to the catastrophe theory of new wealth, we should expect that the next growing season for the new rich would be the Great Depression of the 1930's. In fact, this was the case.

The accepted version of the Great Depression is the version of the great majority to whom it was a period of personal disaster. As Frederick Lewis Allen, whose historical works faithfully reflect the conventional wisdom, put it, the Depression "marked millions of people — inwardly — for the rest of their lives. . . . Here were failure and defeat and want visiting the energetic along with the feckless, the able along with the unable, the virtuous along with the irresponsible." And, to a point, he is right. I have often had occasion to remark how different the *Weltansicht* of my own generation is from that of the generation that came before ours. We who emerged from college during World War II are insane optimists whose lives are guided by the conviction that tomorrow, or next month, or next year will be better. The generation of the 1930's, quite contrariwise, are insane pessimists, convinced that the woods around them are filled with gins and snares and mantraps. I am thinking mainly of our economic behavior, but that inward marking of which Allen wrote makes itself known in other ways as well.

The conventional view of the Great Depression as an unmitigated tragedy and disaster to the entire population, however, does violence to some hard and little-known facts. Between 1930 and 1933, while the number of taxpayers who made more than $5000 a year fell precipitously from 810,000 to 330,000, the number of millionaires was increasing; in 1932, only

20 Americans reported incomes of over a million, but by the next year the figure had more than doubled to 46. The road back to the halcyon days of the 1920's was a long one, but clearly some men, shrewder or clearer-eyed than the rest, had found ways to prosper. As John Chamberlain, the uncritical historian of the American business genius, has put it, "What the fog of conventional history tends to conceal is that the thirties were also a period in which vast new industrial enterprises were spawning."

Whenever a rich man reports that he has been wiped out, it is well to inquire more closely into his precise circumstances. A typical case in point is furnished by the wealthy inventor J. J. Mascuch, an extraordinary fellow not without a certain dour charm, who described the collapse of his fortunes to an interviewer. "In 1929, when I was worth about six or seven million dollars, the market collapsed and I was almost wiped out," Mascuch said. Then he went on, "Well, I wasn't wiped out completely. I just wasn't as rich. I probably wound up with a million bucks or so."

Nor were the rich universally obliged to place their butlers on the relief rolls and send their children onto the streets to peddle matches. Tony Cromwell's allowance was cut from $36,000 to $20,000 a year, but for many life went on much as it always had. In 1934, Walter P. Chrysler contributed to the gaiety of the nation by bestowing on his son a custom-built $20,000 car equipped with a bar, a picnic set, and a $3000 leopard robe. Earlier, in 1930, young John F. Kennedy had written home from school, "Please send me the Litary [sic] Digest because I did not know about the Market Slump until a long time after, or a paper."

The Catastrophe Theory of Wealth

There is no particular personal reason why the thirteen-year-old Jack Kennedy should have been aware of the Depression, for his father was the archetype of those men who managed to advance their fortunes while around them arose the dismal chorus of the ruined.

At his leisure, Kennedy plucked bargains from the wreckage.
— *Richard J. Whalen*

Although Joseph P. Kennedy's biographer is referring to his subject's activities during the collapse of the Florida land boom in 1926 under the dual assaults of mortgage foreclosures and hurricanes, the sense of the quotation suggests itself at a number of occasions in Kennedy's life. The founding father of the Kennedy clan is clearly one of the most remarkable men of our times, although hardly a lovable one. Whalen has described him as hard, unforgiving, and arrogant, and the judgment is borne out by his financial career. The story of the Harvard-educated Boston Irishman exhibits in pure form many of the classic features of the common experiences of the Great Big New Rich.

Having both a gift for handling money and a dedication to its accumulation, Kennedy at 25 became the youngest bank president in Massachusetts and is reported to have taken a solemn oath to make himself a millionaire by 35. In 1917, when the United States entered the European war, his course was suddenly diverted in a way that is reminiscent of the earlier generations of the rich. While his Harvard classmates went to the war, Joe Kennedy was persuaded by Guy Currier, a lobbyist for Bethlehem Steel, to become assistant to the general manager of Bethlehem's Fore River Shipyard. Although, as we have already noted, Bethlehem did exceedingly well during the war, Kennedy was on a salary of $10,000 and his profits came largely in the form of what he learned. Among the other lessons of the war, the chiefest, apparently, was that a young man interested in making large sums of money should engage himself at a place where money is handled. The matter has never been put more concisely than by that folk hero Willie Sutton, who, when asked why he robbed banks, replied, "Because that's where the money is." Instead of returning to his bank, however, Kennedy went into another business where the money was and became manager of the stock department of the Boston office of the brokerage firm of Hayden, Scott and Co.

Until Franklin Roosevelt appointed him chairman of the Securities & Exchange Commission and then Ambassador to the Court of St. James, Kennedy's career was characterized by a succession of those brilliant strokes of the dedicated moneyman that inspire not only our admiration but also our fervent thanks that we are not as they. The grave robber may be loved by his wife and children but he does not have a large circle of admirers, and financial grave-robbing was the field in which Kennedy's particular genius lay.

Richard Whalen tells an anecdote that is revealing not only of Kennedy's business ethics but of the business ethics of the generality of the Great Big New Rich. In 1924, after he had acquired a reputation as a formidable operator in the stock market, Kennedy was visited by a midnight caller who begged him to rescue the Yellow Cab Company, whose stock had slid

Joseph P. Kennedy when he was U. S. Ambassador
to Britain. WIDE WORLD PHOTOS.

in a month from 85 to 50 and threatened to go lower. The diagnosis was that Yellow Cab had been singled out by a pack of bears whose wicked machinations were driving the stock down to their own great profit. Hearing the stern call of money, Kennedy tore himself away from his wife, who was imminently expecting the birth of her sixth child, and set himself up in the Waldorf in New York with a battery of telephones and a ticker. From this headquarters, he covered the country with orders to buy and sell, and after an arduous campaign established the price of Yellow Cab firmly above 50. Kennedy went back to Boston a month after his first daughter, Patricia, had been born.

But this is not the point of the story. Months later, Yellow's stock fell again, and John D. Hertz, the founder of the company, was heard to threaten to punch Kennedy in the nose the next time he saw him. Whether rightly or not, Hertz was convinced that the most recent break in his stock had been engineered by Kennedy himself. As Whalen puts it antiseptically, "To those who knew Kennedy, it would not have been unthinkable for him to switch sides and take advantage of Yellow Cab's weakness. His mind always detected the remote gains in immediate tasks."

Just before the crash, Kennedy removed himself from the movie business and retired to Palm Beach for the winter with some $5 million in profits. After having had his shoes polished by the ominous bootblack, he sold all his stocks and put the cash proceeds in a safe place. When the big break came, Kennedy, together with a handful of other farsighted men, was prepared to cope with the circumstances. Unlike such men as Bill Danforth and Ben Smith, who tended to hunt in packs,

Kennedy had the reputation of being a loner, not often found in the war councils of the other shrewd and canny operators whose fortunes rose in exact proportion to the extent of the general disaster. Of one occasion when he did take part in a bear-raid, the story is told that he was approached in the Harvard Club by Senator Burton K. Wheeler, who remarked that Anaconda Copper looked like a bargain at twenty dollars a share. Kennedy answered, "If I find you buying Anaconda, I'll kick you in the pants. It will go to five dollars before we're through with it." It did. Kennedy's profits during the Depression are estimated at anywhere from a million to $15 million.

Ironically, the larger part of the Kennedy fortune was made because of a miscalculation. During World War II, Kennedy, who as ambassador had taken a gloomy view of England's chances, acted on the hypothesis that there would be a financial crash after the war. With the thought of cutting his losses he went into real estate, trading Manhattan properties to great profit. The war, however, was followed not by a crash but by general prosperity, and Kennedy, even though he had bet on the wrong horse, was turned into a winner in spite of himself. His greatest single coup occurred in 1945, when he bought Marshall Field's Merchandise Mart in Chicago for almost $13 million, of which $12.5 million had been borrowed from an insurance company. Over the next twenty years, the Mart's value rose to $75 million and its annual rentals to $13 million, or more than its original price. In the meantime, Kennedy had become among the richest of the Great Big New Rich, with a personal fortune estimated in 1968 at somewhere in the neighborhood of a quarter-billion dollars.

The chronicle of Joseph P. Kennedy and the family he founded may someday furnish material for a great work of literature in the American grain. Such a book will not, however, be a simpleminded inspirational story of a Boston Irish lad who made good, but of an exceedingly complex and unsympathetic man whose pathological drive for money indirectly contributed to some of the deepest-cutting moments in our experience in this century.

> It looked as if everybody and his brother was out to get the Government in the lush war years.
> — Lindsay Warren

Some twenty years after World War I, Gerald Nye earned for himself an honorable place in the history of public scandals by convoking a committee that brought into the light some of the bonanzas earned by patriotic industries during that war. Biding his time less patiently, in the summer of 1946 Senator James M. Mead of New York presided over hearings of an investigating committee that looked into the profits that had been made in the war that had been over less than a year. Yet, as Lindsay Warren, Comptroller General of the United States, told the committee, it was already too late. Angrily reminding the committee of the "reckless abandon" and "nefarious practices" that had prevailed, Warren told the senators that the door had been closed forever on $65 billion of war contracts that had already been settled.

For the press and the public at large, the ripest scandal uncovered by the Mead Committee was that involving the association between Andrew Jackson May of Kentucky, chairman of the House Military Affairs Committee, and the brothers Garsson, Henry and Murray, who had been awarded $78 million in war contracts for the contributions made to the defense of democracy made by two largely imaginary corporations. Diverted by the revelations that were to ruin May, the committee never managed to do justice to its broader purpose, which would have involved more illustrious persons than the Garssons and more patriotic corporations than their Erie Basin–Batavia combine.

Lindsay Warren's testimony, however, made clear that the ancient affair between war and prosperity in the United States had not been suspended between 1941 and 1945. Warren's General Accounting Office had been charged with auditing and reviewing the cost-plus contracts that were then the style. Without any real power, the GAO had been expected to "whitewash almost any conceivable cost." The required reviews were so perfunctory, Warren said, that they could have been carried on by a "ten-year-old moron." He went on to say that war contracts had been rewritten to avoid audit and protect profits, the customary invocation being the overriding necessity of carrying the blessings of freedom to the four corners of the world.

In spite of the straitjacket within which it was obliged to function, the GAO had managed to recover in the last year of the war more than $100 million in illegal payments to such corporations as Boeing, Lockheed, Consolidated Vultee, Curtiss Wright, Bell Aircraft, and Ford. Even this laudable activity had been carried out against obstacles not unfamiliar in our other wars. Officials who exercised too much diligence in protecting the public interest were, Warren testified, frequently and effectively transferred to other jobs.

In the fall of 1946, the House Merchant Marine Committee made public some provocative statistics concerning the profits enjoyed by the best known of the new rich of World War II, the late Henry J. Kaiser. The GAO's chief attorney, Ralph E. Casey, testified that six shipyards owned or controlled by Kaiser had made profits of more than $192 million on a total investment of $2.5 million. Kaiser, who had attained a sort of secular sainthood by causing industrial miracles to happen, answered quickly and positively that Casey was wrong. His profits should be compared to his production volume and not his investment, and, in any case, a good many of his wartime enterprises had suffered patriotic losses. The matter was let die.

The definitive history of the Gold Rush of 1941–1945 has yet to be written. Let us note, however, that none of the Great Big New Rich grew poor during the war. The oil men — Getty, Hunt, Mecom, Smith — were among the most blessed of our citizens in this great war of oil. Ludwig emerged as the owner of a great fleet of war-built ships. Hughes acquired $60 million of contracts without delivering a single plane. Kennedy bought real estate that was to escalate most profitably in the postwar boom. Thanks to wartime food shortages, even Simon profited, his Hunt's label becoming known across the nation.

> Every war has produced a new crop of "war profiteers" and the Vietnam War is no exception.
>
> — James Reston

Since the days of Lindsay Warren's bitterness, another and finer-sounding agency has been set up to ride herd on the making of extravagant profits during wartime. In 1951, at the height of the Korean War, the Renegotiation Board was set up by law, with its mission being to review government contracts and "renegotiate" those which appeared to contain too much fat. Some $800 million was recovered in this way from Korean War contracts. A laudable effort, surely, and yet the astonishing thing is that it is such a trifling sum — less than the personal fortunes of any one of four of the Great Big New Rich.

The truth of the matter appears to be that we Americans have become almost indifferent to the great obscene spectacle of old men growing rich while young men are dying. Our capacity for indignation has become blunted, and we accept the most outrageous phenomena as being simply in the nature of things. Let a single bureaucratic statistic register our lack of concern: In 1952 the Renegotiation Board had 550 employees; in 1968, in the midst of a much viler and more expensive war than Korea, the Board has been reduced to about 150 employees.

There is no reason to think that this corporal's guard is overworked. At a time when, as Vice Admiral Hyman G. Rickover has testified, "defense" contracts are producing about $4.5 billion in profits a year, there is no public concern at all that the old, shameful drama is being played out again. There is not even a program to the show. As James Reston reported in the spring of 1968, in spite of the new Freedom of Information law and in spite of the prestige of the New York *Times*, his efforts to get details of war profits had repeatedly been "turned aside." We are in this matter an indifferent people, and the piling up of bloody dollars appears to us as no more than one of our great national sports, like caber-tossing in Scotland or fighting fish in Thailand.

As always, the Great Big New Rich have not suffered from the Vietnam War. D. K. Ludwig is building even greater tankers to carry the oil that fuels the machines. Colonel Henry Crown owns a substantial part of General Dynamics, which produces aircraft (including the controversial F–111), submarines, surface ships, missiles, and guided missiles. Charles B. Thornton's Litton Industries is involved in an astonishing variety of war-related products, from nuclear submarines to microwave ovens to cook the troops' food. James J. Ling's LTV makes aircraft and missiles, command and control systems, reconnaissance and surveillance systems, and missile components. Howard Hughes' Hughes Aircraft, which acquired a virtual monopoly of certain types of airborne electronic gear during the Korean War, manufactures missiles for the Air Force. The oilmen continue to enjoy both the blessings of the depletion allowance and their war-guaranteed profits.

An echo of the Mead Committee hearings can be heard in an AP story from Washington that went out on the wire on Veterans Day, 1968. The lead paragraphs read:

"The Defense Department does not obtain full information on profits realized by contractors receiving more than $22 billion a year in military orders, Comptroller General Elmer B. Staats said yesterday.

"He told a Senate subcommittee on government economy, 'We know of no complete and comprehensive study that has ever been made on profits actually realized by defense contractors.'

"Sen. William Proxmire, D-Wis., chairman of the subcommittee and its parent Joint Economic Committee, said:

" 'In other words, we just don't know what the real profits of defense contractors are.' "

SEVEN

Gallery Three: Savings-and-Loan Tycoons

> What's made it go is the old philosophy of three drugstores on a corner. Competition. Out here you're competing with the champs.
>
> — *Howard Ahmanson*

With the possible exception of Dallas and Houston, Los Angeles encompasses within its far-flung and meandering city limits the most notable accumulation of new private wealth in the country today. When I visited Los Angeles to look into this phenomenon, I found not just an accidental accumulation of several wealthy men but a community of rich entrepreneurs such as emerged in New York, Pittsburgh, Chicago, and San Francisco in the latter part of the nineteenth century. I do not think we shall see their like in this country again.

It is not hard to identify the Los Angeles rich — in fact it requires some ingenuity to escape from their presence. As I approached the Ahmanson Gallery of the Los Angeles County Museum of Art, I walked across the Mr. and Mrs. Norton Simon Sculpture Plaza and, inside, admired exhibits hung in the Amelia and Mark Taper Gallery, the Mr. and Mrs. Harry Chandler Gallery, Pauley Hall, the Mr. and Mrs. Edward William Carter Gallery and the Jane and Dustin Dart Gallery. (On somewhat different sociological levels were the Bob and Dolores Hope Gallery and the Della Mulock Mudd Memorial Gallery). That evening I attended a dance concert in the Ahmanson Theater, which shares a hilltop site with the Dorothy Chandler Pavilion and the Mark Taper Forum. The next day I visited Bart Lytton in the Lytton Center of the Visual Arts. I could go on, but I think the point is clear.

One understands something real about the culture of Southern California — more real than swimming pools and dark glasses and fat ladies in slacks — when one understands that the greatest source of new wealth in Los Angeles is not the movies and TV (Bob Hope is the only Great Big New Rich actor), nor oil, but the New Technology and a complex of financial empires that prosper by making it possible for all but the most deprived citizen to build or buy his own suburban bungalow. The savings-and-loan firms (which are generally called S&L's in the trade) have grown prosperous because a great many people have been moving to California. A great many people have been moving to California not only because the climate is often pleasant but also because there are a great many jobs there. There are a great many jobs in California because it is a garrison state whose industrial output is largely directed toward supporting our various wars and threats of war.

The three tycoons of the S&L business at the time of my visit in 1967 were as different in their personal styles as they were similar in the source of their wealth. Howard Ahmanson, who owned a hundred percent of the country's largest S&L until his death in June 1968, was an extrovert Middle Westerner. Mark Taper, who controls the country's largest publicly owned S&L, is a more formal man who speaks with an English accent. Bart Lytton, a onetime screenwriter who operated Lytton Savings and Loan until he was deposed in April 1968, fails to qualify as Great Big New Rich but makes up for it in sheer *brio*, even in his current exile from the big money.

Home Savings & Loan has one stockholder. Me.

— *Howard Ahmanson*

A weatherbeaten, gray-haired, handsome man in his early sixties, Howard Ahmanson looked like exactly what he was — a prosperous yachtsman with a cultivated taste for Scotch who had once been a member of the Republican National Finance Committee and was a loyal alumnus of the University of Southern California, from which he earned a B.S. in 1927. He was a trustee of U.S.C. as well as of the Kennedy Center for the Performing Arts and the Los Angeles Museum of Art. The main thing, however, that set him apart from his fellow members of the Newport Harbor, Santa Monica, and Los Angeles yacht clubs was the measure of his prosperity. Ahmanson was president and sole stockholder of Home Savings & Loan, the

Howard Ahmanson, the nation's richest savings-and-loan man until his death in 1968. ROTHSCHILD PHOTO.

country's largest. Figures that have appeared in print encourage my belief that Ahmanson's personal fortune was somewhere between a quarter-billion and a half-billion dollars. If Ahmanson paid himself at the same rate he paid his depositors, his income fell into the range of $15 million to $20 million a year, which is about what the presidents of, say, General Motors or Ford can expect to earn during their entire working lives.

I talked to Ahmanson in the morning room of his baronial house in the Hancock Park section of Los Angeles. Among his domestic servants were a butler and a chef, which attributes in themselves set him apart from the rest of the Great Big New Rich. The high-ceilinged, paneled rooms were hung with old masters. (It should also be recorded, however, that the Ahmanson lawns are broad but the grounds are not vast. A couple of blocks away, schoolchildren cross streets and walk toward houses in which you and I might live.)

Ahmanson was born in 1906 in what he describes as a "comfortable Midwest home in a happy family." His father, a well-to-do insurance man, gave him a small brokerage account when he was twelve or thirteen and was pleased when the boy did better than he did himself. Ahmanson also recalled, however, that his future was not always pictured to him as rosy. At Omaha's Commercial Club, where his father used to take him on Saturdays, there was much gloomy shaking of heads over the income tax. "Howard's a nice young fellow," the worriers would say, "but there certainly isn't any future for him."

When he was twenty-two or -three, William K. Vanderbilt offered Ahmanson an "incredible" job handling insurance. "I turned down something any sane person would have taken,"

Ahmanson told me. Instead, he continued his business in Los Angeles, writing insurance for banks and mortgage companies. When the crash came in 1929, he was already out of the stock market, with his cash safe.

When I remarked that it seemed to me that an extraordinary number of today's very wealthy men had seemed to exhibit a sixth sense about the market in the summer of 1929, Ahmanson lighted another cigarette, squinted at the half-models of his racing sloops on the wall, and answered, "It wasn't quite that glamorous. At U.S.C. I'd written an awesome and witty thing called 'The Great American Debacle.' I'd found out that workers were spending 122 percent of what they made. Everybody had a college chum on the wire to New York.

"Well, when I came back from a trip to San Francisco I found out that my secretary had had my broker buy two hundred shares of an insurance company I'd never heard of even though I'd been brought up in the insurance business. I found out from my broker that the company had started the week before and had already gone up from $30 to $44. It takes a long time before an insurance company begins to show a profit. I said to myself, well, you wrote that article, you great big goose. I went back to my broker and told him to sell everything I had.

"I'm not sure but that the people you're talking about all made their decisions for prosaic reasons like this."

The only stock Ahmanson held on to was that of the National American Insurance Company, his father's firm. During the Depression, Ahmanson specialized in insuring foreclosed properties, an experience he describes as having made him feel like an undertaker in a plague. Whatever discomfort he may have felt about his role was compensated for by his growing prosperity.

In 1943 Ahmanson, an experienced blue-water sailor, went into the Navy. When he came out as a lieutenant in 1945 he took another look at the S&L's, which he had previously scorned, and decided that with new government controls, they had turned into a more reliable sort of animal. In the next years, Ahmanson put together Home S&L in a series of intricate deals that involved buying up other firms. "We never merged," he told me. "That would have diluted ownership."

California S&L's: The Boom the Bankers Knock

— *Fortune*

The institution of the S&L is not a Southern California invention, but it has burst into its finest flowering there. In essence, an S&L is a specialized bank that attracts savings by offering higher interest rates than do the commercial banks and lends the money out to citizens who want to buy houses or to developers who want to build houses. "The S&L's come from British building societies and German lending institutions that aren't quite as old as banks but are very ancient," Ahmanson told me. "They didn't amount to much in New York. Twenty years ago a New York banker thought that somebody who attracted savings and loaned money on real estate wasn't a banker. A. P. Giannini changed that." The postwar building boom in Southern California has turned several S&L's into multibillion-dollar enterprises.

The prosperity of an S&L rises and falls with the spread between the rate at which it pays interest to its depositors and the rate of interest it receives from its borrowers. In recent years this margin has sometimes become uncomfortably thin, with the borrower paying as low as 6.25 percent and the depositor of a bonus account getting up to 5.75 percent. (A bonus account is usually defined as one of at least $5000 which is left intact for thirty-six months.) Since a spread of 1 to 1½ percent is considered necessary for comfort, a tremor of chill runs through the S&L community whenever Home & Fireside S&L announces it is raising its depositors' rate by a quarter-point.

The fierce competition for both loans and deposits has generated some practices among the S&L's that have attracted some exceedingly sour looks from Eastern bankers. Part of this is due to the S&L's merchandising practices and their somewhat more liberal loan policies, but most of the glumness is probably inspired by the aggressiveness with which the California S&L's have gone after Eastern money, placing ads in such media as the New York *Times* to trumpet their higher dividend rates.

Ahmanson told me, "Advertising is what makes the New York banks sore. I didn't advertise, but it wasn't for moral reasons. [The reason was that he didn't have to.] The West has always been short of money and has paid higher rates. Too much money accumulates back in New York. The end isn't in sight, but someday before long we'll be operating on the same level."

He went on. "We were the biggest tract-loan company in the country when we got out. All S&L's were lending 100 percent or 110 percent at 6 percent and two points to builders. The situation had become so competitive they were throwing their money away. We enlarged our staff to make loans to people, like a life insurance company. This is the hard way to make money. The competition has gone berserk."

These misers — I call them that to their faces — Getty and Ludwig aren't having any fun out of life. They think they're going to live forever.

— *Howard Ahmanson*

In his personal style, Ahmanson came closer to the traditional picture of the rich man than did almost any of his peers. He clearly enjoyed himself, whether it was through the medium of his ten-meter yacht *Sirius*, his collection of paintings, his civic activities, or, even though he suffered from gout, his chef.

"I've noticed that really rich men have a notable lack of hobbies," he told me, and then laughed. "I guess I won't amount to much." Although after a heart attack in 1956 he quit racing *Sirius*, he still sailed a great deal; not long before I saw him he had come back from a cruise through the Mediterranean. His navigator calculated that he had sailed 11,000 miles in two-and-a-half years.

Ahmanson estimated that he spent sixty percent of his time on civic affairs. Preeminent among these undertakings was his support of the new Los Angeles County Museum of Art, a white extravaganza built amidst the La Brea tar pits, and the Music Center on top of Bunker Hill, downtown, where the Ahmanson Theater seats 2100 cultured Angelenos. He lunched regularly with Dorothy (Buff) Chandler of the Los Angeles *Times* dynasty, another prominent partisan of culture in Los

Angeles, and Ahmanson and his wife took part in those culture-tinted affairs that make up much of the rather sere social life of Los Angeles. Tangentially he remarked to me, "I haven't had an office in ten or eleven years. My secretary is back in the bowels of the house. Civic affairs are just as important as running a business."

Once an active Eisenhower Republican, Ahmanson professed little interest in current politics when he talked to me (it was in the fall of 1967), but, perhaps surprisingly, volunteered the information that he was an outright dove. "We had better reasons for fighting in Cuba, ninety miles away. I've spent some time in the Far East and I don't think we have any business out there. It's ridiculous. A solution has to be reached. Those extra billions are the frosting on the economic cake. It's artificial, and when it's gone . . ."

In an economic vein, he went on, "I'm one person who thinks we should be worrying about deflation. Inflation is inherent in democracy. You have to have inflation. The only way you can have democracy is to have inflation. But I feel it in my bones that things are static."

As he accompanied me to the door, we detoured through the rooms where his paintings are hung. Among the artists were Rembrandt, Vermeer, Tintoretto, Breughel the Elder, Titian, Monet, Millet, Delacroix, Franz Hals, Courbet, David, Velasquez, and John Singer Sargent.

As I left, I was reminded of the answer Ahmanson had made when I'd asked about the motivation that causes men to make large sums of money.

"Motivation?" he'd said. "It's just like winning yacht races."

We are the Mecca, the paradise and dream of the world, and
it is a wonderful thing to share in the fabulous life we are
living here.

— *S. Mark Taper*

Sydney Mark Taper was born in Poland and reared in
England, where he achieved prosperity as a builder and mortgage banker. He came to the United States with his wife and
three children in 1939, intending to retire, but went back into
business two years later as a building developer in Southern
California, an enterprise he followed with notable success until,
some years later, he turned his attention to the S&L's.

Taper is a rather stiff-looking, sparely built man whose white
hair, bushy dark eyebrows and magisterial air are reminiscent of
the late Henry Luce. I interviewed him in his spacious office on
an upper floor of a bank building on Wilshire Boulevard in
Beverly Hills.

"I, of course, came from England," he told me. "I felt the
need for better housing. In 1941 I went about planning to fulfill
the need. If you're going to supply anything, it should be better
than anyone else can supply, and in the form the public wants.
In 1941 the public wanted a house with only two bedrooms,
one bath and a one-car garage. Since then there has been con-
tinuous progress. As the years went on we found to our great
surprise that what people wanted was a house with three
bedrooms and a two-car garage, giving the children one bedroom each, or at least one bedroom for the boys and one for the
girls. Then from three bedrooms, one bath and a two-car garage
we went to three bedrooms, two baths and a two-car garage — a

S. Mark Taper, the country's richest savings-and-loan man.

tremendous step forward. Abundance. In a short time we couldn't sell anything with one bathroom."

Taper closed his eyes as if to collect his thoughts, put the tips of his fingers together, and then went on speaking clearly, in a well-organized and almost formal fashion. "In my particular activity not only was I enthused at filling a need, but I also felt I was doing a patriotic job. There was something else than financial gain. I felt that I was doing good, providing citizens with a stake in our country. Every house we sold made a better American citizen. Communism cannot grow where people have a stake in our country. They're participating in the American way of life."

A little later, having detoured through the *modus operandi* of the S&L's, Taper returned to what was evidently one of his favorite themes. "Those who have achieved some measure of success have the duty to help others. The United States has become the most powerful country in the world because more people have a higher standard of living than since the world began. If we are to maintain this, we still have an enormous amount to do.

"Riots are an effect of too large a part of our people not enjoying the benefits and standard of living that the majority have. While the percentage in the U.S. is less, it is still there. Until we solve this problem there will be frustration and discrimination. The only solution is a mammoth program of education, job training, and the opening of opportunities.

"Over sixty percent of U.S. citizens own their own homes. Sixty percent of U.S. citizens have a stake in their country. They are capitalists. Their stake continues to grow bigger. Yet we have houses available unsold in areas that could be occupied by Negroes, Mexican-Americans, and others. But because the minority groups do not qualify for credit underwritten by the FHA and the VA, the people who need it most don't have the opportunity to buy the houses that are standing unoccupied. We need an immediate change in direction on the part of these government agencies so that they will grant loans to minority groups on a different basis than to others. It would cost us as taxpayers much less. They could solve the problems of the minorities by providing FHA and GI loans under liberalized requirements so that every member of a minority group could be housed decently.

"The time has come for immediate action. Relief must be granted. In 1947 I sensed a need for housing for Negroes and Mexican-Americans. Between 1947 and 1953 I built about 3500 houses. These were sold to young men out of World War II and out of the Korean War, and these areas are just as good as areas occupied by Caucasians. These people are sharing in the American way of life and their children will take part equally. The home is the first place — a garden to play in, not a ghetto or a rat-infested slum. Otherwise, there will be frustration and despair, and we know what that leads to.

"I stopped building in 1955 because I saw I could do more for the state and nation in another field, because there was a greater need for financing."

Taper had first entered the S&L's in 1950, when he bought the Whittier Building & Loan Association. He is now founder, board chairman, and president of the First Charter Financial Corporation, which is the largest publicly owned S&L holding company in the country, with over $2 billion in assets. Last year the value of Taper's personal holdings in First Charter was estimated at over $150 million.

When I left Taper's office, I was considerably under his spell, even though the loftiness of his discourse had made it rather hard for us to establish any personal rapport. Sometime later in the day, in talking to another man prominent in the S&L's, I mentioned Taper's statesmanlike avowals of responsibility for citizens less fortunate than himself.

The other S&L man looked at me quizzically and then said, "Mark Taper's all right, but don't you forget for a moment that that man's absolutely ruthless."

> Sure, I'd rather join them, but if I can't, then I'd rather lick them. At present, you know, I am loath to return to the petty pleasures of group concordance.
>
> — Bart Lytton

Until his sudden although not entirely unexpected excommunication from the savings-and-loan business in the spring of 1968, Bart Lytton of Lytton Financial Corporation was the most galling of all the S&L men to conservative bankers both in the East and the West. A onetime screenwriter and publicity man, Lytton entered the Los Angeles S&L's in 1959 and rose to near the top of the heap when he put together an empire holding assets of three-quarters of a billion dollars. Whether he was punished by the gods for his rampant hubris or whether the causes of his downfall were more mundane, Lytton's career holds the elements of a seriocomic epic of our peculiar times.

A gifted talker who could charm a baby kangaroo out of its

mother's pouch, Lytton once offered the opinion that money could be merchandised like girlie shows and then set out to prove that he was right. The flavor that was distinctive of his operation can be tasted in his account of how he lured customers into the shop when he had only a single office: "We bought all the pans and junk we could find and we advertised our country store. We even had a barrel of pickles — a free pickle for the July reinvestment period. Employees wore armbands and eyeshades. We did sensationally in that period." When the state outlawed S&L premiums costing more than $2.50, Lytton gave away sixty thousand paperback books. As he recalls it, "We ran Dell Publishing dry. We gave a book to anyone who walked in."

Although his principal former competitors, Ahmanson and Taper, could mingle in a crowd of New York or Boston bankers without any protective personal coloration, Lytton is all Southern California. A New Castle, Pennsylvania, boy and the son of a well-to-do lawyer, Lytton made his way to Hollywood in the Forties as a press agent for Warner Brothers. He was also a scriptwriter, with such movies as *Bowery to Broadway* and *Hitler's Madmen* to his credit. (He has said of this period of his life, "I'm a lot prouder of some of the mortgages I've written.")

Lytton's Hollywood career languished after he was expelled from the Communist Party as a suspected agent provocateur, FBI plant, and enemy of the people. (He later testified as a friendly witness before the House Un-American Activities Committee.) Lytton thereupon abandoned the dramatic arts, in which he had once labored as a $24-a-week director in the WPA theater, and went where the money was. He acquired a mortgage company in settlement of a public relations debt, entered the S&L's in New Mexico and Nevada, and in 1959 organized the company that bears his name and that he built into the fifth-ranking S&L in the country.*

> Some are born to fame. . . . Others have it thrust upon them. . . . At the moment I control the best part of a billion dollars — this staggers even me.
>
> — Bart Lytton

As he rose in the S&L business and began to count his personal wealth in the millions, Lytton acquired a nimbus of anecdotes. A characteristic one concerns the time he had himself electronically accoutered at a garden party so that whenever his guests tired of their own conversations they could listen to loudspeakers that carried Lytton's discourse. (Other guests at cocktail parties at which Lytton has been present have remarked that he needs no artificial amplification.) A more recent story describes how, when he walked up to the speakers' platform at an affair to raise money to save a historic monument, he had clenched between his teeth a check for $800,000. Taking the check out of his mouth, Lytton explained that he was responding to criticism that not many supporters of the preservation effort were prepared to put their money where their mouths were. (His philanthropy, while commendable, was not

---

* Lytton Financial Corporation is frequently confused with Litton Industries. Lytton once composed a letter to a young lady who had made this mistake: "Dear Miss D— : Iou have hurt me to the quyck. Yf iou don't know y, then one of us has slypped veri badli in our publyc relatyons. . . ." Since Lytton's deposition, the company he founded has changed its name to LFC Financial Corporation.

Bart Lytton, the once-tycoon of Lytton Savings and Loan of
Los Angeles.

entirely disinterested. Lytton was at the time engaged in planning a $2,375,000 condominium complex on the property around the monument, which was the Walter Luther Dodge house, designed by Irving Gill.)

Lytton's style was not calculated to endear him to the rest of the financial community. He was regularly described as the maverick of the S&L tycoons, although he himself suggested that "piranha" might more accurately convey a generally received opinion. He has referred unabashedly to his "delicious talent for effrontery" and has never been suspected of modesty, false or otherwise. At the height of his success, when his personal fortune was said to be rising to the neighborhood of $30 million, Lytton's name appeared in large letters on the Los Angeles buses, his portrait in a movie-star pose appeared in the advertising pages of the financial sections, and he became the progenitor of the Lytton Center of the Visual Arts, a museum which stands next to the corporate headquarters just inside the Los Angeles city limits from Beverly Hills and a couple of blocks from the fleshpots and skin-joints of the Sunset Strip.

A confirmed believer in traveling first cabin, Lytton scattered money in the proverbial fashion, and when in London parleyed on equal terms with Getty. In Los Angeles he traveled in one of two limousines that were piloted by Rufus Martin, who for twenty-four years had worked for Clark Gable. Lytton was once reported to maintain a wardrobe of thirty-odd suits and thirty pairs of shoes. In 1957 he paid $125,000 for a house on a one-and-a-quarter-acre lot in Holmby Hills. He subsequently spent $400,000 on improvements that included turning the existing swimming pool into a dance floor and building a new and grander pool. The annual maintenance of the house was $18,000. Three or four times a year, the Lyttons invited more than a thousand people to parties that were said to cost up to $20,000 each.

In addition to the income from his share of Lytton Financial, Lytton drew a salary of $216,000, sweetened by an expense account variously estimated between $200,000 and $400,000. With his characteristic *chutzpah*, Lytton once told his stockholders, "I don't think my salary is enough. We can't live on it."

Although he supported Ronald Reagan for governor of California, Lytton is a prominent Democrat, and one year was reported to be the highest individual contributor to the party coffers. His usual annual political contributions ran between $30,000 and $40,000, but in 1960 he gave $200,000 to John F. Kennedy's campaign. A wing of his handsome and well-furbished office was hung with photos of Lytton with HST, Lytton with Adlai, Lytton with JFK, Lytton with Jackie, Lytton with LBJ. An amateur of architecture, Lytton was appointed to the rank of visiting professor of architecture at Stanford. Besides Stanford, he has at various times also addressed students at Harvard, Yale, and the Wharton School of Finance at Pennsylvania.

On the day I talked to Lytton, he was wearing a blue blazer and flannels and, with his curly gray hair and noble-Roman face, looked entirely the picture of the successful alumnus who still thinks of himself as a big man on campus. (He attended Westminster College and the University of Virginia.) As we drank a Scotch in his office together with two vice-presidents of the firm, Lytton expanded on his affinity for students. "The students," he told me, "get a chance to talk with a personality of known achievement. Most of all, the student wants to ask, *How do I live?* The people they ask have to be people with a certain charisma."

He gestured toward a family picture and laughed. "Did I get a banker for a son-in-law? No, I got a guitar player. He'll be studying with Segovia." Then he returned to his main theme. "At Stanford, the kids tend to reject business. They think there's no challenge, no excitement. They think everything is fixed and ordained."

For Lytton himself, it has always been clear that business held a full measure of challenge and excitement and that the boundaries have never been fixed and ordained.

> I once told Bart he was a morning glory, blooming early and fading fast.
> — *Howard Ahmanson*

Lytton's downfall was not entirely unheralded. He had already suffered one setback when, in 1965, the Federal Home Loan Bank board obliged him to sell the Beverly Hills S&L, which divested him of a salary of $105,000 and an expense account of appropriate dimensions. (The unfavorable judgment had come after four years of bitter dispute over whether or not he had acquired the firm in a proper manner. The decision was that S&L's couldn't be bought and sold.)

I was reminded by a Los Angeles philanthropist that Lytton's name had been chiseled from a building at the art museum when he had been unable to make good on the entire amount of his pledge of three-quarters of a million dollars. I heard rumors that Lytton continued to be short of cash and that his ebullience covered a good deal of insecurity. A long-time observer of the Los Angeles scene told me of a fracas on a television show that Lytton sponsored, an affair that led to a quarter-million-dollar suit being brought by Drew Pearson against Lytton for nonperformance of contract. The same man advanced the theory that Lytton might turn out to be the Insull of the S&L's.

Lytton's ill-wishers were legion when, in the spring of 1968, the first hard evidence of trouble became public. In a general way, the trouble came about because Lytton had insisted on expanding in a declining real estate market and an atmosphere of tight money. Ironically, the success of Lytton's promotional efforts put him in a painful bind because as the savings in his S&L's increased he was required by Federal regulations to make a commensurate increase in their capital reserves. This he could do only by pumping money from Lytton Financial into his two S&L's, leaving the parent company short of cash to meet its debts. In 1966 and 1967 Lytton had to dump foreclosed property at a loss of $11 million. Lytton Financial showed losses of $2 million in 1965, $7.6 million in 1966, and $3.2 million in 1967.

The debt which finally broke Lytton was an unsecured note for $2 million held by the United Auto Workers and due in October 1967. In October, when the debt had been reduced to $1.6 million, a new note was arranged with Lytton stock as collateral. The new note was due April 2, 1968, but was extended to April 26. In March, feeling the pressure of personal debts, Lytton sold about half his holdings in Lytton Financial (some 334,449 shares worth about $2 million) to the Union Bank of Los Angeles, giving Union Bank a 13 percent interest in Lytton Financial and reducing his own holdings to 8 percent. Lytton stoutly maintained that he was still at the helm, but the illusion was to last only about a month.

I wasn't thrown out. I wrote my own exit music.
— *Bart Lytton*

He was pretty statesmanlike.
— *Preston Martin*

The meeting that deposed Lytton began at 5:30 on the morning of April 26, the date the UAW note was finally due, and was presided over by Preston Martin, the California S&L commissioner, who acted in effect as an arbitrator between Lytton and his creditors. It was a clean sweep for the creditors, and, under the circumstances, it could not have been much else. Lytton asserts that he was offered the chairmanship as a consolation prize but that he declined to stay on without executive authority, which of course was precisely what his creditors were determined to divest him of. Lytton told his creditors he would "go away quietly" and resigned as chairman, president, and chief executive officer, retaining only his stock and a tenuous connection with the firm as a consultant, with a fee of $500,000 to be paid over ten years. The severance agreement also required Lytton to stay out of S&L's for at least seven years. A new board of directors representing the creditors took over and

Charles A. Wellman, formerly president of Mark Taper's First Charter, was installed as Lytton's successor.

Lytton went into seclusion for two days and then, haggard but still jaunty, assembled a press conference, which he told, "I'm a tiger. I wasn't thrown out. I'm no less a tiger for having been treed. I'm not a rich man any more but I'm probably still a genius."

> I've been a tycoon once and I don't need to be one again.
> — *Bart Lytton*

The financial columnist of the San Francisco *Chronicle* offered as Lytton's epitaph, "The fall of Bart Lytton is unlikely to elicit even many crocodile tears from his fellows in the savings and loan industry of California." If his onetime competitors had hoped to see Lytton reduced to ignominious poverty they were to be disappointed. Still holding a substantial share of Lytton Financial stock as well as other property, Lytton emerged from the catastrophe with a fortune still on the order of a million dollars and was assured of an annual income of about $100,000 a year.

Lytton's program of domestic retrenchment was not calculated to cause him more than passing regrets for the style he had once maintained. He switched to a smaller cigar, thereby cutting his monthly tobacco bill from $300 to $250. He decided to keep on Rufus Martin, but thought about letting go his number-two chauffeur. He sold his condominium apartment and his Holmsby Hills house, but hung on to the six-bedroom beach house in Malibu. He considered whether or not to sell his 1962 Cadillac, but decided to keep the other four cars.

Lytton said confidently, "We'll continue to dine in the best restaurants — Chasen's, Perrino's, La Rue's and the like — but maybe only once or twice instead of three or four times a week. And when we're out with people, I trust the check won't fall in my lap with quite the certainty of the past."

In the weeks following the catastrophe, Lytton reported that he had various offers, including invitations from two publishers to write his autobiography, a proposal for a weekly talk show on a TV network, and an offer to write and direct a movie — "a sort of latter-day 'Executive Suite.' "

Three weeks after the deluge, Lytton spoke to an audience at the Stanford Graduate School of Business. His topic was, "Neither a Borrower nor a Lender Be."

Of the rich men I have talked to, I found Bart Lytton to have the most compelling charm and I would accept another invitation to lunch with him with pleasure. In any case, I would be reluctant to risk any money on the proposition that, given his protean talents and his conviction of genius, Lytton will not rise again, a well-tailored and irrepressible phoenix soaring upward with raucous cries of triumph from the ashes of his savings-and-loan career.

Los Angeles is a state of mind.

— *Old folk saying*

Although there is quite a distance between an uninhibited moneyman like Bart Lytton and such virtuosi of corporate organization as Charles B. Thornton and Norton Simon (both of whom we shall meet later), the very rich men of Los Angeles do form a visible community of interest. The Southern California power structure is not an abstraction but consists of a recognizable group of rich and usually capable people who see each other both at private affairs and at the public ceremonials that are the folk-rituals of a growing city. Ahmanson, Taper, Thornton, and Simon, together with such of their equals as Simon Ramo (of TRW), the Chandler family (of the Los Angeles *Times*), Daniel J. Haughton (of Lockheed) and Edward Carter (department stores), have spent much of their time in the public eye working on enterprises they believe to be good for their city. Their financial support of museums and concert halls are not their only good works: Ahmanson, as we have noted, estimated that he spent sixty percent of his time on civic affairs while Taper, besides contributing the Mark Taper Forum to the Music Center, has been repeatedly honored for his contributions to Jewish causes.

All of this is not intended to suggest that the Los Angeles rich live in a civic garden of shared ideals and mutual admiration. Off the record they are capable of brutal frankness, with the word *ruthless* playing an operative role. Furthermore, although the cultural monuments on Bunker Hill and out Wilshire Boulevard represent the attainment of a common goal, the accomplishment has not been without its price. Notably, the distinguished director of the Museum of Art, Dr. Richard Brown, was forced out in a power play that was reported to have revolved around his refusal to hire Ahmanson's choice of architect or to hang Ahmanson's old masters. More impor-

149

tantly, the Great Big New Rich, like the leading citizens of every Western community since the Gold Rush, seem to be laboring under the odd belief that what Los Angeles stands most in need of is Culture. Now and then the news reports from their city have suggested otherwise.

EIGHT

Billionaires, Aristocrats, and Managers

The Americans have, as they repeatedly assure Europeans, "a great deal of Aristocracy," and, in general, a very nice taste for artificial distinctions; a circumstance which, as yet, is but little known to the great bulk of the European public, who still imagine them to be a set of savages.

— *Francis J. Grund, 1839*

By definition, the Great Big New Rich are neither aristocrats nor hired managers. Yet, since the Great Big New Rich have money, as most aristocrats do, and wield corporate power, as most managers do, the lines are not always clearly drawn between the three classes.

To take up the matter of aristocracy first, the general question of whether or not an aristocracy has grown up — or can grow up at all — in the United States is one that has exercised some powerful thinkers. In the course of an exchange of letters in the fall of 1813, Thomas Jefferson wrote to John Adams, ". . . I agree with you that there is a natural aristocracy among men. The grounds of this are virtue and talents. . . . There is also an artificial aristocracy, founded on wealth and birth. . . ."

Adams replied, "Though we are agreed in one point, in words, it is not yet certain that we are perfectly agreed in sense. Fashion has introduced an indeterminate use of the word talents. Education, wealth, strength, beauty, stature, birth, marriage, graceful attitudes and motions, gait, air, complexion, physiognomy are talents, as well as genius, science, and learning. Any one of these talents . . . gives to the man who possesses it the character of an aristocrat."

The problem that engaged these two great men is still with us, for we are still torn between a philosophical commitment to the political equality of all men and a persistent yearning to admire and bow down before superior men. Jefferson's aristocracy of virtue and talent does not appear to be entirely satisfying to this latter need, and probably for the reason that the aristocracy of talent only rarely perpetuates itself. Conversely, the claims of ancient lineage alone appear to be insufficient when they are not reinforced by titles of nobility. Many American families can trace their ancestors in this country back for two or three hundred years; one would, however, be seriously mistaken in starting his search for an American aristocracy among the members of the Society of Mayflower Descendants or the Daughters of the American Revolution.

Let us, then, propose a definition of three parts. First, the· quality of being an aristocrat, John Adams to the contrary, is based less on personal characteristics than on the idea of family distinction. Second, the aristocratic family is distinguished by a certain ancientness, although the precise degree of this ancientness is hard to fix. Third, the aristocratic family controls an amount of wealth above the average — although, again, the precise amount is hard to define and the phenomenon of the impoverished aristocrat is not unfamiliar.

The natural progenitors of an American aristocracy — the Founding Fathers — largely disqualified themselves by their lack of distinguished issue, or of any issue at all. There are no latter-day Washingtons, Jeffersons, or Franklins, no Madisons, Hamiltons, or Monroes who are deferred to as the recipients of the mysterious mana of their ancestors.* Almost alone among the families of Revolutionary statesmen, the Adams family persisted in throwing up men of uncommon distinction: John Adams himself; his son John Quincy; John Quincy's son Charles Francis, our minister to Great Britain during the Civil War; Charles Francis's sons, Charles Francis, junior, the economist and historian, and Henry and Brooks, the writers.

Other families of comparable distinction suggest themselves. The Lees of Virginia sprang from the loins of Richard, who settled in the New World in 1642. The generations of his descendants included not only Francis Lightfoot Lee, who signed the Declaration of Independence, but also his distin-

---

* When descendants of the Founding Fathers do appear, the occasion is often considered newsworthy because of its rarity. In August 1968, for example, the 135-ton research submarine *Ben Franklin* was christened at West Palm Beach, Florida, by Miss Louisa J. Castle of Wilmington, Delaware, who was identified in the press as the great-great-great-great-great-granddaughter of Poor Richard.

guished brothers Richard Henry (also a signer of the Declaration) and Arthur and their cousin General Light-Horse Harry Lee. Light-Horse Harry sired Robert E. Lee, who in turn sired William Henry Fitzhugh Lee.

In Philadelphia, the Biddles trace themselves back at least to Clement Biddle, the Quartermaster General of the Continental Army, and Nicholas, who was official historian of the Lewis and Clark expedition as well as president of the second Bank of the United States. Other relatively ancient families can point with honest pride to comparable track records: the Lowells of Massachusetts and the Roosevelts of both Hyde Park and Oyster Bay come first to mind.

If there is such a thing as an American aristocracy, it is surely embodied in the combination of family identity, talent, and personal style that is found in genealogies such as these.

> The elite of power, wealth and celebrity are not the elite of culture, knowledge and sensibility. Moreover, they are not in contact with it, although the banalized and ostentatious fringes of the two worlds do overlap in the world of the celebrity.
>
> — C. Wright Mills

I confess I find myself prejudiced in this matter, but I do not think I am alone in finding it difficult to accept the present-day Vanderbilts and Rockefellers as aristocrats. Their ancestors were too mean; their origins in the noxious industrial wars of the past century too immediate; their accomplishments, in spite of the public careers of the current generation of Rockefellers, too insignificant. It is too hard to describe these families and their peers as "distinguished."

The eagerness with which the new rich everywhere, and in particular the new rich in America, have rushed forward to assume the rights and privileges of aristocracy almost before they can tell an oyster fork from a butter knife has been the subject of considerable comic comment, and rightly so, for the shifting conditions of its actors is one of the eternal givens of the human comedy. One of the historic milestones in this department was Mrs. William K. Vanderbilt's memorable fancy-dress ball of 1883, at which Mrs. Vanderbilt concluded a cease-fire and truce with Mrs. William Astor.

Mrs. Astor, though only two generations removed from the old scoundrel John Jacob, had by a combination of innate talent and "the acclamation of society itself" been installed as the queen of New York society — a society which had been carelessly defined at the Centennial Ball as the Four Hundred. (The real number was closer to six hundred.) Mrs. Astor, secure in her ancient lineage and queenly role, had neglected to call upon Mrs. Vanderbilt, whose father-in-law, William H. Vanderbilt, had haggled over scowloads of manure with the old "Commodore." In return for this studied oversight, Mrs. Astor was not invited to Mrs. Vanderbilt's party. As the preparations for the affair went ahead, it became apparent that it was to be a ball of such supreme lavishness that the absence of the queen would present a serious social difficulty. Aware of her obligations to her peers, Mrs. Astor at last did the decent thing, called upon Mrs. Vanderbilt, and in return was invited to the party.

Josephson's account of the affair cannot be improved on:

155

"For this memorable evening, fulsomely described in the press of two continents, Mrs. William K. Vanderbilt was costumed as a Venetian princess, Mr. Cornelius Vanderbilt as Louis XVI, and his spouse as 'The Electric Light,' in white satin trimmed with diamonds, and with a superb diamond headdress. In the drawing-rooms of the Vanderbilt palace, with its cluttered interiors in Japanese or in French style, hung with flowing masses of pale red velvet, drapery which was embroidered with foliage and jeweled butterflies, the noble throng ate, drank, and danced through the night. For the six quadrilles which represented the high moments of the ball, the dancers formed in the gymnasium on the third floor, moved down the grand staircase of Caën stone (fifty feet high), and swept through the great hall (sixty-five by twenty feet) into a drawing-room (forty by twenty feet whose whole wainscoting of carved French walnut had been torn from a French château and hauled across the ocean). A memorable evening which, as it broke the last barriers between the Astors and Vanderbilts, also broke all bounds for 'conspicuous consumption.' "

Among the established industrial families, only the Du Ponts can lay serious claim by reason of ancientness and origin to a condition of aristocracy, and it is not inappropriate that they established their claims in the Old World. The founder of the American line, Pierre Samuel Du Pont de Nemours, was a man of quite formidable talents. An economist and historian, he took part in drafting the Treaty of Paris, which brought an end to the American Revolution. He was, in addition, an author and a successful publisher but when his plant was destroyed during the French Revolution (he was a constitutional monarchist), he fled to the United States with his sons Eleuthère Irénée and Victor Marie. Du Pont did not arrive as a lonely and penniless immigrant, for Jefferson and Franklin were already friends and correspondents of his.

Since then, the prosperity of the Du Pont family has to a large degree rested on the profitable exploitation of wars, a line of development which was set when Eleuthère and Victor Marie, noting the inferior quality of the local product, established a gunpowder mill on the banks of the Brandywine. In the popular phrase, the Du Ponts have been merchants of death; at the same time, their family history has hewed closer to the classic notion of aristocracy than other American industrial dynasties such as the Mellons, Dukes, Rockefellers, Astors, Vanderbilts, McCormicks and Whitneys. Yet, given their talent for profiting from catastrophes, the Du Ponts are hardly a national treasure.

As Mills points out, the elite of power, wealth, and celebrity have not, since the early days of the Republic, coincided to any significant extent with the elite of culture. If this is true of the Robber Barons and their descendants, it is even more true of the Great Big New Rich. Except for the collecting of expensive paintings, there has been little in their careers that shows any leanings toward the aristocratic pleasures or vices. They are typically private men, the texture of whose lives is not calculated to evoke the recognition of superiority that lies at the base of any definition of aristocracy. Their wives, even, appear indifferent to formal society; there are no great hostesses among them. Unlike the Vanderbilts and Astors, they do not promote the marriage of their daughters to titled youths from Europe. Their sons become not playboys but business executives.

Most of the people in the top management of American business are promoted clerks, engineers, and salesmen.

— J. Paul Getty

Today we can observe the rise of a class of engineers, salesmen, minor executives, and social workers, all engaged in actually running the country's temporal affairs.

— Thurman Arnold

The most romantic view one can take of the Great Big New Rich is that they represent the last flowering of the tough, practical, individualist spirit that, as the saying goes, made this country great. It is a tempting hypothesis, and one that is not without merit, particularly when one compares the Great Big New Rich with the engineers, salesmen, and promoted clerks who, by the accounts of both J. Paul Getty and Thurman Arnold (strange bedfellows!), are now managing the daily affairs of the United States. But as we shall see, both Getty and Arnold have failed to note that these are engineers, salesmen, and promoted clerks of a very special sort.

As we will recall, the main thrust of the Lytton theory of tycoonery was to point up the difference in quality between the tycoon and the shogun — the tycoon being an imperial figure and the shogun a hired commander of a territory. (I am obliged to add that the distinction cannot be supported etymologically: In Japanese, *taikun* is a synonym for *shogun*.) The theory is a useful and meritorious one when it is applied to those few industries in which genuine tycoons can still be found. It fails entirely, however, to explain the true nature of the great bulk of American business enterprises.

We are obliged again to enter, with all due caution, that fascinating and dangerous land in which the beguilements of folklore seduce the traveler bent on fighting his way through to some accommodation to reality. It requires only a slight talent for exaggeration to argue that the bulk of Americans would accept Stewart Holbrook's vigorous description of the Robber Barons as still descriptive of American business leaders: "They were tough-minded fellows, who fought their way encased in rhinoceros hide and filled the air with their mad bellowings and the cries of the wounded; while their determined womenfolk badgered them into erecting monstrous houses that were much like the ennobled bathrooms of ancient emperors."

As we shall see, the facts are considerably otherwise. We can properly describe the men in charge of our greatest business undertakings neither as tycoons nor as shoguns but as mandarins.

> Not for a generation have people outside Detroit and the automobile industry known the name of the current head of General Motors. In the manner of all men, he must produce identification when paying by check.
>
> — *John Kenneth Galbraith*

The name of the current president of General Motors is Edward N. Cole.

Mr. Cole is about as thoroughly a company man as one could possibly imagine. He has worked for General Motors since 1933, when he went on the payroll as a lab assistant in the

Cadillac division. (He was 58 when in the fall of 1967 he was elected president.) His degree is a B.S. earned from the General Motors Institute. As an executive vice-president, his main impact on the industry had been the development of the Corvair automobile. He no longer flies a private plane but tinkers, grows orchids, hunts ducks and pheasants, and skis. He was divorced from his first wife and remarried. Otherwise, he is the perfect mandarin, handsome but faceless, well known but anonymous, powerful but powerless.

> Whatever our national hopes, the business leaders of America are a select group, drawn for the most part from the upper ranks. Only to a limited extent may it be said that every man's chances are as good as the next man's, for birth in the higher occupational levels improves these life chances considerably.
>
> — W. Lloyd Warner

Horatio Alger to the contrary, the road that leads to great success in business does not lead from rags to riches by grace of luck and pluck, but from riches to riches by grace of Yale and the Harvard Graduate School of Business Administration.

It is a curious fact that whereas the sociologist C. Wright Mills used the comparatively neutral term "business elite" to describe the governors of our greatest corporations, W. Lloyd Warner, who is much more sympathetic than Mills to the mystique of commerce and industry, calls them a "birth elite." And, as he demonstrates in his studies of eight thousand leaders in all varieties of business, Warner's phrase is a precise and accurate one.

Warner's general argument is that, although latter-day Horatio

Alger heroes can, as we have seen, still be found, the chances of a boy's reaching the top level of the corporate hierarchy are vastly improved if he chooses a father who is already a success and who can afford to send him to the right schools. Of the business leaders Warner surveyed, something over half had been born into business. Of these, eight percent of their fathers owned large businesses, 15 percent were major executives, 18 percent owned small businesses, 8 percent were minor executives, and 3 percent were foremen. Of those born outside the parish of business management, the sons of professional men accounted for 14 percent. Less than a third of these upper-level executives (32 percent) were born to families headed by a clerk, a farmer, or a laborer. Opportunity surely still exists, but it is heavily qualified by the odds.

The birth elite tend to pass through the schools of the Ivy League and several of the better state universities. The school which is the most diligent in training business leaders is Yale, followed in order by Harvard, Princeton, Cornell, Pennsylvania, Illinois, M.I.T., Michigan, N.Y.U., Minnesota, Williams, Berkeley, Chicago, and Columbia. The graduate schools of Harvard and Columbia add the final polish. (As a footnote to Warner's scholarly endeavors, let me add my own amateur finding that, judging from the twentieth-anniversary directory of my class at Yale, a truly remarkable number of my classmates hold positions of eminence in firms bearing their family names or associated with family dynasties, such as the Watsons of IBM. As Warner observes, there is an elite within the elite, and the sons of big businessmen dominate the chief executive positions.)

The importance of the birth elite varies from business to business. Older, slow-growing businesses are heavily populated by Ivy League types who "tend to value social graces, manners, and other qualifications not directly or obviously connected with the job." Prominent among such "closed" businesses are brokerage and the chemical and paper industries, in which about three-quarters of the executives are college graduates. At the other end of the scale, the railroads and highway transportation offer more opportunities to bootstrappers; a fifth of their executives dropped out of high school.

As we have seen, the Great Big New Rich resemble in their educational careers the executives of "open" industries. Unlike the majority of upper-level management in industry as a whole they have not been trained for their jobs. Quite on the contrary, they take pride, even in the case of the Harvardman Edwin Land, in having been too impatient to have stayed on for their diplomas. Whereas graduates of Yale tend to dominate the world of corporate management, the record does not reveal that a single one of the Great Big New Rich ever set foot in New Haven.

In terms of their geographic origins, there is not much to choose between the Great Big Executives and the Great Big New Rich. The single exception is that the South has produced a larger proportion of the executives than of the entrepreneurs. In both cases, the Atlantic Seaboard and the Middle West are overrepresented when compared with the distribution of the general population. Few top executives and even fewer of the Great Big New Rich were born on the Pacific Coast (Norton Simon, it will be recalled, is the sole Westerner on our panel).

Before putting down the West as a land of happy lotus-eaters, however, we are obliged to remind ourselves that the West Coast was a considerably different and much less populous place before World War I. Another generation will have to pass before we will be justified in the conclusion that the currently well-populated, affluent, but leisure-oriented culture of the West is not a fertile growing ground for business leaders.

We have already had occasion to note that even the most well-rewarded corporate executive is rich according to an entirely different scale than the Great Big New Rich. Our lower threshold for great wealth was set at $100 million. At a conservative 5 percent, this capital would yield an annual income of $5 million. Not even the greatest and most powerful corporation pays its chief executive officer more than a fraction of this minimum.

In 1967 the highest paid industrial executive in the United States was James M. Roche, the chairman of the board of General Motors. Mr. Roche received only $200,000 salary (an amount that H. L. Hunt is said to take in every day). Although his salary did not compare with the $331,475 paid Samuel Bronfman of Distillers Corp.–Seagrams Ltd., or the $325,000 paid Neil H. McElroy of Procter & Gamble, Mr. Roche's bonus and stock options and other benefits, such as GM's contributions toward his pension, brought the total figure close to, but still below, a million dollars.

The managers are better trained for the modern world . . .
The entrepreneurs are survivals of an earlier age.

— *David T. Bazelon*

The great theme of American business history in this century has been the progressive bureaucratization of industrial and commercial enterprise. As always, recognition lagged well after the fact. It was not until 1941 that James Burnham's *The Managerial Revolution* — one of those books whose title has probably had more influence than its contents — announced the great change. Thirty years later, our rhetoric still honors the rugged virtues of the free market and the entrepreneurial spirit even while, as John Kenneth Galbraith has demonstrated in *The New Industrial State*, the great bureaucracy of industry daily firms up its working alliance with the great bureaucracy of government, and in which such dissonances as antitrust actions are little more than lovers' spats.

The bureaucratization of enterprise is of course not an isolated phenomenon, but one that has been taking place within a general worldwide movement toward the rational organization of human energies. The Chinese civil service under the Manchus was a prototypical example of bureaucratization in which mandarins were created by virtue of rigorous competitive examinations open to young men without regard for family origin. (Practically, of course, the mandarins were usually the scions of the birth elite, who could afford for their children the proper preliminary training. Similarly, in our own time, as we have observed, Yale College and the Harvard Business School offer a superior training for a business mandarin while Harvard College and Harvard Law prepare the governmental mandarin.) Seventy years ago Max Weber was analyzing the process of bureaucracy and predicting its inevitable and irreversible victory. We are only now beginning to admit that what has happened is indeed the case, although, as we have already seen, the reactions to Professor Galbraith's recent book suggest that the emotional resistance is still powerful.

Lloyd Warner has put the matter well in *Big Business Leaders in America*. After demolishing the popular image of the business leader as a two-fisted but brilliant laborer who worked his way up from the shop or the production line or as a salesman who began with a tiny capital which he caused to flourish and multiply, Warner goes on to say, "The typical career pattern is a bureaucratic one in business today, just as the typical business organization is primarily bureaucratic. Careers are built largely on formal education, acquisition of management skills in the white-collar hierarchy, and movement through the far-flung systems of technicians and lower-level management personnel into top management. Traces of the legendary patterns remain, and spectacular examples of the type exist; they tend to be unique."

And this, of course, is our point. The Great Big New Rich are precisely those spectacular and unique types that are more familiar in legend than in the actual business world of today. D. K. Ludwig was a mechanic who worked his way to the very top. W. Clement Stone was a salesman who caused a tiny capital to multiply more than a million times. Charles Allen, Jr., was a Wall Street runner. Joseph H. Hirshhorn was an immigrant boy from Eastern Europe. If these men were great figures in the public eye, we could conclude that their greatest service has been to preserve the useful illusion that great opportunities are still open to all. As it is, they have remained shadowy figures, whose anonymity bears witness to their essential lack of importance.

It was not long ago that the high-ranking executive took on the personal style of the entrepreneur. Now, the entrepreneur will often take on the protective coloration of the executive. If this has tended to make them rather obscure men, it is also true that none of the Great Big New Rich are hated as the Robber Barons were.

NINE

Gallery Four: Conglomerate Men

At its present rate of growth, by 1970 Litton Industries will cover three-fourths of the earth's surface.

> — *A Wall Street insider*

Everybody loves Tex, but nobody really knows him.

> — *Dorothy (Buff) Chandler*

Charles B. (Tex) Thornton is very likely the most gifted business manager to emerge since the end of World War II. Unlike other noted exponents of scientific management — his friend and onetime colleague Robert McNamara, for example — he has also become one of the Great Big New Rich. Thornton's business success can be measured by his achievement in raising Litton Industries, which when he acquired it in 1953 was a small firm manufacturing microwave tubes, to a billion-dollar conglomerate corporation, said to be the fastest-growing business organization in American history. Litton's 188 plants in 31 states and 24 countries produce nine thousand products, of which half were unknown five years ago.

Thornton is a virtuoso in at least three areas: First is his ability to seduce productive results from the currently fashionable management metaphysics that goes under the name of systems analysis; second is his ability to organize the manufacture of products of the New Technology; third is his command of the subtleties involved in corporate mergers. Furthermore, although Thornton is a friendly and personable man* who hardly fits the image of a man of disaster or a campfollower of catastrophe, it is clear that the direction of his subsequent career was set by World War II and that Litton Industries would be a much different sort of firm if it were not for the requirements of the Cold War and the preparations for the greater conflict to come.

> I'm an industrialist, not an in-and-outer in the stock market.
> — *Charles B. Thornton*

When I went to see Thornton, who is now chairman of the board of Litton, I was struck by the contrast between the firm's activities and the atmosphere of its headquarters (across from the Beverly Hills city hall), where, in offices furnished in wormy

---

* Another view of Thornton is apparent in a confidential report prepared by a Wall Street accounting firm and quoted in a recent issue of *Ramparts* magazine: "Tex Thornton — good abilities along a few lines but not a good all around man; is unprincipled, ruthless, and is universally disliked; cannot be trusted."

oak and hung with Revolutionary War prints in carved frames, executives confer about the development, manufacture, and distribution of nuclear submarines, desktop computers, or sophisticated materials handling systems. (Roughly a third of Litton's revenue comes from defense and space contracts, a third from business machines, and a third from specialized industrial and professional contracts that range from running a Job Corps camp to preparing programs for the economic development of Greece and Portugal.)

Thornton is a solidly built, ruddy man in his middle fifties with shrewd eyes and the remains of a Texas drawl. He was born in 1913 in a small farming town in Knox County in the north-central part of the state. Thornton's childhood presents a textbook case for the psychoanalysis of the entrepreneur. His father departed the family circle soon after young Charles was born, and tried to find his fortune blowing out oil-well fires with nitroglycerin. He never caught up with his luck and died unfortunately, murdered by a couple to whom he had given a lift in his car.

In the meantime, Thornton's mother, Alice, set her son firmly on the road whose signposts are individual responsibility and the value of sound investments. Charles earned money and bought land, and it has been reported that by the time he was fourteen he could cash a check in any store in town. He left home to study engineering at Texas Technological College in Lubbock, but left in his third year for Washington, D.C. As Thornton recalls his decision, "It was a pretty grim outlook in the Thirties, especially in Texas. I borrowed fifty dollars and left in 1934. I remember seeing fences covered up with sand, right there on the edge of the Dust Bowl. No, there was opportunity then, and there was more later, and there's never been opportunity like today.

"When I was in college, I was told by businessmen, lawyers, architects, anybody, don't follow *this* profession, you'll starve to death. And so I wound up in business administration," Thornton told me. He earned a business degree at George Washington University while working as a clerk in the Department of the Interior. A report he wrote caught the eye of Robert Lovett, then Assistant Secretary of War for Air, who offered him a commission as a second lieutenant if he would try to make sense out of the business practices of the Air Corps. Thornton stayed a second lieutenant for forty-eight hours. He came out of World War II a 32-year-old chicken-colonel and the leader of a group of nine other young business-oriented officers who proposed to apply methods of statistical control to peacetime industry. Henry Ford II accepted a proposal Thornton made to him in a brash telegram. (Thornton's salary when he started at Ford was $16,000.) Somebody at Ford derisively called Thornton's group the Quiz Kids, which later became Whiz Kids. Two of them, including Robert McNamara, became presidents of Ford, and four others became division chiefs.

Thornton left Ford after two years and went to Hughes Aircraft as vice-president and general manager. Although his tenure at Hughes saw the company's sales shoot upward from $2 million to $200 million, Thornton was not universally beloved by Howard Hughes' associates, and in 1953 he left as part of a general exodus of Hughes Aircraft's top management.

Thornton and Roy Ash (who had been a Whiz Kid and a

Charles B. Thornton, chairman of the board of multi-circuited Litton
Industries of Beverly Hills. LITTON INDUSTRIES NEWS BUREAU.

colleague of Thornton's at Hughes Aircraft) went to Lehman Brothers, looking for $1.5 million. "I told them that I wanted to start a company that would become a strong blue chip in the scientific and technological environment of the future. It would be a balanced company — not just engineering, not just manufacturing, not just financial. You can't win a ball game with only a pitcher and a catcher, and you can't have a strong company unless it's balanced." Lehman Brothers found the money by selling packages of stocks and bonds worth $29,200 each. Ten years later each package was worth $3.2 million.

Thornton's formula for a balanced company evidently worked, for within these ten years Litton had prospered so exceedingly well that *Time* called it "an amorphous giant with interests and appetites as broad as the universe."

In the last quarter of 1967, however, Litton's profits went into an alarming decline, apparently reflecting management decisions of less than Olympian wisdom and giving some comfort to businessmen still operating more on intuition and less on systems analysis. Thornton's own holdings of stock fell in value from $147 million in October to $79 million in March. The goat, or possibly the scapegoat, was senior vice-president William McKenna, who had headed the hard-hit business-equipment division. (McKenna resigned to become chairman and chief executive officer of Norton Simon, Inc.)

In commenting on Litton's "repeated and seemingly elementary mistakes in production, cost estimates, and pricing," *Fortune* observed that the company's bad fortune had cast some shadows on the notion that "talented general managers, applying modern management techniques, can effectively over-

see diverse businesses in which they have no specific experience." Yet, as 1968 went on, Litton recovered and seemed
certain to go on growing — either because of or in spite of its
management philosophy.

> Roy and I and the rest of the people don't work for money.
> There are other things.
>
> *— Charles B. Thornton*

The incongruity I had noticed in the colonial furnishings of
Litton's headquarters turned out to have a personal parallel.
Tex Thornton is a paradox, and one that is typical of the business community of our time in that, notable entrepreneur that
he is, his personal style and philosophy identify him with the
corporate bureaucrats and professional managers. *Management*
and *executive* are key words in his vocabulary; *entrepreneur* is
also a key word, but it was not until we had been talking for
some time that I recognized that we were using the word in
quite different ways.

Curious to find out what this wealthy and successful entrepreneur thought of the decline of entrepreneurship in the
United States, I explained that it was my impression that few
young men of my acquaintance burned with a consuming fire to
set up their own businesses and drive through the competition
to make their first, second, and hundredth millions. Instead, their
wildest ambitions reached about as high as comfortable vice-
presidencies at, say, Xerox, IBM, or Litton.

Thornton reacted vigorously to this suggestion. "Litton is
built on the idea of entrepreneurship," he said. "The executive
at Litton is an organizer and implementer and not just a sal-

aried manager. His responsibilities and abilities are the same as if he were running a separate corporation. In this way, the executive can more completely use his total management capabilities. We want to keep the virile strength of our own industrial base, to preserve the incentive system within the structure of a large corporation."

It took me a while to get back to my definition of entrepreneur, which is of a man who has had the original vision and taken the original risk, but after Thornton suggested Secretary of Defense McNamara as an outstanding example of the entrepreneur it became clear we were operating on different wavelengths and we went on to other things. This is, I think, a point worth recording, for *entrepreneur* is a key word in the theology of the American business community and, in the best tradition of the ecclesiastical establishments, the word is being modified to meet the new generation. *Predestination* doesn't carry the same meaning to a modern Presbyterian as it did to John Calvin; *entrepreneur* no longer invokes a vision of Cornelius Vanderbilt or Henry Ford but of the leaders of that new class of scientific manager who are in the process of taking over the world of industry.

In his personal style, Thornton is consistent in his role as being primarily an executive rather than primarily a rich man. He and his wife Flora live well but not ostentatiously in a ranch-style house in one of the more expensive residential districts in Los Angeles. (They also own a ranch less than an hour's drive away.) One of the Thornton sons went to Stanford and the other to Harvard; both went on to the Harvard Business School. ("We forget the tremendous pool of responsible young men coming up," Thornton told me. "This new generation is an exciting group.")

Thornton rises early and, after orange juice, begins to telephone the East, where the working day is already well under way. He smokes a great many cigarettes during the four hours or so he spends on the telephone every day. He is not a big spender, and cabbies and waiters have been reported to wince at his notion of largesse. Money, simply, appears to be not very much on his mind.

For relaxation, Thornton takes a horse on a thirty- or forty-mile ride along the mountain trails north of the city, or flies over the bleak but dramatic Southern California landscape. "I often marvel at what the pioneers did coming across undeveloped country to California," he told me after one of these flights. "How they made it I'll never know. Not long ago I followed the California Trail by plane. I did it in two hours. Two hours a distance that had taken the pioneers six weeks! Maybe that was an outlet for the hippies of those days — at least the haircuts had something in common. We've got other challenges now. Maybe part of the trouble is that those who don't feel or see the challenge are the articulate ones. They're the ones you hear."

> Horatio Alger used to be typical of America, but we don't talk about that sort of responsibility the way we used to.
> — *Charles B. Thornton*

In a cover story about Thornton, a writer for *Time* theorized that, with his father gone chasing will-o'-the-wisps, it was his mother who molded Thornton's essential philosophy, preaching the gospel of responsibility until "it enveloped him like a Sunday suit." This too is thoroughly in the American grain.

Whatever the source of his basic orientation, the most interesting thing to me in listening to Thornton philosophize about the world of business and the world at large was a beguiling mixture of naïveté and sophistication. For him, as for others of the Great Big New Rich, Horatio Alger still lives. (As if proof were needed, in 1964 Thornton was one of ten citizens — including Gene Autry, Pearl Buck, and the architect Minoru Yamasaki — who received awards in memory of Horatio.) Hard work, thrift, early-to-bed, and a little luck — these, we are assured, are the ingredients of which great successes are made. It is, of course, not so simple. And yet Thornton has said a great deal about becoming rich in five words: "I can't stand useless leisure."

In his explicit philosophy, Thornton tends to return again and again to three touchstones: the healthiness of the profit motive, the continuing opportunity offered in America, and the social responsibility of the businessman. "I don't know what's evil about paying a profit if you can get a job done for a third less," he said, and bummed a menthol cigarette from me. "Bob McNamara has been encouraging the idea of increased profits and decreased costs. But there's this political idea that you shouldn't let them make profits. We ought to go back and study the growth and expansion of America. Let's not kill the thing that's given us our growth."

He went on, "One thing that bothers me about America is that we don't talk as much as we used to about the great opportunities that exist. I'd like to see more discussion. The opportunity for young men was never greater. We don't have a Gold Rush or Indians to fight, but the young man with ability can get just as excited by the opportunities today.

"And, you know, I don't find many young men who really feel that everything's done and that there's no way to break in. They just think they'll do a better job. I used to think that too. Now, I'm a little more restrained."

In the traditional style of the businessman, Thornton views the intellectual community with some uneasiness: "I don't care how smart anybody is, you've got to bring that smartness to bear. The trouble with some intellectuals is that they often have other degrees of judgment. You have to have intelligence, but you have to have the judgment to go along with it."

In an article in *Harper's* in the fall of 1967, Michael Harrington wrote with some distress of the emergence of the "social-industrial complex." The danger was not, he wrote, that the "social industrialists" were greedy profiteers engaged in a conspiracy against the common good, but that "when business methods are sincerely and honestly applied to urban problems, with very good intentions, they still inevitably lead to antisocial results. It is exactly when crass concerns are not paramount that the real problem — the inapplicability of business methods and priorities to the crisis of the cities — emerges most clearly."

Harrington's concern reminded me strongly of Thornton's response when I inquired after his thought on solutions to the cruel and pressing urban problems of Los Angeles. Thornton's credentials are not unimpressive. "I'm on the President's Commission on Civil Disturbances — what's usually called the 'riot commission.' You've got disciplined management in tens of thousands of business corporations, but these resources aren't being brought to bear. Some people have the notion that businessmen aren't compassionate. Sure they are. They're as compassionate as anybody else. They do get discouraged when they deal in areas the government has usurped. The government should be mainly concerned in creating an atmosphere where things can happen. The government and the intellectuals have their hearts in the right place, but you can't accomplish things just by the huge appropriation of funds. What we're missing is the creativeness we could harness by getting American business and industry involved."

There's really no place to stop. We will never reach our destination.

— *Charles B. Thornton*

The construction of conglomerate companies is the hottest game in U.S. business today.

— *Newsweek*

Time has called Litton Industries the fastest-growing organization in American business history; *Newsweek* has called Ling-Temco-Vought of Dallas the fastest growing major company in the world. Whatever discrepancy exists here is not particularly important, for the fact is that both Litton and LTV have been growing in the same explosive way and that both are in the same sort of business — the business of building huge and widely diversified corporations by merging with other corporations. (The antitrust people are stern about horizontal or vertical mergers, involving companies that are in the same business or that have a supplier relationship, but do not frown on the merging of dissimilar enterprises — hence the conglomerate corporation.) *

Although few other merger-minded corporation presidents have practiced their specialty with quite the skill and élan of Tex Thornton and LTV's James J. Ling, the phenomenon is a widespread one: the Radio Corporation of America owns the Hertz car-rental company and Random House; the W. R. Grace shipping company brews Miller's High Life beer; Westinghouse Electric bottles Seven-Up; and the Reynolds Tobacco Company cooks Chun King Chinese foods. By 1965, Litton had absorbed fifty other corporations, including Royal McBee (typewriter), Ingalls Shipbuilding (nuclear submarines), Monroe Calculating Machines, and Hewitt-Robins (materials handling). The total has risen since then, with an important acquisition being Stouffer Foods, whose line of frozen products fitted neatly into Litton's development of microwave ovens. Similarly, in 1967 LTV's Jimmy Ling, who is ten years younger than Thornton, engineered the acquisition of the giant Wilson company (meat, sporting goods, and pharmaceuticals) to add

---

* The first really large conglomerate merger occurred in 1952 when E. R. Squibb became part of Olin Matheson. Merging as a major business strategy has been picking up steam ever since. The biggest merger up to now occurred in October 1968, when the Xerox Corporation and CIT Financial said their vows and set up housekeeping in a union that boasted assets of $3.4 billion. In the week following, five mergers involving corporations worth more than $100 million each were announced. The reaction of the Federal Trade Commission to conglomerate mergers sometimes provokes thought. For example, although holy water was sprinkled on the merger of Pepsi-Cola and Frito-Lay (corn chips), it was with the solemn proviso that the two products could not be advertised together for five years.

to his subsidiaries already engaged in manufacturing missiles, aircraft, electronic gear, radar and sound equipment, and electrical cable.

Diversification of this sort is not merely insurance against a sudden decline in the sales of a single product; it also creates a favorable climate for the entrepreneurial spirit that in the last century went into the creation of great railroad or financial empires. As Thornton explains it, "We have never acquired companies as such. We have bought time, a market, a product line, a plant, a research team, a sales force. It would take us years to duplicate all this from scratch." Ling is somewhat breezier: "People ask, where's the magic, where's the pixie-dust? I suppose we're complex compared to a bread-and-butter maker, but it's still uncomplicated. Every one of our divisions has prospered."

In the world of the mergers, the greatest coup of all was Ling's acquisition of Wilson. It was, as *Newsweek* pointed out, an act rather like Jonah swallowing the whale — Wilson's annual sales were about a billion, while LTV's were only half of that. This act of legerdemain was accomplished with Rothschild money that Ling found in London with the help (like Thornton) of Lehman Brothers.

Wilson stock was quietly acquired on the open market. Wilson's president, Roscoe Haynie, first learned what was going on when he was paid an unexpected call by one of Ling's top men. Haynie recalled later, "The meeting lasted just twenty minutes, about half of which was taken up with the weather and things like that. He told me he always played with Wilson golf clubs, but I knew damn well he hadn't come all the way to Chicago to get his golf clubs repaired."

Meanwhile, other LTV men had been visiting other Wilson directors, who saw the advantages of accepting Ling's offer. Even Haynie, who was at first angry and alarmed, accommodated himself gracefully and now works for LTV as president of Wilson meat packing. Yet, in spite of the atmosphere of good feeling, a decided flavor of Robber Baronism lingers on.

Ling puts it another way. A student of Field Marshal Erwin Rommel's campaigns, he has said, "He is one of my teachers. The message is mobility and the quick strike."

> Don't tell me how hard you work, tell me how much you get done. A racehorse can get around a track a lot faster than a jackass.
>
> — James J. Ling

Like Thornton, Ling is an early riser and a light breakfaster (toast, orange juice, coffee). Unlike Thornton, who paid only $250,000 for his Holmsby Hills house (which he bought from Mrs. Nancy Sinatra), Ling awakes in a scene of considerable opulence. The master bedroom of his pillared, porticoed and befountained French Provincial mansion on the north edge of Dallas is about as large as the main living room. Among the other features are a bathtub hewn out of a single block of Italian marble ($14,000) and a two hole golf course with 230-yard fairways. The entire layout cost him some $1.5 million.

After reading the *Wall Street Journal*, Ling (who is six-foot-two, 200 pounds) enters his Lincoln limousine for a 20-minute drive to his office, on the fourth floor of the LTV tower downtown. By 7:45 he is at work. Like most of the other Great Big New Rich, he works hard, putting in a 90-hour week. He is well tailored in an upper-level-executive style. He has an extraordinarily good-looking wife and three children.

Ling (his name is Bavarian, not Chinese as some unfriendly Dallas jokes had it when he was on the way up) was born in Hugo, Oklahoma. After his mother's death when he was twelve, he lived with an aunt in Louisiana. He attended a Catholic high school in Shreveport, and then, after four *Wanderjahre* in Oklahoma and Texas, he joined the Navy, in which he served under fire in the South Pacific.

After the war, he started an electrical contracting business, which he built into a prosperous concern. Deciding to go public, "I developed my own prospectus and gave it to a lawyer to put the holy water on it. I got an associate to sell some of the stock from a booth at the Texas State Fair. I sold 25 percent of the stock myself, to friends." Having raised enough cash, he performed his first merger, buying a West Coast electronics company. Since then he has built LTV into a giant concern that is listed No. 38 on *Fortune*'s 1968 compilation of the 500 leading U.S. corporations, and that with $1.8 billion in annual sales is six numbers and $200 million ahead of Litton.

Ling has great ambitions for his company, both at home and abroad. Speaking of the prospects for 1970, he said recently, "I'll say here and now that if we're not closer to five billion dollars than four, then my name won't be associated with this company. Maybe by then we'll have finished working on the Pill. Not pills for women. This is a pill for man's eternal problem of virility. We want to enable you to be what you

James J. Ling, youngest of the Great Big New Rich.

would like to be when you're seventy or eighty. After 1970 — well, if I told you what we'd be doing then, you'd think I had been on LSD."

The conglomerate men, who include not only Thornton and Ling but also such operatives as Charles Bluhdorn of Gulf & Western Industries, Fred Sullivan of Walter Kidde & Co., Dr. Henry Singleton of Teledyne, and Rupert Thompson of Textron Inc., have of course attracted a great deal of attention in the business community and in governmental agencies, not all of it admiring.* Each year, fewer and larger corporations control a larger slice of the American economy. It has been estimated that the two hundred largest U.S. companies controlled 30 percent of manufacturing assets in 1947; controlled 55 percent in 1967; and may well control 67 percent by 1975.

So far as the function of the conglomerate corporation in producing new members of the Great Big New Rich goes, their most prolific days may well be over. If Bart Lytton's theory of tycoonery is more than a pleasant lunchtime conceit, it would seem that the conglomerates have about had their fifteen to twenty years of fertility. In that case, Tex Thornton may well turn out to have been one of the first of his kind while Jimmy Ling may well be the last.

---

* The Federal Trade Commission announced in the summer of 1968 that it was going to investigate the conglomerates. Ling fired back promptly in a public speech that the FTC was lowering itself to "business McCarthyism or witch-hunting."

TEN

The Pathology of Money

Last month you reported 1,119 bungs. Ten thousand were
sent you at the beginning of the month. You have used 9,527
this month. You report 1,102 on hand. What has become of
the other four hundred and ninety?

— *John D. Rockefeller*

In spite of the original Rockefeller's great philanthropies, the
picture of him that will endure is of the counter of bungs and
drops of solder, the old skinflint with the face of an Egyptian
mummy whom the publicist Ivy Lee taught to pass out shiny
dimes in the hope that he would miraculously become loved
and no longer suffer from the knowledge that he was the most
hated man in the United States. Swift, the meatpacker, made it
a habit to rise at daybreak to check the waste grease at his
slaughterhouses. The incredible Hetty Green, though she en-

joyed a personal income of $7 million a year at a time when the average American made less than $500, lived in unfurnished rooms where she did her own cooking, wore a black dress for such a long time that it turned green, and carried graham crackers in her purse to save her the cost of restaurant meals. When she was convalescing from a stroke, her son (who spent about a million a year himself) was obliged to ask her nurses to dress as housemaids, for he knew that the sight of a nurse's uniform in the house might be more than his frugal though desperately ill mother could bear.

Anecdotes of the prodigious meannesses of the great rich of the last century are many and are diverting, but can be matched, story for story, by our own Great Big New Rich. Of these, the late S. S. Kresge, a farm boy of Swiss descent who became a great potentate in the world of the dime store, contributed more than his share. Kresge regularly salvaged worn-out shoes by lining them with paper, discouraged his valet from pressing his clothes for fear of wearing them threadbare before their time, and was divorced by two wives for a variety of complaints, among which was simple stinginess. In middle age he was persuaded to take up golf, but he lasted only three rounds, most of which he spent hunting balls he had driven into the rough. Then he quit, explaining that, considering the number of balls it used up, the game of golf was too expensive for him.

Another engaging specimen is Howard Hughes, the landlord of Las Vegas, who like many others of the rich manages to combine in his temperament strains that allow him to be simultaneously a great plunger and a great skinflint. The story has been told that when on the set of one of his films Hughes saw a Mexican actress chewing a piece of chicken as called for in the script, he called the property man aside and demanded, "Did you have to get a *whole* chicken?"

H. L. Hunt, whose oil holdings are so vast that even Getty sometimes defers to him, is the despair of lunchtime visitors, who are lucky to get a drugstore sandwich while Hunt lunches out of a desk drawer on dried prunes, a wedge of low-calorie cheese, and a slice of bread baked from wheat grown in Deaf Smith County in the Texas panhandle. The visitor's napkin may be typewriter paper. The great tycoon's office is furnished with chairs upholstered in cracked leather, a display for Gastro-Majic, a stomach nostrum that Hunt manufactures and promotes, and a dime-store American flag.

We shall return to the life styles of the Great Big New Rich later on. For the time being, the point of these observations is to establish the proposition that many of the very rich are as irrational in their attitudes toward money as are the very poor.

> The love of wealth is therefore to be traced, as either a principal or an accessory motive, at the bottom of all that Americans do; this gives to all their passions a sort of family likeness and soon renders the survey of them exceedingly wearisome.
>
> — de Tocqueville

For once, the great Frenchman who anatomized the Republic of the early 1800's with the flair and skill of an expert prosector before a class of medical-school freshmen, was wrong — or, at least, wrong for now, deficient in the capacity for uttering eternal verities with which he has often been credited.

Yet his observation that we Americans are nothing but a race of money-grubbers, laying waste our powers in feverish getting and spending, is still firmly implanted in the folklore, and not only in the folklore of our friends and enemies beyond our borders but also in the most important folklore of all, the folklore that we cherish about ourselves.

The liberal, with his characteristic genius for self-humiliation, will triumphantly announce that this once-fair country, the home of Emerson and Thoreau and the James family, has been thoroughly corrupted, that Mammon rules over all, and that goodness is gone from the land. The lunatic militiamen of the Right rally to the defense of money, decorate themselves with earrings, tie clips, and assorted gilded gimcrackery fashioned in the shape of the dollar sign, and declare through their seeress Ayn Rand, "Money is the root of all good."

The argument here is largely a paper one, concerned more with asserting ancient pieties than with asserting the truth about the changing functions of money in our world.

Money is the most important thing in the world. It represents health, strength, honor, generosity, and beauty as conspicuously and undeniably as the want of it represents illness, weakness, disgrace, meanness, and ugliness. Not the least of its virtues is that it destroys base people as certainly as it fortifies and dignifies noble people.

— George Bernard Shaw

"Dear me, I wisht I had money," said Mr. Hennessy. "So do I," said Mr. Dooley. "I need it."

— Finley Peter Dunne
("Mr. Dooley")

And is this not it? Unless we are infants or wards of the state we need money to live at all. For most of us, to live with dignity and pleasure requires more money than the average man can earn. (Ergo, the average man does not live with dignity and pleasure.) As Shaw pointed out in the *Intelligent Woman's Guide,* money lets us get what we want instead of what somebody else thinks we want. Within limits, the love of money is surely as healthy as the love of well-prepared food, of handsome clothes, or of comfortable and aesthetically pleasing surroundings.

There is another fact about money that must not go unregarded. Our attitudes toward money are undergoing radical changes and it is probably no exaggeration to say that money is regarded more lightly in the United States in this year of our Lord than since the Industrial Revolution. I suspect that this is one of the few benign influences of the computer revolution: More Americans than ever before have broken through to an understanding of the great truth that our individual hoards of money are not silver and nickel and copper and paper imprinted in tasteful shades of green which the banker keeps locked up for us, but are nothing more than sequences of numbers printed out on machine-generated statements of a variety of sorts.

Although I have a friend who once carried $26,000 cash to Brazil in his hip pocket, few of us ever equip ourselves with much currency; instead, we carry our checkbooks and credit cards. The great bulk of educated and articulate but non-rich Americans have at last discovered what the rich have known all along, that money is almost a pure abstraction, an entity to which an actual physical presence is pure irrelevance. As H. L. Hunt himself once put it, "Money is nothing. It is just something to make bookkeeping convenient." This might have been the epigraph of a recent article in the *Harvard Business Review* in which the authors demonstrated the practical possibility of turning over our entire personal economy to the computers, with a master credit card replacing not only our cash but our checkbooks too.

It is easy to represent the upper level of the corporate bureaucracy as men driven by their lust for ever-larger salaries, bonuses, and stock options. It is also, of course, quite wrong. The spur is neither fame nor money but the passionate need to identify oneself with an organization, a theme that John Kenneth Galbraith has explored with great success in *The Affluent Society* and *The New Industrial State.* No matter how many vice-presidents sweep the path before him, no matter how many million automobiles or toasters or pork chops he midwives into the world each year, the corporate executive of our time is moved by something quite distinct from the sequences of numbers that represent his annual income or the amount of stock he has on option. He is moved by the urgent need to live within a family of similarly motivated people. This may be pathetic, but it is neither trivial nor ignoble.

In the upper levels of the Technostructure, the monetary rewards are considerable. For the most part, however, the professional manager's regard for money is in the Shavian and Dooleyan sense a healthy one. Even an income of $100,000 or $200,000 a year represents a real response to a real need, for this much may be necessary for a man to live in the style appropriate to his position at a time when it is quite possible to go broke on $50,000 a year.

Even among the Great Big New Rich there are men who seem to have accumulated their wealth almost accidentally and without any passionate interest in money for its own sake. One of the richest men in Los Angeles remarked to me once that even if personal income taxes were to rise to 99 percent, he doubted that Tex Thornton would slow down at all. When I repeated this remark to Thornton, he laughed and said it was quite true. It wasn't the money that counted but the game itself.

Yet there are others among the Great Big New Rich whose lives demonstrate in an almost clinical sense the pathological love of money not for what it can buy but for its own sake.

> Let me tell you about the very rich. They are different from you and me.
>
> — *F. Scott Fitzgerald*

> He remembered poor old Scott Fitzgerald and his romantic awe of them and how he had started a story once that began, "The very rich are different from you and me." And how someone had said to Scott, Yes, they have more money.*
>
> — *Ernest Hemingway*

Now at last we can settle for all time the right and the wrong of this celebrated literary putdown. Fitzgerald was clearly right,

---

* The quotation is rendered as it appeared in the first publication of "The Snows of Kilimanjaro" in *Esquire*, August 1936. After Fitzgerald wrote him a "somewhat indignant letter," Hemingway changed the name to Julian before publishing "The Snows of Kilimanjaro" in *The First Forty-Nine Stories*.

and Hemingway, who in any case displays a sad carelessness in getting a quotation quite right, was wrong. Many of the rich — the very rich — are different from you and me, and for that matter, they are different from Tex Thornton. The difference is not that they have more money but that they feel differently about it, and the difference of their feelings is so extreme that the healthy majority can only regard it as pathological.

A splendid case history of the characteristic pathology of the very rich is furnished by the first two generations of the Vanderbilt family. The old "Commodore" Cornelius Vanderbilt, the loutish onetime Staten Island ferry boy, untutored and uncouth, amassed his vast fortune by gaining control of the New York ferry system, then expanding into coastwise shipping, and finally making himself master of the New York Central. His manners were vile and his tactics would have shamed a Turkish bandit chieftain, but he acquired the first industrial fortune in the world, something more than $100 million.

Yet this "golden luminary" of his time, this "magnate of unprecedented wealth and power" practiced at home such a fierce parsimony that his unfortunate wife (who earlier in their marriage had run a New Jersey tavern) was at length committed to the Bloomingdale Asylum. The Vanderbilt home at No. 10 Washington Place was small, the carpets were shabby, and the "Commodore's" twelve children were treated as cruelly and indifferently as the mother who bore them. The vicious-tempered old buccaneer himself wore the plainest of black suits, watched the domestic food budget as if he were the overseer of an orphanage, and though he gave millions to the university.

that bears his name and to Columbia's medical school, never relaxed his passionate attention to the individual dollar.

Vanderbilt's regard for money became so intense that, as Gustavus Myers describes it, "it far passed the line of a passion and became a monomania." Even on his deathbed he remained true to this unedifying description. A familiar anecdote about the old man tells how, when the attending doctor recommended a daily bottle of champagne to ease the dying man's discomfort, Vanderbilt moaned, "Champagne! I can't afford champagne. A bottle every morning! Oh, I guess sody water'll do."

The fierce passion for money that has always possessed many of the Great Big New Rich is not always passed on to the succeeding generations, which in fiction have often been portrayed as lambs and butterflies by comparison to the wolves and lions of the first generation. From old Vanderbilt's loins, however, sprang a son, William Henry, who was his true scion, rivaling and sometimes surpassing the old man in his pathological regard for the dollar saved.

William Henry's true talents were not immediately apparent. Exiled to a farm on Staten Island, frequently addressed by his fond parent as an idiot, the unprepossessing William H. bided his time until he was well into his forties, meantime tending his farm assiduously, driving his men hard, and swooping down on them whenever he detected a momentary slackening of their energies.

Then a critical incident occurred. After picking up from his father's stables a scowload of fertilizer, he tricked the old man into agreeing to a price of $4 per load, which to the older scoundrel represented a fine price for a wagonload. When, the next day, Vanderbilt *pere* saw another scow loaded with manure ready to leave for Staten Island, he asked how many loads it represented.

"One, of course," was the answer.

"One! Why, there's at least thirty!" protested the "Commodore."

William Henry answered, "No, father, I never put but one load on a scow — one *scowload*. Cast off the lines, Pat!"

It was, according to the family historian, this gentle family transaction that persuaded the old man to give his late-blooming son a place in the New York Central.

Although cautious where his father had been bold, and methodical where his father had been inspired, William Henry Vanderbilt succeeded so well that he managed in eight years to double his inheritance to almost $200 million. ("I am the richest man in the world," he told a friend. "In England the Duke of Westminster is said to be worth $200 million, but it is mostly in land and houses and does not pay two percent.") Even after this great success, the younger Vanderbilt's parsimoniousness became as notorious as his father's; he haggled, huckstered, and pursued pennies. He lived, it is true, in baronial splendor in a great brownstone mansion on Fifth Avenue between Fifty-first and Fifty-second streets, which he filled with a mixture of fine art and odds and ends from foreign parts, providing a considerable contrast to his Staten Island farmhouse, with its lean-to on one end for a kitchen. Even though he ate when at home in a lofty dining room wainscotted with carved English oak and with hunting scenes painted on the ceiling, when he was in the congenial atmosphere of his office he was capable of paranoid meanness. As W. A. Crofutt, the admiring family historian, told the story:

"When in active control of affairs at the office he followed the unwholesome habit of eating the midday lunch at his desk, the waiter bringing it in from a neighboring restaurant.

"He paid his bills for this weekly, and he always scrutinized the items with proper care. 'Was I here Thursday?' he asked a clerk at an adjoining desk.

" 'No, Mr. Vanderbilt; you stayed at home that day.'

" 'So I thought,' he said, and struck that day from the bill. Another time he would exclaim, sotto voce, 'I didn't order coffee last Tuesday,' and that item would vanish."

Thanks to his practiced closefistedness, Vanderbilt spent only about $200,000 a year out of his income of more than $10 million. The point to observe is that in spite of his passionate attention to money, Vanderbilt plainly did not *need* 98 percent of his income.

The pathological temperament, of which both Vanderbilts partook, was also displayed in its classic form in the second and even the third generations of the Goelet family, in whose well-provided childhoods one could find no rational springs for miserliness. Owners of a great tract of farmland in what is now midtown New York, the original Goelet brothers advanced to the rank of millionaire when that word was still new. Peter Goelet, a grandson of one of the brothers, was outstanding for his parsimony in even this parsimonious family. He kept needle and thread in his office in the Chemical Bank and was known to sew up his coat personally when it needed attention. He methodically saved old letters and envelopes, which he used for his own correspondence. His house was well supplied with tools which the multimillionaire — a sort of premature do-it-your-selfer — wielded to avoid the expense of carpenters and plumbers, while he acquired a substantial law library to enable him to do the lawyers out of *their* fees. In his stable was a cow which he sometimes milked himself.

It is only infrequently that one of these classic misers manages to exhibit traits of humanity that move us to feel at all warm toward him. Peter Goelet loved fine animals. Stephen Girard, the great shipping merchant and banker, was a bitter and ferocious shark of a man who lived more meanly than the clerks in his countinghouses; in his will, however, he left bequests to each of his relatives, annuities to his servants, and five hundred dollars apiece even to his apprentices. Large sums went for civic improvements in Philadelphia and New Orleans, and some six million for the establishment of the college for orphans that is now called Girard College.

A considerable tension between the peculiar impulses of the moneymaker and the humane impulses was displayed by Nicholas Longworth, the largest landowner in Cincinnati, a merciless and tightfisted man who was yet capable of creating local scandals by his impetuous and unseemly displays of generosity. The best story about Longworth tells how a beggar made his way into Longworth's office to show the millionaire his ragged shoes. Longworth kicked off one of his own shoes and told the beggar to try it on. When it fit, he gave the beggar his other shoe. Afterward, he sent a boy down the street to buy him a new pair, but with the instruction not to squander more than a dollar and a half.

The Pathology of Money

Freedom from scruple, from sympathy, honesty and regard for life may, within fairly wide limits, be said to further the success of the individual in the pecuniary culture.

— Thorstein Veblen

Except among those citizens who are most smitten with the moral grandeur of the profit motive, it is no secret that many of the most successful capitalists have displayed precisely that spectrum of strengths that are exhibited by the lower-class delinquent: shrewdness, ingenuity, ruthlessness, a contempt for the law, and the abiding conviction that the rest of society exists to be plucked. The chief difference between the delinquent and the millionaire, Veblen suggested, is that the millionaire possesses a keener sense of status and the capacity of working more consistently and toward a remoter end.

Accounts of the rapacity of the Robber Barons of the late 1800's fill a library of fat books. The epitome of their gang-mystique is contained in a letter which the elder Vanderbilt wrote to some of his colleagues who had ill-advisedly tried to seize control of his properties while he was vacationing in Europe.

Gentlemen:

You have undertaken to cheat me. I will not sue you, for law takes too long. I will ruin you.

Sincerely yours,

Cornelius Van Derbilt

And, the story ends, he did ruin them.

The mystique reflected in Vanderbilt's letter is precisely the mystique of the outlaw, and that word is used in its literal meaning. It is the world-view of a mafioso, of a Chinese river pirate, of a gunslinger, of a Mexican bandit. The lawlessness not only of the Vanderbilts but also of John Jacob Astor, of Jay Gould, of Russell Sage, of Pierpont Morgan, of Jim Fisk and of Daniel Drew has been too thoroughly chronicled to bear telling again. Perhaps never in the history of man has the world seen such a remarkable collection of successful swindlers, blackmailers, corrupters, and cheats as flourished in the United States in the nineteenth century.

In any case, the lesson here is that there is no truth in the pleasant conceit that many very rich men have ever attained their distinction by superior virtue, thrift, probity, sobriety, piety, or patriotism. No, these are the virtues of the unsuccessful, of the salaried man, the bureaucrat, the people who run the mom-and-pop stores and who from the beginning of civilized society have consoled themselves with the thought that although they aren't rich they are honest.

With honorable personal exceptions, many of the very rich at all times and in all places have been propelled by motives that are in an exact clinical sense pathological. Or, to put it another way, the energy of the very rich man chasing after still another million is healthy in the same sense that the rosy cheeks of the tubercular, the high spirits of the maniac, and the ambivalent beauty of the homosexual are healthy.

> If ye had nawthin' but money ye'd have nawthin' but money.
> Ye can't ate it, sleep it, dhrink it, or carry it away with ye.
>
> — *Finley Peter Dunne*

198

The Pathology of Money

I now have 275 marbles.
Counted my stamps — 305.

— J. Paul Getty, aged 11

The classic explanation of the characteristic sickness of the very rich was, as everybody knows, first formulated by Sigmund Freud, who in 1908 published in *Psychiatrisch-Neurologische Wochenschrift*, to the jeers and ribaldry of his colleagues, the theory that persons who had taken unusual pleasure in anal sensations during their infancy were likely to develop in later life the traits of orderliness, miserliness, and obstinacy. Whether or not the toilet experiences of the infant Vanderbilts and Goulds and Gettys had anything to do with their adult behavior need not particularly concern us. The grand truth here has less to do with the etiology of the impulse to collect large sums of money than with the perfection of the metaphor Money — Feces. Freud will surely be remembered as a poet long after his psychological theories have gone the ways of the four humors or animal magnetism.

An examination of our language soon confirms the poetic rightness of Freud's metaphor. The word *possession* comes from the Latin *possidere*, which in turn comes from *port*, towards, and *sedere*, to sit. A possession is something one sits on; the defecatory posture is suggested, even if subliminally. The argument is strengthened by such clichés as "filthy lucre," "stinking rich," and "rolling in money." These examples have become so commonplace that they are, I suppose, known to every bright schoolchild. The really astonishing thing is how often the equation is generated and regenerated by people with no particular expertise in the dark mysteries of psychoanalysis. Not many months ago I found in my morning paper the following dispatch from Germany:

"Some politicians in Bonn are calling this the Great Constipated Society. . . .

" 'The trouble is that we Germans have short memories of the old days and have become more gourmand than gourmet. . . . The result of such gourmandizing is a constipation of plenty.' "

The most consistently useful and understandable explanation of the drive to collect money that I have found appears not in Freud's works, however, but in an essay by Otto Fenichel in a thirty-year-old issue of the *Psychoanalytic Quarterly*. After observing that the drive to amass wealth is partly a biological instinct and is partly socially determined, Fenichel goes on to identify five motives for making money.

First comes the entirely rational motive of making money in order to satisfy one's needs.

Second, money is a weapon giving one power over others.

Third is the passionate desire for possessions, in which money, according to the psychoanalyst, plays the part of an extension of the body, of an arm or leg or breast or penis.

Fourth is that characteristic of our economic system which compels the capitalist to make as much money as he can under penalty of his own destruction.

Fifth and finally, the making of much money is held up before the lower classes as a life-ideal, just as the ideal of a marshal's baton was kept before the privates of Napoleon's armies.

Clearly, the only completely rational motive for acquiring money is the first, but with the acquisition of money, as in every other human activity, the dividing line between sanity and insanity is not clearly drawn. Instead of clear differences in kind, we must learn to cope with differences of degree, not with sanity and insanity, but with what Karl Menninger has called orders of dysfunction. In these terms, a low order of dysfunction exists when money is regarded operationally and is valued for what it can do, while a high order of dysfunction exists when money is valued primarily for what it represents.

Fenichel refers approvingly to Charles Odier's extension of the Freudian equation: Money does not equal feces alone, but everything that can be taken or given — milk, food, mother's breast, intestinal contents, sperm, child, potency, love, protection, care, passivity, obstinacy, vanity, pride, egoism, and so on, ad infinitum.

Now that we are free from the narrowly orthodox interpretation of Freud's metaphor, we can at last propose a hypothesis explaining the drive that propels a man to pass up the really enjoyable things of this world to spend the greater part of his waking hours thinking about how to make money that he doesn't really need, worrying about keeping money that he will never need, and grieving over the loss of money that he never really needed. In spite of Freud's original proposition and the suggestive example of the Vanderbilts' scowload of manure, in its symbolic aspect money represents everything desirable. On the healthy side of the spectrum, it is money that makes possible love, pleasure, independence, creation, and life itself; on the other side of the spectrum, where the orders of dysfunction increase, money becomes not the medium that makes things possible, but a substitute, a surrogate for everything desirable. The means becomes the end.

In spite of this generalizing, the sexual component continues to loom large. Money often means manliness, and the common drive which moved Astor, Vanderbilt, Gould, Fisk, Morgan and the others of the classic American millionaires was the compelling necessity to prove to themselves that they were not effeminate weaklings. It is all there — the deliberate coarseness, the indifference to others, the passion to collect things, the stubbornness, the displays of ferocious temper, the unsatisfactory marriages, the cultivation of the virtues of criminality, the reckless expenditure of energy, and the erection of great palaces. Seen in this light, the Robber Barons were not supermen but emotional cripples, grown men governed by the fears that properly belong to an adolescent boy peering in his mirror for the signs of a moustache.

A most striking anecdote in support of this thesis is the story told of Clint Murchison, who had one of the bedrooms of his house equipped with eight beds "so a group of us boys can talk oil all night." The point is that the oil business is surely the most sexual of all businesses. There is first the business of drilling, drilling, drilling, a sort of economic Don Juanism in which the Earth itself represents the desired women but in which only a minority of affairs are satisfactory. The striking of oil becomes a graphic analogue of the orgasm, notably in the case of a gusher. The symbolism of the derricks and the well-shafts hardly needs comment, nor does the rhythmic rocking of the pumping machinery. Then, just in case we doubt the truth of this interpretation, along comes Murchison to give the whole game away. Of all places, it is the bedroom in which these night-long orgies of talk take place, substituting the oil business for the bedroom's proper business. Instead of a female companion, Murchison's bedroom is occupied by seven other men who, in Texas at least, are not embarrassed by a situation that elsewhere might be regarded as rather equivocal. Finally, there is that ubiquitous word *boys* — the fraternity password of the American who refuses to grow up.

The pursuit of money is a game, but a game touched with a fine glint of madness.

ELEVEN

Gallery Five: Paranoiacs

$$$$$

par·a·noi·a (par'-ə-noi'-ə), n. *Psychiatry.* mental disorder characterized by systematized delusions and the projection of personal conflicts, which are ascribed to the supposed hostility of others; the disorder often exists for years without any disturbance of consciousness.

— *Random House Dictionary*

It can hardly be an accident that the three richest Americans of our time — Getty, Hughes, and Hunt — are not merely not lovable men but also share a style that is compounded partly of the traits of the classic anal-erotic personality and partly of outright paranoia. The world is full of other such withdrawn, suspicious, grasping, mystery-loving, and illiberal people who have not become immensely rich; one looks for some other ingredient. In the cases of Getty and Hughes, the other ingredient may have been money itself, since both began their ascents to the stratosphere equipped with inheritances on the order of half a million dollars. (Hunt, who began with nothing, is a phenomenon unto himself.)

Unlike Clement Stone, who in his characteristically naïve-shrewd way has contributed much money to worthy causes, or Howard Ahmanson, who gave millions to the cultural elevation of Los Angeles, or Tex Thornton, who contributed his energy and intelligence to the Kerner report on racial disorders, no activities for the public good have been associated with the richest three. Getty appears to be the most innocent of any such tendencies. As a friendly commentator, Goronwy Rees, once put it, "There are no great public acts of charity associated with Mr. Getty, as there are with so many other men of great wealth, and he carries his liking for simplicity and thrift to such a degree that in a man of his fortune it may seem to amount to meanness." (Elsewhere, Rees has referred to one of Getty's "rare, slightly wolfish smiles, that have a certain wintry charm of their own.")

If questioned on the extent of his largesse, Hunt would no doubt point to the millions that he has put into the activities of the now-extinct Facts Forum or his Life Line Foundation, which is a mainstay of the radical Right, working mightily to save the country from communism and to preserve it for the unfettered capitalist ethic and the oil-depletion allowance. (We shall return to Hunt and the Life Line Foundation later.)

As for Hughes, although in 1953 he assigned the profits from the Hughes Aircraft Corporation to the Howard Hughes Medical Foundation, there is a characteristically Hughesian mystery about the precise activities of the foundation and its positive contributions to the frontiers of medical science. Furthermore, the sole trustee is Howard Hughes. (Hughes has also promised $6 million to the establishment of a state medical school in Nevada; perhaps uncharitably, there have been public comments that this openhandedness was not unrelated to his application for Las Vegas gambling licenses.)

In personal styles, the denominator that is common to these three men is the gift for taking great gambles combined with remarkable personal stinginess. Hunt has been known to wager $300,000 on a single World Series game, but he trims his own hair. In the days when Hughes was the hottest pilot in the world, he used to drop into Manhattan nightclubs wearing sneakers and sometimes hiding his identity under the alias of Señor Gomez. Getty has spent millions for a distinguished collection of paintings and sculpture, but as his friend Penelope Kitson once recalled, "When his eldest boy, George, got married . . . I had to badger him to send a present."

Once I happened to meet at a cocktail party an Englishman who turned out to be a don at Getty's college at Oxford. When I mentioned the rich man's name, he laughed and recalled an anecdote. Getty's response to an appeal for funds from the alumni of St. Catherine's was a check for precisely £100. Another alumnus, hearing of this, offered the college £150 if he could preserve this evidence of the scale of munificence practiced by the richest man in the world.

Although none of these three are, strictly speaking, Great Big New Rich, they are not Old Rich either. Getty, who is now 76, was the earliest; after giving up ambitions to serve in the foreign service, he began wildcatting during World War I and by 1923 was worth around $3 million. After his mysterious beginnings as a barber or ranchhand, Hunt, who is in his eighties, went broke in the cotton market in the early Twenties and did not strike it rich until he entered the East Texas oil fields in the 1930's. By the time World War II was over, Hunt owned more oil reserves than all the Axis nations together. Hughes, who is now 63, inherited in 1924, when he was 19, a three-quarter share of the Hughes Tool Company, which was worth about $600,000. His great personal success in business (if, indeed, that is how his progressive wealthiness can be described) did not come until a couple of decades later.

As a case study in the characterology of the very, very rich, Hughes presents the most promising field for our further investigation.

There is nothing mysterious about me.

— Howard Hughes

The greatest mystery about Howard Hughes is the puzzle of accounting for how he became as rich as he is. His inheritance — hardly more than a half-million — was not large enough to set his feet automatically on the road to vast wealth. There is little in his personal characteristics either as a human being or as a business operator that can explain why this young man of relatively modest fortune drove triumphantly past so many other young men even better equipped for the pursuit of money. In trying to find some pattern in the history of Hughes' accumulation of great riches, one is pushed slowly and firmly

207

toward the proposition that, given a fortuitous and unpredictable combination of circumstances, money will tend to multiply itself without rational control and even in spite of gross errors and eccentricities that outrage not only every accepted principle of good business management but also the advice of common sense. (And, in fact, these two often come down to the same thing.)

Alone among the very rich men to whose careers we have been attending, Hughes' life presents no consistent theme, no clear set of character, no thread that can be easily recognized in each of the enterprises in which he has engaged himself. D. K. Ludwig has embarked on undertakings even more diverse than those of Hughes. In spite of the shyness he shares with Hughes, Ludwig's driving motive is quite clear. He is the entrepreneur par excellence, the enterprise-driven man whose entire life has been subordinated to making a fortune through the deliberate organization and manipulation of businesses in which he sees opportunities for profit. Hughes is an entirely different species, and some of his greatest strokes of moneymaking appear to have been accomplished in spite of his own bad judgment, carelessness, and a management philosophy based on paranoia.

Hughes' career as a maker of money is obscured at every point by the other guises in which he has presented himself. There is the aviator who flew the fastest plane in the world and who lifted the largest plane in the world into the air for a brief flight. There is the lover whose affairs with Katherine Hepburn, Ava Gardner, and Lana Turner are only the most widely noted of an extraordinary emotional life. There is the leader, the innocent idol of Hughes-for-President clubs. There is the great

Howard Hughes, mysterious and elusive billionaire.
WIDE WORLD PHOTOS.

man, of whom the *New Republic* once wrote, "Simple in manner, careless in dress, unconscious of social distinctions, he devotes his superior capacities to the conquest of new difficulties." There is the paranoid who conducts business conferences while riding around in a battered, anonymous sedan and who once signed a great contract at midnight in a municipal dump.

> The nearest he ever came to making a pass at me was offering me a bite of a cookie.
>
> — *Jean Harlow*

To the vulgar mind, enjoying the love of a succession of beautiful women is surely one of the most attractive prerogatives of commanding a very large amount of money. Jean Harlow's testimony to the contrary, Hughes is the only one of the Great Big New Rich who qualifies as a womanizer. As one of his biographers has written in a passage that skirts the fine edge of libel, it was one of the duties of Johnny Meyer, who for years was Hughes' man-of-all-work, to suggest to women who caught the rich man's eye that "it would be quite profitable to perform sexual services in a certain bedroom at a certain hour for a certain Hollywood producer and industrialist."

Hughes married early and conventionally, taking as his wife Ella Rice of the family that founded Rice Institute, which Hughes was attending at the time his father died. Hughes was nineteen. Taking his bride to Hollywood, Hughes plunged into the making of motion pictures, the earliest of which are mercifully forgotten. Ella was entranced neither by Hollywood nor by her husband's unpredictable working hours, and during the

filming of *Hell's Angels* returned to Houston alone. An un-
contested divorce followed, with Mrs. Hughes receiving a property settlement of a million dollars.

In the thirty years between the divorce and Hughes' marriage
in 1957 to Jean Peters, he was known to be on more than
friendly terms with women whose seductive forms on the silver
screen inspired only the fantasies of less fortunate men. In the
years immediately after the divorce, he was reported as being
involved with Billie Dove, Lillian Bond, June Collyer, and Ida
Lupino. At the time of his round-the-world flight in 1938, his
great friend was Katherine Hepburn, to whom he sped after
escaping from the ticker-tape parade. In the 1940's his atten-
tions turned to Lana Turner and Faith Domergue, a teen-age
starlet whose contract he bought from Warner Brothers. In the
1950's his name was associated with those of Linda Darnell,
Yvonne DeCarlo, Elizabeth Taylor, and Ava Gardner. Oddly,
the two women who have convincingly denied any off-studio
friendships with Hughes are the two whose names and bodies
he made into national symbols of passionate and willing sex —
Jean Harlow and Jane Russell.

It was, consequently, with understandable disbelief that
Hollywood learned that Hughes had married Jean Peters, an
actress of great facial beauty but homey habits. According to one
account, the announcement itself was made in Hughes' characteristic style, by way of a phone call to Louella Parsons in
which he instructed that lady to announce merely that he and
Jean were married. Hughes declined to give Miss Parsons any
further information, and in fact nobody has been able to find

out precisely where and under what circumstances the ceremony took place.

As Miss Ohio State University, Jean Peters had won the obligatory trip to Hollywood and screen test. Unlike most winners of beauty contests, she was offered and signed a seven-year contract. Her films included *The Captain from Castile*, *Three Coins in the Fountain*, and *A Man Called Peter*. She acquired a reputation for being rather withdrawn and mildly bookish. Virtually her only act that fitted thoroughly into the Hollywood mold was her one-year marriage to a Texas oilman. Two months after her divorce came her marriage to Hughes.

Since then, so far as anybody can tell, Hughes has, in his own curious fashion, been a faithful married man.

He said he didn't want me bringing other customers' germs into his presence.

— *Eddie Alexander*

Hughes' passion for privacy — he hasn't given an interview since 1954 — has not served to obscure his other idiosyncrasies, which include a morbid fear of germs, a fear of being poisoned, and a profound suspicion of the good faith of all other human beings.

Hughes is said to drink water only from a sealed bottle that must not be opened until he is ready to drink. At the Beverly Hills Hotel, where he maintained a $100-a-day cottage for his convenience when in Los Angeles, his food was carried from the kitchen by one of his own employees. It has been reported that in the kitchen of their house in Bel Air, separate refrigerators were maintained for food intended for Hughes and for Jean Peters. While staying at Las Vegas in the 1950's, a request came from Hughes' suite for more blankets. According to a hotel executive, the blankets were hung over the windows to keep out the germs.

Anecdote after anecdote has been told of Hughes' practice of keeping employees and other people with whom he has business "on the hook" indefinitely until Hughes is ready for them. His longtime barber Eddie Alexander was once asked to keep himself ready until Hughes called. The barber stood by for a month until the call came and he gave Hughes a haircut that cost him $1200. In his biography *Bashful Billionaire*, Albert B. Gerber has also told the possibly apocryphal story of the employee who was directed to check in at a hotel and stay in his room as much as possible until Hughes called. As Gerber tells the story, "The unfortunate employee remained in his room awaiting the call from his boss. He had meals sent in and day after day, week after week, he stayed in his room, waiting for the phone call that never came. On the day he had checked in he had noticed in a tree outside his window a small bird building a nest. He watched the bird bringing twigs and grass and filler and saw the nest completed. He observed the bird settle down in its nest and lay its eggs. He saw the bird sit on its eggs, watched as the baby birds broke the shells and emerged into the world. And when the maturing babies tested their wings and finally flew away he was still sitting by his window. It is quite probable that Mr. Hughes did indeed remember the waiting man; he just wasn't ready yet to contact him."

An even odder story is told by Hughes' other biographer,

John Keats. A girl named Gail Ganley, tapped by Hughes for stardom that never came, used to collect her expense money by driving to Hughes' personal headquarters at 7000 Romaine Street in Hollywood and sounding her horn three times. Thereupon a second-story window would open and somebody would lower an envelope on the end of a string. Miss Ganley would then take her money out of the envelope, sign a receipt, and watch the envelope go back up to the second story.

Some curious working conditions were required of the staff in the office on Romaine Street. Nobody was allowed to go out for lunch. Although lipstick was permitted, typists were discouraged from wearing nail polish or perfume. Each girl was segregated in a private office, where she wore rubber gloves while typing or handling papers. When composing a letter, Hughes would dictate directly to two typists. The work had to be perfect. If a mistake was made, the letter was torn up and Hughes would start over again. One secretary recalled, "One night he spoke the same two sentences over and over and over again from midnight to 7 A.M. I must have typed it two hundred times."

> I find it very difficult for me to be standing up here on this platform, for I realize that if it were not for you men and women and your diligent work, I would probably be pushing a plow.
>
> — *Howard Hughes*

The picture of Hughes behind a plow is so thoroughly preposterous that one can only credit this pretty conceit to a publicity man dipping once again into the grab bag of our conventional rhetoric. Yet, there is a measure of poetic truth in the conceit, for Hughes' management of his affairs has, by any rational judgment, been consistently and abysmally wrong-headed. If there has been a theme to his career as a tycoon of ever-increasing wealth and power, it will be found in the strategy of snatching great profits from disasters of his own making.

Hughes' career in the movies began in 1925, when he came with his bride to Hollywood, where his uncle, Rupert, was writing scripts. Without calling on the advice of anybody who knew anything about films, Hughes, who was then twenty, formed an outfit called Caddo Productions and personally produced and directed a movie called *Swell Hogan*. It was apparently a dreadful movie, for nobody has ever seen it.

In the years that followed, Hughes' films became somewhat more expert and considerably more profitable, although few of his products were to be distinguished for their artistic quality. The two most remarkable were *Hell's Angels* and *The Outlaw*. *Hell's Angels*, which occupied Hughes from 1927 to 1930, was the World War I airplane opera which turned a blonde extra named Harleen Carpenter into Jean Harlow. Hughes cut no corners in the production, buying 80 planes and one Zeppelin (which was shot down on camera), and hiring more than a hundred stunt pilots. At one point 24 cameramen were simultaneously shooting battle scenes; the consumption of film as well as of money set a new record for Hollywood. The general critical reaction after *Hell's Angels* opened at Grauman's Chinese in June 1930 was that the flying scenes were great but that the rest was pretty dull stuff.

215

Between *Hell's Angels* and *The Outlaw* there came a succession of films, some of which are remembered and some of which are not — *Cock of the Air, Sky Devils, Age for Love, Scarface, The Front Page.* Although the latter two are his best films, Hughes will probably be longest remembered for *The Outlaw,* which he made in 1940 after an eight-year interlude devoted to aviation.

The Outlaw was not the worst picture ever made although it can make a strong claim in some areas. It was, of course, the film that was built in equal parts of the legend of Billy the Kid and the breasts of a buxom but rather straitlaced dentist's receptionist named Jane Russell. It was by all accounts a thoroughly deplorable movie, although anybody of a liberal disposition can only admire Hughes' rugged determination to defy the Hays office (which withdrew its seal of approval) over such lines as "tit for tat" and the advertising slogan, *How Would You Like to Tussle with Russell?* Among the mildly gamy anecdotia of the filming of *The Outlaw* is the account of how Hughes, dissatisfied by the artistic effects of a scene in which Miss Russell was spread-eagled between two trees by leather thongs attached to her wrists, remarked that the proper suspension of her celebrated breasts was a simple matter for a man qualified in aeronautical engineering, and devised an ingenious and satisfactory brassiere on the spot. The only virtue the more persnickety critics could find in the movie was its unconscious humor, but Hughes had not been betrayed by his estimate of the colossal mammary fixation of the great American public. The picture was a great success and the original print is preserved in a lead-lined vault.

Gallery Five: Paranoiacs

The Outlaw had been made under the banner of RKO, a controlling interest in which Hughes had bought from Floyd Odlum in 1948 for almost $9 million. Hughes' management of the company was characteristically eccentric; during the first five years of his ownership, RKO lost $20 million and the services of talented movie people including Dore Schary. Hughes was sued for some $30 million by unhappy stockholders. In 1952 Hughes began what turned out to be an abortive attempt to sell out and cut his losses; instead, he hung on and two years later divested himself of RKO at a nice profit.

This happy outcome was due less to any foresight, courage, and good judgment on Hughes' part than to the circumstance that the television industry had developed a voracious appetite for old movies. Hughes first became sole owner of RKO by writing a personal check for $23 million. He then entered into negotiations with Thomas Francis O'Neil, president of a chain of television and radio stations. O'Neil was lured to the Beverly Hills Hotel, where Hughes kept him in discussion for three days and nights. When the documents for the transfer were finally drawn up, Hughes insisted on having them signed in Nevada rather than in California. O'Neil found himself aboard one of Hughes' planes, piloted by the great man himself. The story is told that somewhere over the desert Hughes suggested that O'Neil take over control, and left the cockpit. No flyer, O'Neil presumably told his beads until Hughes came back and took over, remarking casually, "Well, Tom, you're a great pilot."

O'Neil bought RKO Radio Pictures, Inc., for $25 million. Hughes kept RKO Radio Pictures Corporation, which he merged with Floyd Odlum's Atlas Corporation, receiving stock worth about $10 million. His final profit after eight years of mismanaging RKO amounted to something in the neighborhood of $10 million, all honest capital gains.

An even more profitable variation on the Hughesian theme of success-through-disaster was repeated in 1966, when the creditors of Trans-World Airlines forced Hughes to sell his 75 percent interest in the firm. Hughes emerged from the debris of his airline venture with a cash profit after taxes of about a third of a billion dollars. This was five years after the management of the firm had passed from Hughes to Charles C. Tillinghast, Jr., a period during which TWA stock had risen from about $10 a share to almost $100, reflecting the conversion of a $15 million loss under Hughes in 1961 to a $50 million profit under Tillinghast in 1965.*

For a final demonstration of the death-wish quality of Hughes' methods of management, we shall now turn to the affairs of the Hughes Aircraft Corporation.

Hughes Aircraft: The High-Flying Might-Have-Been
— *Fortune*

The Hughes Aircraft Company was formed in 1934 as a subsidiary of the Hughes Tool Company for the specific purpose of designing and building the fastest land-plane in the

---

* In September 1968, Herbert Brownell (who had been attorney general in the Eisenhower administration), acting as special master for the U.S. district court in New York, recommended that Hughes pay TWA $137.6 million for mismanaging the airline. The main point at issue was that Hughes had delayed in acquiring jet aircraft in the 1950's. Tillinghast said he was "gratified." Hughes said nothing.

world, the H-1. Its plant consisted of a rented hangar in Glendale where Hughes and his colleagues did in fact produce the plane in which in 1935 Hughes set a new transcontinental record of 9 hours, 27 minutes, and 10 seconds. (There have been suggestions in print that the Japanese Zero fighter was derived from the H-1, but there is a faint whiff of apocrypha to this story.) Later, it was through Hughes Aircraft that Hughes contracted to produce a plane that would be larger than any other in the world, a plywood monster that would lift 700 troops and their equipment into the air.

The story of the *Hercules* (or the "Spruce Goose" as it was more familiarly known) has passed into legend and it need not concern us at length here. As with others of Hughes' ventures, the work dragged on. In the fall of 1943 Hughes confidently offered to post a half-billion-dollar bond that the *Hercules* would be ready by the end of 1944. It was as well for Hughes that his offer wasn't taken up, for *Hercules* was not ready then or at the end of the next year, or the year after that. The original contract of $18 million for three such planes was cancelled and then reactivated, but for one plane only.

In 1947, when Senator Owen Brewster launched an investigation of the manner in which Hughes had received a total of $60 million of war contracts without producing a single plane, *Hercules* had still not flown. Hughes appeared tieless in a dirty shirt and a badly fitting jacket borrowed from his butler-valet, and testified that Brewster had suggested to him that the heat would be off if he would agree to merge TWA with Pan American Airways. Brewster's political career was cooked as a result (he was not renominated) but his original proposition about the $60 million still stood. (A year later when Hughes bought RKO, he sent Brewster a wire reading: "I hereby offer you a job as a motion picture actor at a salary of $300 a week. This is twice the usual starting salary, but you are no amateur.")

In November 1947, during a break in the Brewster hearings, Hughes flew *Hercules* for a distance of about one mile in Long Beach harbor before an audience of dignitaries. The big ship has not flown again, although work has gone on; as of 1962 it was reported that *Hercules* had cost Hughes $50 million.

Despite its name, Hughes Aircraft became large, powerful, and profitable not through aircraft at all but through the manufacture of sophisticated electronics equipment for the Air Force. This departure from Hughes' original conception of his company came about in the late 1940's when the scientists Simon Ramo (of CalTech) and Dean Wooldridge (of Bell Telephone) joined the company as part of an infusion of new blood that included Tex Thornton as vice-president and effective general manager of a team that operated independently of Hughes, and Noah Dietrich, who had been his second-in-command since 1924. (An accountant, Dietrich performed much the same function for Hughes that the moneyman William Wagner does for D. K. Ludwig.)

In 1948 Hughes Aircraft contracted with the Air Force to develop and produce fire-control systems for its combat planes. After the outbreak of fighting in Korea, Hughes became practically the sole supplier of these vital systems. The annual sales of Hughes Aircraft had been $2 million in 1948; they had risen to $200 million five years later. This hundredfold increase had been brought about by the remarkable combination of brains on both the management and technical side that had been brought together in Culver City. The impetus to go heavily into electronics had come from Hughes. Neither he nor Dietrich were able to keep their hands off the well-functioning machine that had been created in his name. Particularly after he moved to Las Vegas in 1951, Hughes became more unreachable than ever and no less capricious. On one occasion, when weighty management decisions hung in the balance, the Culver City team was instructed to prepare an accounting of what happened to the proceeds from the plant's vending machines. When Ramo and Wooldridge recommended an expansion of the research lab, they were told the expansion should take place in Las Vegas.

The palace revolution which destroyed Hughes Aircraft as it existed in the early 1950's and from which the firm has never fully recovered appears to have been almost single-handedly brought about by Noah Dietrich. The company was most evidently prospering and promising even greater profits in the future when Dietrich, whose prime allegiance was to Hughes Tool (Aircraft's parent company), felt obliged to take a place in the game. He implied fraudulent management of a parts inventory amounting to some $500,000 and attempted to impose his notions of management on the Culver City plant.

In the summer of 1952, General Harold L. George, the president, Thornton, Ramo, and Wooldridge had had more than they could take of Dietrich and signed a manifesto directed to Hughes protesting that Dietrich was trying to seize power at the risk of ruining the company. Hughes' reaction was characteristically oblique. Three months went by before, prodded by another manifesto, he met with the management team. In spite of the refreshments and the personal charm he dispensed to them at his cottage at the Beverly Hills Hotel, he offered them no real comfort. The outcome of the meeting was that Thornton, Ramo, and Wooldridge flew to Washington to tell the Defense Department that Hughes Aircraft was in serious trouble and could not meet its commitments.

Internecine warfare went on into 1953. In September, Ramo and Wooldridge walked out to found the firm that now, as TRW, is one of the phenomena of the New Technology. They were followed by General George and by Thornton, who, as has already been recounted, went on with Roy Ash (who had been assistant controller at 'Hughes) to acquire Litton Industries. It has been reported that on the night after Thornton and George left, their office furniture was cleaned out and the locks changed on their doors.

After surveying the wreckage at Culver City, Harold Talbott, Secretary of the Air Force, told Hughes, "You have made a hell of a mess of a great property and, by God, as long as I am Secretary of the Air Force, you're not going to get another dollar to do business."

Hughes answered, "If you mean to tell me that the government is prepared to destroy a business merely on the unfounded charges of a few disgruntled employees, then you are introducing socialism, if not communism." The mind reels.

As for Dietrich, poetic justice waited four years. In May 1957, Dietrich and Hughes broke over a question of financial policy complicated by disagreements over the arrangements for

Dietrich's retirement. Arriving at the Beverly Hills Hotel to discuss the retirement matter in person, Dietrich was offered only a telephone conversation with Hughes. The conversation ended with Dietrich quitting. When he arrived at the Romaine Street headquarters the next day, Dietrich found that his office had been padlocked during the night. (Dietrich sued for $2 million, but the case was settled out of court when he agreed to give up a book about Hughes that he had in mind, the price for abandoning his literary ambitions being one million dollars, dispensed at a rate of $50,000 a year.)

Hughes Aircraft has come a long way back since the disaster of 1953, but its sales are far below those of either Litton or TRW, which in a sense are its illegitimate sons. After the debacle Hughes divorced the aircraft company from the tool company and assigned the profits from Hughes Aircraft to the Howard Hughes Medical Foundation, with himself serving as sole trustee. The patient's convalescence was encouraged when, in 1960, Hughes got his first contract with NASA. A rapprochement with the Air Force brought a number of contracts, notably for the Falcon air-to-air missile. Other Hughes products have included the Syncom communications satellite, the Early Bird satellite, and the Surveyor spacecraft.

With ten plants in Southern California and a missile plant in Tucson, Hughes Aircraft is currently prospering under the direction of Lawrence A. Hyland, who has been allowed to manage its affairs without interference from Hughes and with no Noah Dietrich. Hughes himself appears to be occupied with his new career as the first citizen of Las Vegas, having acquired the Desert Inn, Sands, Frontier, and Castaways casino-hotels as well as other real estate, including 30,000 acres of desert.*

In the early summer of 1968, Hughes appeared to have decided to branch out into the communications industry. For sixteen days his agents acquired stock in the American Broadcasting Company, finally gathering 34 percent of ABC's common stock as the result of a tender offer that turned Wall Street on its ear. Then, unexpectedly but characteristically, Hughes withdrew the tender. In the financial community his retreat was put down to the Federal Communications Commission's active interest in Hughes' plans, the stubborn opposition of ABC's management to being taken over, an unfavorable court interpretation of the tender offer, and Hughes' own recognition that it would be a mistake to become involved again with a publicly owned corporation, as he had with TWA.

As *Fortune* pointed out recently, Hughes missed his chance some sixteen years ago to turn his aircraft company into the General Motors of the New Technology. Given the peculiar qualities of Hughes' character, this is surely an outcome for which the rest of the nation can only be grateful.

---

* Hughes' involvement with gambling casinos instead of the New Technology has in fact evoked fulsome gratitude from Nevada dignitaries, who credit him with raising the Las Vegas gambling operation to a higher ethical level. In November 1968 Governor Paul Laxalt said, "A general business increase and creation of a better public image, particularly with the advent of Mr. Hughes, have had a decided effect. There no longer is the fear, fancied or otherwise, that some hood is going to take your money away from you."

TWELVE

The Rewards of Money

. . . affairs with stage favorites, love nests aboard oceangoing yachts, private railroad cars, racing stables, vast retinues of domestics, collections of bogus old masters . . . titled sons-in-law, custom-made motorcars, cottages at Newport and mansions on Fifth Avenue, a nice taste in Madeira and fêtes champêtres around swimming pools . . .

— *Lucius Beebe*

The late *arbiter elegantiae*'s catalogue of the classic hallmarks of wealth and character carries as powerful an air of a long-departed culture as does a menu for a feast in Herculaneum. In these degenerate days darlings of the silver screen are seldom found in the amorous clutches of Texas oil barons or even of Los Angeles savings-and-loan tycoons. The oceangoing yacht is in decline both as a means of transportation and as a floating house of assignation, while its closest contemporary equivalent, the private jet, travels at a velocity that discourages the decent and leisurely consummation of an affair. With some notable exceptions, few of the new rich are excited by horseflesh. While the servant problem may not trouble the spouse of the very rich man in quite the same way it does the suburban housewife, it nonetheless exists; some millionaire households are known to struggle along with a part-time cleaning woman. Titled sons-in-law, Newport cottages and Fifth Avenue mansions strike our sensibilities as quaintly as does a nice taste in Madeira. The swimming pool has descended to the middle classes. Virtually the only items in the catalogue that still exercise the powerful magic of symbols of great wealth are expensive automobiles and collections of old masters, bogus or otherwise.

This is not to say that the Great Big New Rich are entirely indifferent to possessions nor that there are not among them men with the peculiar flair for spending money to no good purpose that, in the last century, inspired such great foolishness as C.K.G. Billings' celebrated horseback dinner at Sherry's, at which a score of tailcoated guests ate and drank in the saddle, a conceit that set the host back about $250 per.

Today this sort of splendidly insane gesture seems to have become localized in the *haute monde* of Houston and Dallas. It has, for example, been reported on good authority that in the latter metropolis of wealth and culture, the wife of the oilman Jake Hamon once entertained the guests at her annual costume party by making her entrance on an elephant. (The Hamons also once gave a Christmas-in-July party, complete with snow.) In 1957, a fellow-Texan, D. D. (Tex) Feldman spent about

$120,000 on a New Year's Eve party at Romanoff's in Beverly Hills, at which 300 guests were entertained by Edith Piaf. (As conspicuous consumption goes, $120,000 is surely a respectable sum of money; yet, to put it into perspective, it is well to recall that thirty-three years earlier, when Clarence Mackay entertained the Prince of Wales, the flowers alone cost five thousand dollars more than Mr. Feldman's entire party.) Another pair of Texans, Mr. and Mrs. A. B. Lawrence, whose money comes from ranching, have been reported as regularly arriving at the Houston Fat Stock Show in His and Her Cadillacs, white and pink; their luggage contains a couple of dozen changes of Western clothing. The existence of the Fat Stock Show as a social affair of the first water is itself a commentary that needs no comment.

Perhaps the most widely circulated example of conspicuous consumption was offered to the world by the 1960 Neiman-Marcus catalogue, which listed His and Her airplanes, at $149,000 and $27,000 respectively. (Let Easterners beware of regional pride: Tiffany's offered its customers one Christmas not long ago a 14-carat gold putter for $1475, less impressive in scale perhaps than the Texas airplanes, but also less rational.)

Even the automobile only occasionally produces the effect it used to. The millionaire inventor J. J. Mascuch once declared, "I bought a Rolls-Royce several years ago for fifty thousand plus. Then I started to tinker with it. I sent it over to Italy and had those fine Italian coachmakers put an entire new body on the Rolls. I had a toilet installed in the back seat, and a television set, and . . ." A year or so later Mascuch, a deceptively severe-appearing gentleman, presented himself, clad in a gorgeous brocade smoking jacket, at a television show presided over by David Susskind. Under Susskind's artful questioning, Mascuch revealed that the Rolls-borne toilet had been fitted with a grille and was now in use as an ice bucket.

There is a moral of general application in another story, reported not long ago in West Coast newspapers, of the man who had the chromework of his Cadillac plated gold at a cost of $15,000 or so. The point of the story was that this big spender had thriftily bought the Cadillac secondhand. Mascuches are in the minority among our modern multimillionaires; most of the rich are inclined to hedge, even when it comes to gold-plating their Cadillacs.

> Prestige involves at least two persons: one to claim it and another to honor the claim.
>
> — C. Wright Mills

Perhaps no symbol of the prestige that accompanies great wealth has excited such universal admiration among the vulgar as the possession of an oceangoing yacht. We have all been educated by J. P. Morgan, who said, "Nobody who has to ask what a yacht costs has any business owning one." Although a full-size passenger airplane (such as the Boeing Stratocruiser that Glenn McCarthy — the onetime king of the wildcatters — bought for $2 million) rivals a yacht in capital investment and upkeep, the ownership of an airplane, no matter how splendid, fails entirely to confer the cachet that automatically went with the ownership of a yacht of more than approximately 150 feet length overall. The popular fascination with the yacht as a symbol of high life was surely associated with the opportunities it offered for delightful wickedness. The word *yacht* is encrusted with a rich and lovely patina of licentious associations: beautiful and willing young women, muscular and willing young men, bottomless jeroboams of champagne, ortolans on toast, an unending orgy of every sense.

The great age of the American yacht opened on May 20, 1853, when the crewmen of Cornelius Vanderbilt's *North Star* cast off the lines and the captain set a course eastward across the Atlantic. At 270 feet length overall, *North Star*, whose interior decor was that of the age of Louis XV, was an appropriate advertisement of Vanderbilt's great wealth, but even this splendid vessel was overtaken both in size and lavishness by later entrants in its class. Among the seagoing Robber Barons and their descendants were William K. Vanderbilt (*Alva*, 285 feet), William Backhouse Astor (*Nourmahal*, 233 feet) Morgan the Elder (*Corsair I*, 165 feet; *Corsair II*, 205 feet; *Corsair III*, 302 feet), Morgan the Younger (*Corsair IV*, 313 feet), and Jay Gould (*Atalanta*, 250 feet).

Lucius Beebe has described how "Guests were conveyed from the landing to *Atalanta's* gangway by cutters manned by ten oars uniformed in the Gould colors of white and blue and were piped over the side in naval style and ceremony. Oriental rugs, plush, rare boiseries, gold-monogrammed velvets, costly draperies, and opulent furniture vied for the admiration of the beholder with a truly fine library, for Gould was a discerning reader, and a built-in upright piano in the music room. In the galley, supervised by an English chief steward who had seen service with the Earl of Rosebery, French chefs labored over culinary masterpieces for Gould's guests while a specially gifted pastry cook from Vienna dedicated his entire time to the confection of the ladyfingers which were the sole delicacy permitted Gould himself by a rigid diet." Beebe goes on to tell how, when Gould was denied admission to the New York Yacht Club, he founded the American Yacht Club, using the same stratagem with which he and others of the new rich built the Metropolitan Opera House to challenge the old-money pretensions of the Academy of Music.

When, in 1900, James Gordon Bennett replaced his aging and modest *Namouna* with *Lysistrata* (named "for a Greek lady reported to have been very beautiful and very fast"), the bill came to $625,000, the equivalent of something better than $2 million in our present coin. *Lysistrata* carried some of the most extraordinary accommodations and fittings of any of the great yachts, her most noteworthy features including three complete owner's suites, one on each deck, a full Turkish bath where Commodore Bennett was ministered to by his masseur, and, most extraordinary of all, a padded stall designed for the high-bred Alderney which produced one of the necessary ingredients for milk punch.

It was none of the great names of robber barony who built what Beebe called the "most pretentious of all private vessels," however, but Mrs. Richard Cadwalader of Philadelphia, whose *Savarona* was built at Kiel at an initial cost of about $5 million, but with an immediate added bill for another million for last-minute changes demanded by the owner. The story of the rebuilding of *Savarona* is instructive of the grandest and most dreadful style of the very rich. *Savarona* — which at 408 feet was almost half as long as the world's only battleship, the *New*

Jersey — was fitted with gold-plated plumbing fixtures, Gobelin tapestries, and a two-story-tall pipe organ, but was discovered to lack an elevator. Mrs. Cadwalader insisted that one be installed, and it was, though it required major structural changes in the ship, which accounted for the last million dollars of the yacht's cost. Unwilling to pay U.S. taxes on her ship, Mrs. Cadwalader kept *Savarona* under foreign registry and had to travel by other means at least as far as Bermuda to board her yacht. (In the 1930's, *Savarona* was sold to Kemal Atatürk for a mere million.)

A pleasant hour can be spent with *Lloyd's Register* trying to identify the descendants of these gold-plated vessels. Although more Americans own boats of some description than ever before (eight million according to a recent estimate), fewer Americans own really grand vessels than ever before. A search of a recent Lloyd's turned up only six American yachts over 200 feet long, and two of these, the presidential yacht *Williamsburg* (228 feet) and the late General Doctor R. L. Trujillo Molina's *Angelita* (254 feet), belong to a somewhat different category.*

The others included D. K. Ludwig's *Danginn* (257 feet 5 inches, registered to National Bulk Carriers), *Elpetal* (206 feet, with her owner hidden behind registration to the Concordia Navigation Co. of New York), Horace E. Dodge's *Delphine* (251 feet), and, the largest of all, the *Moineau* of New York

---

* Unfortunately outside our purview is 1968's yacht-of-the-year, the 325-foot *Christina*, on which Aristotle Socrates Onassis carried off his bride. *Christina*, once the Canadian frigate *Stormont*, was turned into a yacht at a cost of $2.5 million and is navigated by a crew of fifty. Among its amenities is a mosaic bathtub modeled after that of King Minos at Knossos.

(283 feet), registered to a lady with the exotic but not widely known name of Mme. Lucienne Benitez Rexach.

Although all of the Great Big New Rich easily meet Morgan the Elder's criterion for the ownership of a yacht, there has clearly been a decline in the value of a yacht in the status game. It is hard to imagine, say, W. Clement Stone ensconced in the grand salon of a yacht half the length of the *Queen Mary*, dispensing twenty-year-old liquors to a merry company of fast women and moneyed men while a battery of chefs prepare Tournedos Héloïse and the wine steward uncorks the Romanée-Conti. The times are simply not congenial to the great yacht; it is perhaps not a mere accident that when, some years back, the Texas oil tycoon John Mecom acquired Astor's *Nourmahal*, the yacht burned and had to be abandoned. Although it will probably not cause keen regret to many readers, the great yacht has clearly been replaced, even among the very rich, by power vessels of such modesty that their sisters are owned by assistant vice-presidents, successful shopkeepers, and dentists.

The yacht still survives, though only barely; the other great possession of the nineteenth-century rich, the private railroad car, appears to have disappeared entirely.

Never really competing as a capital investment with the yacht, the price of a private railroad car manufactured by Pullman or one of its competitors ran from $25,000 in the 1870's for Leland Stanford's *Stanford* (acquired as a birthday present from Mrs. Stanford) up to the most expensive of all, Mrs. James P. Donahue's *Japauldon*, which was manufactured by American Car & Foundry for $350,000.

Beebe, with his nostalgia for both the great age of spending and the great age of railroads, wrote lyrically of the last stand of the private cars in the 1920's, when he saw them "drawn up twenty deep in the private railroad yard of the since vanished Royal Poinciana Hotel in Palm Beach." Now, in an age when many young people have never set foot on a train, owning a private railroad car (as Beebe himself did) seems as curious an affectation as owning a coach-and-four.*

Cadillac owners look a little younger these days.

— *Advertisement*

The great age of the motorcar as the visible symbol of wealth virtually ended about the time of the First World War when manufacturers began to market models that were not beyond the resources of the merely well-to-do. In those simpler days the mere possession of a Mercedes or Darracq, a Rolls, Napier, Pope-Hartford, Packard or Lozier was in itself proof of uncommon prosperity.

The democratization of the automobile in the years since then has had some curious results, not the least of which is the ubiquitousness of the Cadillac as *the* car of the self-conscious new rich, whether they be billionaires, surgeons, or big men in Harlem. The truly great and interesting cars — such as the Daimler, Isotta-Fraschini, Cord, and Duesenberg — have passed into the hands of *aficionados*, who tinker and polish,

---

* Incurable romantics are happily still among us. Three years ago Hastings Harcourt, publisher and entrepreneur-at-large, bought a private Pullman with the austere name of *Car 11* for $34,000. Alas, in the fall of 1968 Mr. Harcourt was reported to be planning to auction it off as an elegant nuisance.

polish and tinker, and whose motives well from entirely different sources. Otherwise, except for an occasional very rich man who amuses himself with a Jaguar or Ferrari, the rich, and particularly the new rich, do appear to have an unreasonable partiality for the Cadillac above all other makes of automobile. (In a remarkable display of loyalty toward another manufacturer, the Houston oilman R. E. (Bob) Smith has maintained as many as four Lincolns at a time.)

As a visible symbol of wealth, however, the Cadillac recommends itself most highly to men who are not entirely sure of their own success; its ownership implies either uncertainty or lack of imagination. In any case, among the really rich there is probably a lower per capita count of Cadillacs than among, say, the members of the dental association of Sherman Oaks, California.

I was once given a lift by Bart Lytton in a limousine equipped with a communications system of such awesome proportions that I neglected entirely to make a note of the make of the car while I admired the switchboard at Lytton's command. Later, I found that I had been riding in a customized 1963 Cadillac limousine, and that Lytton also owned at that time (the summer of 1967) a 1962 Cadillac, a 1957 Mark II Continental, a 1962 Thunderbird, and (for Mrs. Lytton) a 1962 Continental. Although Lytton (who was once severely injured in an automobile accident and doesn't like to drive) employed two chauffeurs to pilot this fleet, the comparative antiquity of his automobiles provokes thought.

With the exception of such sports as J. J. Mascuch with his Italian-bodied Rolls fitted with a toilet–ice bucket, many of the really rich appear to have only a perfunctory interest in their cars. H. L. Hunt is reported to move about in a sedan of undistinguished make, while Tex Thornton has been seen at the wheel of a Ford and Clint Murchison in a middle-aged Plymouth. Ralph E. Schneider, the founder of the Diners Club who has acquired a fortune somewhere in the early millions, once bought a Cadillac and hired a chauffeur but sold the car and fired the man within six months because he felt it made him seem pretentious.

The ambivalence that obtains among even the new rich in the matter of cars can be summed up with a listing of the cars owned by some of the men who qualified for entry in *The New Millionaires*, a book edited by the *Wall Street Journal*:

> Cadillac and Jaguar convertible
> Imperial Ghia
> Cadillac, Thunderbird, and Chevrolet wagon
> Cadillac, Chevrolet, Ford
> Oldsmobile sedan, Oldsmobile wagon
> Two Buicks and a Chevrolet
> Cadillac and custom-built Thunderbird
> Two Cadillacs and Thunderbird

To continue would be tedious.

house (*n.*, *adj.* hous; *v.* houz), *n.*, pl. hous·es (hou'ziz), *v.*, housed, hous·ing, *adj.* — *n.* 1. a building in which people live; residence for human beings.
— *Random House Dictionary*

With its forty master bedrooms and quarter-million-volume library, Biltmore, which George Washington Vanderbilt (grandson of the "Commodore") erected on a 130,000-acre tract near Asheville, was the greatest private house of them all. Biltmore was also one of the most extraordinary enterprises of any kind undertaken by a rich American. Vanderbilt prepared himself for the challenge by studying architecture, forestry and landscape gardening. Biltmore employed more people than the entire Department of Agriculture did at the time. Vanderbilt provided a hospital and a church, schools, and shops for his employees. Gifford Pinchot, who was later to become governor of Pennsylvania, was superintendent of Biltmore's forests, carrying out there the first professional forestry work in the country.

Biltmore surpassed even Jay Gould's gothic Lyndhurst at Irvington-on-Hudson, from which he commuted by steam pinnace to New York and where he raised eight thousand orchids in a complex of greenhouses, or William K. Vanderbilt's Long Island estate, where twenty chauffeurs and mechanics were headquartered in a garage that accommodated a hundred automobiles. Another contender among the great houses was William C. Whitney's 530-acre estate at Westbury, also on Long Island; Whitney's pride was a $2-million stable, whose 68 stalls each had immediate access to the outside in case of fire. (The grooms were not so thoughtfully provided for.)

A rich man's house, whether a mansion in town or a country estate, exercised a large part of its function as a symbol of high standing by providing a setting for great potlatches. (The potlatch is a ceremonial affair carried on by the Indians of the

Northwest, at which presents are distributed and property willfully destroyed with the object of demonstrating the great-heartedness of the host.) Besides such grand affairs as Mrs. Vanderbilt's 1883 ball and C.K.G. Billings' legendary horseback dinner, there were other affairs of less decorous and less awe-inspiring nature, given by younger and hotter bloods among the Great Big New Rich of the time. Preeminent among these was the Awful Seeley Dinner of 1896 (the Seeleys were heirs of P. T. Barnum) at which, in spite of police intervention, Little Egypt danced in the nude and gentlemen guests made free of the lady performers' dressing rooms.

But enough of scandal, which is not our purpose. The point to be recorded is merely that among the rich of previous generations, both homes and entertainments were conceived on a grand scale that few of our own Great Big New Rich find at all congenial.

> I have discovered that I cannot spend more than five hundred dollars a week. . . . When I spend five hundred dollars a week, I'm wasting a great deal of money. . . . What I'm trying to say is that after a certain point, increased earnings will not raise your standard of living.
> — *William G. Riley, 1964*

> Will anyone undertake to demonstrate that there is better taste involved in the consumption of soft drinks and patent breakfast foods than champagne and *foie gras?*
> — *Lucius Beebe*

It is a curious irony that in the present development of our society — which Galbraith has called affluent, R. H. Tawney called acquisitive, and C. Wright Mills called overdeveloped —

237

being rich has become a lost art. Even where there is display, it is often fatally touched with the dominant middle-class style. Only 2 percent of the Cadillacs sold in Texas are models designed to be driven by a chauffeur. The other 98 percent of Cadillac-type Texans presumably drive themselves.

The sense of what William G. Riley (a millionaire who owns a management firm in Chicago) has just been quoted as saying has been commented upon earlier. There are certain physical and physiological limits which automatically impose themselves on attempting to spend money on one's personal needs. Even Hughes, Hunt, and Getty can wear only one suit and sleep in one bed at a time; even by the most diligent effort they each cannot eat more than four or five meals or drink more than a bottle of Scotch a day, or make love to more than one woman at a time. Riley's five hundred dollars a week is surely unduly modest, but his principle is a sound one. As in any other great enterprises the spending of large sums of money requires imagination of a sort that does not flourish in our time.

At one extreme of the spectrum is H. L. Hunt, who lives in an oversize replica of Mount Vernon which needs painting, trims his own hair, and eats brown-bag lunches. Little of Hunt's energies goes into the spending of money either for pleasure or show; instead, he has dedicated his vital energies to the making of money for its own sake and to spreading the doctrines of the Radical Right by means of his Life Line Foundation. Even among the curious personalities that crop up in the ranks of the very rich, Hunt is an eccentric, but one whose eccentricities are not untypical of his class.

At the other end of the spectrum are a corporal's guard of

millionaires who plainly enjoy their money and their posses-
sions. One of the most attractive to the collector is John
Mecom of Houston, the third-ranking independent oilman
(after Hunt and Getty), who has been called the King of the
Wildcatters and whom Stewart Alsop once described as "this
last representative of a dying breed," having in mind the frank
pleasure Mecom takes in his ten airplanes, his ranches in
Oklahoma, Louisiana, and Texas, his thoroughbreds and his
Ferrari, and his 18-room French-style château. It was also
Mecom who bought W. B. Astor's *Nourmahal* from the government, which had requisitioned it for patrol duties during the
war, only to have the great yacht burn almost before he owned it.

> John gambles like a pro. He takes a long careful look at the
> odds, but once he's made his play, he'll back it until your eyes
> bug out.
>
> — *A Texas oilman*

A large man, full of both charm and charisma, John Mecom
was born in 1911 in El Paso and managed to drop out of both
Rice University and the University of Oklahoma before going
to work as a roughneck in the oil fields. Borrowing $700 from
his mother and an old drilling rig from his father, Mecom
turned wildcatter and with two friends tried his luck on oil leases
that had been deemed marginal by the major producers. That
their luck was good is memorialized in the story of the Juneteenth hole. Juneteenth — June 19 — is Emancipation Day in
the South, a holiday that among the colored population ranks a
little ahead of the Glorious Fourth. When they discovered that
their hired hands had abandoned the drilling gear a hundred

yards or so from the intended site and had taken off for premises better equipped for celebration, Mecom and his partners decided to set up the equipment where it lay. The hole they drilled brought in oil, while, as it turned out later, the hole they finally drilled at the original site was a duster.

The partners' luck continued, with twelve successful holes out of twenty attempts. Within three years of his first hole, Mecom sold out for $100,000, which he invested in modern equipment. He went after more old leases and dry wells abandoned by the majors and soon he had production up to a thousand barrels a day.

Mecom's wife Mary Elizabeth, a Houston girl whom he married early in his career, wears a silver pendant with the inscription *With Love from S.S.S.O.B.*, and thereby hangs a pleasant tale. In 1945 Mecom decided to have a try at High Island, a coastal field that had already been worked over, sinking his holes on the north flank of High Island's salt dome, where the received opinion was that oil could not possibly be.

Upon inquiring of a muskrat trapper what was going on on High Island, a curious traveler was informed that "Some silly son of a bitch is looking for oil on the north flank." Sometime later the traveler returned to find considerably greater activity than he had remembered. Returning for information to the same trapper, he was told, "Why, some smart son of a bitch found oil on the north flank."

The story is also told that when the first big strike came, Mecom raced back to the beach cabin in which he was living, threw open the door to discover Mrs. Mecom at a humble domestic chore and roared, "Get up off your knees, Miz Got-rocks, we've struck it rich!"

Like others of the Great Big New Rich, Mecom has branched out in many directions that have no connection with the source of his original fortune. An accounting of his various interests in 1964 included ownership of a New Jersey plant that manufactures plastic dinnerware, two Peruvian fishmeal plants, a Houston construction company, a drugstore, a $100 million residential development near Galveston, the Gran Hotel Bolivar in Lima, a half-interest in the San Francisco Hilton, and ownership of Houston's Warwick Hotel, a decaying caravanserai which he refurbished with Aubusson tapestry and Baccarat chandeliers at a cost of some $12 million. Besides oil ventures in the Arab countries and Colombia (where he was engaged with Standard Oil of New Jersey in building a 120-mile pipeline to Cartagena), Mecom was also considering investments in South Africa, Tunisia, Morocco, and Libya, as well as refineries in the Caribbean and Europe.

In 1966, when Mecom was taking possession of the Houston *Chronicle*, it was said in Texas that Mary Elizabeth had simply asked John to pick up a paper on the way home. As it turned out, the *Chronicle* deal fell through. Mecom offered Jesse Jones' Houston Endowment $85 million for the *Chronicle* and some other local property, putting up a million in cash. He was thereupon elected chairman of the board and chief executive officer and had his offices carpeted in a shade known as "Mecom blue" before he discovered that money was so tight that not even a semibillionaire could lay his hands on ready cash of the magnitude required. Mecom's attempts to raise money

241

involved conversations with Scripps-Howard, the Chandler dynasty of Los Angeles, and Sam Newhouse, which apparently caused bad blood with the Endowment. In any case, when Mecom arrived at the end of his first six months of tenure with a cashier's check for $14 million in his hand, J. Howard Creekmore of the foundation told him coolly that the entire $84 million was due within 48 hours. Mecom walked out the door and out of the newspaper business.

In accounting for his usual run of success, Mecom has said, "I just spot my shots. I like to take promising properties that have been misused or neglected and try to use them the right way. Whether you're talking about an oil field that has been improperly developed, a poorly managed manufacturing concern, or a hotel that's been allowed to go to seed, the principle is the same."

Since our concern in this chapter is the rewards of money, the remarkable thing to note about John Mecom's success is that he has chosen to recreate the constellation of status symbols of the last century — the racehorses, the château, the yacht and other appurtenances more traditional than pink Cadillacs and eight-needle cowboy boots. There are not many like him.

I have one customer on the West Coast who owns ninety-six complete table settings. She has one room on the top of her estate which was built especially for table settings. When she has a dinner party, she simply tells her butler, "I want number thirty-three, or twenty-one."

— Carole Stupell

Although J. Paul Getty is currently living in considerable splendor on a 750-acre estate in Surrey he bought from the

Duke of Sutherland, most of the Great Big New Rich have not particularly spread themselves in the matter of house and chattels. Leo Corrigan, a Dallas real-estate man worth something on the order of half a billion dollars, was last reported living in a $40,000 suburban house with nine rooms and two baths which, as John Bainbridge pointedly observed, "is just sixty-six rooms, thirty-eight baths, and four million, one hundred and sixty thousand dollars less than went into the dwelling that Charles Schwab put up in 1905 on Riverside Drive."

William Randolph Hearst spent some $20 million on the gorgeous vulgarity of San Simeon, not counting his $50 million collection of art. Among our current big rich, the level of grandeur is considerably more modest. A sort of median is offered by the case of Tex Thornton, who, as we have noted, bought his Spanish-style ranch house in an affluent section of Los Angeles for $250,000. A quarter of a million dollars is a fair amount of cash, but as an investment in a house it hardly qualifies its owner to run in the same race as George Washington Vanderbilt, Jay Gould, or William C. Whitney.

The fact is that the possession of a great dwelling place staffed by troops and regiments of servants is no longer part of the style of the rich. Although one is told that it is crushing taxes or the high cost of domestic help that have doomed the traditional rich man's mansion, these seem to be far from the real reasons for its disappearance. The world of post–Civil War high vulgarity to which Veblen directed his attention in the *Theory of the Leisure Class* disappeared with World War I. Our own styles of vulgarity involve less in the way of gaudy display.

There is little conspicuous consumption visible in the houses of the Great Big New Rich. Edwin Land, the inventor of Polaroid and the Polaroid Land camera, was discovered not long ago to be living in an upper-class but not ostentatious house on Brattle Street in Cambridge. Norton Simon, who has made a great fortune reorganizing moribund business corporations, lives in a large and comfortable ranch house on an affluent but not extraordinary street. Clement Stone lives in a quiet house in Evanston.

When I asked Stone to account for this middle-class style, he explained at some length: "First, from practical sense, a few do it from the fear that if they're too conspicuous it isn't so good. Second, getting loyal servants is a thing of the past. Next, it's so easy to get quality by renting. You can rent a château in France if you want. Next, the individual who worked his way up doesn't see the need. The way of life of the American businessman isn't particularly luxury minded."

When I asked Norton Simon the same question, he said, "There's a great change in the sociological climate. People are more interested now in movement and travel. We no longer have a feudal society. If people are interested in movement, they can't sit in their stately mansions. There's a change in society as a whole."

John D. MacArthur, the insurance man who is the brother of the late Charles MacArthur, the playwright, was run to earth by Stewart Alsop in an $18,000 bungalow in one of his own housing developments. When the rich man asked what Alsop would do if he himself had a lot of money, the writer improvised at length. As Alsop reported MacArthur's response: " 'Yes,' said MacArthur, eyeing me owlishly, 'I guess that's what you *would* do, and you'd be a goddamn jackass.' "

In *The New Millionaires*, the staff of the *Wall Street Journal* unconsciously gave the game away, for the extravagances breathlessly described by the newspapermen included such modest possessions as two-year-old Buicks and summer cottages. One of these new millionaires, a Michigan restaurateur named Winston J. Schuler, for example, was described as living (in 1960) in a four-bedroom red-brick Colonial house with a pool, the whole thing being worth about $40,000. Mr. Schuler was driving a current year's Oldsmobile sedan, while his wife drove a year-old station wagon of the same make. Schuler's great extravagance was described as buying one or two suits a month — at a price of $50 to $100 a suit. Even a reporter for the *Wall Street Journal* could probably afford as much if he stretched himself.

Another of the *Journal's* millionaires was Thomas F. Boland, a New Mexico oilman, who owned both a yellow brick town house (bought for $7100 in the late 1940's) and a $100,000 suburban ranch house. Most of the time Boland was living in the town house, without servants except for a part-time cleaning woman. The Bolands ate from blue plastic plates. In the case of Hans Fischer, a consulting engineer from Cleveland, the phrase "trappings of wealth" is spelled out in some detail: a Cadillac, a Jaguar convertible, a forty-five-foot Chris Craft cabin cruiser, and a seven-bedroom Tudor home in Shaker Heights that cost $65,000 in 1953. Alas!

Echoes of the high style of the past are still provided by a few of the very rich such as Getty, with his ducal estate, and

James J. Ling, with his $14,000 bathtub big enough to swim in. Even they, however, like Carole Stupell's customer with ninety-six complete table settings in the attic, seem slightly dated and even a little pathetic.

I can't stand useless leisure.

— *Charles B. Thornton*

Loving his work to the ultimate degree, Ludwig is unable to take much pleasure from anything else.

— *Fortune*

Like Thornton and Ludwig, the other Great Big New Rich as a class do not count themselves among the beneficiaries of the new age of leisure in which bookkeepers, insurance underwriters, and slaughterhouse workers will spend their free hours listening to chamber music, taking extension courses in conversational French, or learning to play squash racquets.

Although I have not run a statistical study on the subject, it is, I think, a safe assertion that among the very rich, golf is the Cadillac of sports, the sport to which they gravitate almost automatically at some time during their rise to riches. Tennis, by contrast, goes almost unmentioned in the biographies of the rich. Hunting, fishing, and driving fast cars are not unknown but do not figure to any significant degree.

The Great Big New Rich are, not unexpectedly, well represented among the members of the more expensive clubs, both in town and in the country. Howard Ahmanson, a formidable clubman, listed membership in the Stock Exchange Club, the Los Angeles Yacht Club, the Wilshire Country Club, the

Newport Harbor Yacht Club, the Newport Ocean Sailing Association, the Trojan Club, the Santa Monica Yacht Club, and both the Shadow Mountain Club and Shadow Mountain Golf Club. By contrast, his fellow Angeleno Norton Simon lists no clubs at all in his biography in *Who's Who*. (Simon owns a sailboat but does not race it. Neither a fisher nor a golfer, Simon goes for long bicycle rides, plays the organ, and goes to the movies.)

J. Paul Getty, before moving to England at least, belonged to the Explorer's Club of New York, the Beach Club of Santa Monica, and the Los Angeles Athletic Club. Tex Thornton also belongs to the Beach Club as well as to the Army and Navy Club of Washington, the Los Angeles Country Club and the All-Year Club of Southern California.

In Boston, Edwin H. Land belongs to the St. Botolph Club and also maintains membership in the Harvard clubs of both Boston and New York. Charles Allen, Jr., belongs to the Downtown Athletic Club and plays golf at the Deepdale Golf Club at Great Neck. (Allen took up the Cadillac of sports after a serious illness.)

The Chicagoan Henry Crown is a director of La Quinta Country Club in California as well as holding membership in the Midday, Standard, Executives, and Tavern clubs. When he is at home in Chicago, John D. MacArthur can sign a chit only at the Lake Shore Club.

John Mecom pays dues to the Houston Country Club, the River Oaks Country Club, and the Ramada Club as well as the Boston Club of New Orleans. James J. Ling, whose participation in such good works as the Community Chest and the

Dallas Symphony is well documented, does not admit to any club memberships in his biography in *Who's Who in America*. With Ling's known dedication to golf as evidence, however, this would appear to be an oversight.

D. K. Ludwig does not belong to any clubs.

Virtually the only exceptions to the prevailing rule of conventional dullness in the recreations of the rich is provided by some of the Westerners. Gambling, which enjoys no good name in the East, is still one of the traditional dissipations allowed a Texan by social if not legal sanction. In Houston, John Mecom has been reported to sit in on games where plus or minus twenty thousand dollars is a good evening's action for a man. (Twenty thousand in winnings or losses, no matter how prodigal it may seem to the rest of us, represents only about half of Mecom's daily take-home income — the equivalent of about fifty dollars to a $25,000-a-year man, enough to annoy one's spouse but not enough to upset the domestic budget seriously.)

H. L. Hunt, who neither smokes nor drinks, bets on horse races and baseball games. Twenty years ago, Hunt kept two employees on his payroll whose work was to follow all the major tracks in the United States via a direct line to Western Union, to place bets for their employer, and to keep up a specialized research library devoted to horseflesh. More recently, a rumor has circulated that Hunt employs a graduate of the Massachusetts Institute of Technology to assist him in the arcane calculations required to figure odds. He is reputed to have lost $300,000 on the Yankees in 1956 but has apparently been luckier with the ponies, for he has been quoted as saying that in a recent year he made a million dollars gambling.

Both Mecom and Ralph Lowe, another prosperous independent oilman, maintain racing stables. Mecom has bought thoroughbreds directly from a Jordanian prince, while Lowe not
long ago spent a million dollars buying horses, including nine
yearlings from the Aly Khan stables. At the trial of a St. Louis
bookie, Lowe testified, "In 1949, I placed $248,593 in bets,
mostly on horses and ball games, and I got back $107,775. I sort
of quieted down after figuring my losses at the end of the
year."

Out in California, where the *hoi polloi* regularly drive over
the mountains to the gambling hells of Reno, Las Vegas, and
Lake Tahoe, the very rich engage in gambling of a more traditional, discreet, and gentlemanly nature. They buy art. The late
Howard Ahmanson, Norton Simon, and J. Paul Getty have
each amassed collections that rival William Randolph Hearst's
$50-million collection at San Simeon. We have already paid
tribute to the Ahmanson collection and will shortly view
Simon's. In this context, Getty can be counted a compatriot of
theirs in spite of his translation to ducal splendor, for he
maintains in his mansion in Pacific Palisades a collection of art
open to the public that has been called his only major act of
philanthropy.

Turning collector in the Depression, Getty bought great
pieces at a fraction of their previous value. His collection of
Greek and Roman sculpture is the only notable one in the
entire West; it includes the Lansdowne *Hercules* and three
pieces from the Elgin marbles. His collection of eighteenth
century furniture has been described as superior to the Louvre's,
while his paintings include Rubens' *Death of Queen Dido,*

Tintoretto's *Toilet of Venus*, Titian's *The Penitent Magdalen*, Veronese's *Bust Portrait of a Boy*, and Gainsborough's *Portrait of Sir James Christie*.

Writing in the magazine of the Los Angeles *Times*, Digby Diehl has summed up Getty's attachment to his collection, undiminished by his absence of seventeen years: "That's the amazing part. Mr. Getty really cares! . . . He really cares because it's uniquely his. Someday, somebody else will be the Richest Man in the World, but no one can ever assemble another collection of art like this one."

THIRTEEN

Gallery Six: Collectors

$$\$\$\$\$\$\$\$\$$$

My hostilities are usually showing. . . . Some people are born with peace of mind. I was not. In the Dostoievskian sense, I am the suffering man. . . .

— *Norton Simon*

On a day in March 1965, the chairman of Christie's auction house in London, Ivan Oswald Chance, knocked down Rembrandt's portrait of his son Titus to Sir David Somerset for $2,166,800. As the auctioneer's gavel fell, a tall American whose deeply seamed face showed extreme agitation jumped up and cried, "I am still bidding, Mr. Chance!" One observer reported that Norton Simon was shaking with rage when he reminded Chance of his instructions: "When Mr. Simon is sitting down he is bidding. If he bids openly, he is also bidding. When he stands up, he has stopped bidding. If he sits down again, he is not bidding unless he raises his finger. Having raised his finger, he is bidding until he stands up again."

Overcome by the force of Simon's argument, as others have been under other circumstances, Chance reopened the bidding, and Simon acquired *Portrait of Titus* for $2,234,400. Chance's own agitation was revealed by a mistake of $30,000 in calling Simon's bid. Simon did not bother to correct the mistake, and Sir David Somerset did not try to top his bid. It was a record price for a work of art sold in Britain.

As has been noted on a number of occasions in the public prints, Norton Winfred Simon's entire career has been devoted to collecting, his possessions including not only three notable collections of paintings and sculpture but also the control of a sizable collection of corporations. Simon's career as collector of art began in 1954, when, having already amassed a fortune of $35 million or so, he bought a Gauguin, a Picasso, and a Bonnard. Since then he has not only put together one of the most notable private collections in the country but has also established two "museums without walls" in the Hunt Foods and Industries Museum of Art and the Norton Simon Foundation, which acquired *Titus*, and which lends art for public showing without charge.

One of Simon's great coups occurred in 1964, when the Foundation bought the entire Duveen Collection, including the building in which it is housed, for something more than $15 million. He was an early and generous backer of the move to replace the stodgy old Los Angeles county museum with the impressive complex of white Southern-California-gothic buildings that are now arranged around the Mr. and Mrs. Norton

Norton Simon, who earned about one hundred million by acquiring and reorganizing ailing corporations. PHOTOGRAPH BY LEIGH WIENER.

Simon Sculpture Gallery. Although at times up to a quarter of the exhibits in this museum have been on loan from Simon's foundation, Simon's relations with the museum and its other directors have been visibly cooling in recent years, the points at issue being matters of policy that need not concern us here.

Simon doubled the size of his house in the Hancock Park district of Los Angeles (where he was a neighbor of Howard Ahmanson's) in order to accommodate more paintings, including works by Caravaggio, Degas, Giorgione, Renoir, Van Gogh, and another Rembrandt, the portrait of Titus's nurse. In his dining room hang three major Picassos. A recent visitor to his office noted a Van Dyck portrait, a Rubens oil, a Gauguin, and bronzes by Barlach and Daumier. Ahmanson, who as we have already noted was himself an avid collector, called Simon the most sophisticated amateur collector of art in the country.

> I think of Norton as a Cézanne or a Picasso — unconventional, constantly probing and testing, constantly dissatisfied.
> — Dr. Franklin Murphy

> Before you can communicate with others, you must learn to communicate with yourself.
> — Norton Simon

Simon was born in Portland, Oregon, in 1907. His father, Myer Simon, had achieved a moderate degree of prosperity as owner of a department store. After the death of his mother when he was fourteen, Simon moved to San Francisco to live with relatives and attended Lowell High — the city's elite college-prep public school — where he was a classmate of the future governor, Edmund (Pat) Brown. Besides various small business ventures and an entry into the stock market, Simon devoted some of his youthful energies to the mysteries of the dice. Pat Brown, another crapshooter, recalls, "It was amazing how Norton could always figure out the odds. He might be playing against half a dozen others, but somehow he kept all the odds in his head." Simon was not a dedicated student, and when he went across the bay to the campus at Berkeley, he stayed only six weeks. Of this experience he has said, "The university was involved with requirements, and I was interested in learning only what I wanted to learn."

Simon went to Los Angeles, played the market, and in 1929, when he was twenty-two, emerged from the disaster with $35,000, of which he invested $7,000 in a bankrupt firm called Val Vita, whose principal product was orange juice. In 1932 Val Vita's sales were $43,000. In 1934 they were better than $500,000. In 1936 they broke a million. In 1939 they were $2 million. In 1942 they were $9 million. In 1943 Simon sold Val Vita to Hunt Brothers Packing Company for $3 million. Simon was thirty-five and a millionaire.

. . . may well be the most unpopular businessman in California.

— Editors of *Fortune, The Art of Success*

. . . one of the most feared businessmen in the land.

— *Time*

. . . the most existentialist personality among those said to have amassed personal fortunes exceeding $100 million.

— *Henry J. Seldis*

The working pattern which Simon has followed throughout his career among the corporations became evident in his acquisition of Hunt Brothers and his subsequent success with the company. John Elsbach, a fabled Los Angeles elegant and financial operator, having noted that Hunt stock, which had a book value of $11, was listed at only fifty cents, suggested that Val Vita be merged with Hunt and rounded up 75,000 shares for Simon, giving him control. Simon gave up the private-label trade that had been Hunt's mainstay, modernized the plant's operations, and earmarked a large budget for promotion and advertising.

In the course of pushing Hunt ahead, Simon managed characteristically to make himself thoroughly disliked. His tactics could hardly have had any other consequence. In 1946, for example, when canned goods were hard to come by, Simon forced buyers to agree to pay the "price at time of shipment." In the fall, OPA ceilings were taken off and prices rose accordingly. Simon declined to modify his contracts, and is said to have collected $5 million more than if he had lowered his prices enough to have left his customers grateful instead of angry. As a result of his indifference to the traditional practices of the trade, Simon managed to alienate the big chains, the wholesalers, and the smaller canners. He also turned Hunt into the country's number-one processor of tomato products, with twenty million pounds a day of tomatoes going through Hunt canning lines at the peak of the packing season. By 1967, Hunt (now Hunt Foods and Industries) had risen to Number 150 on *Fortune's* annual list of the five hundred leading corporations, one place ahead of Time, Incorporated.

To his enemies Simon is a pirate, a brigand, a condottiere, a Viking raider; to his friends he is a creative entrepreneur of formidable intellect and exquisite talent. Although he continues to operate from Hunt's headquarters in Fullerton (to the south of downtown Los Angeles), he is as well known in New York and Pittsburgh as he is at home.

Simon is not a proxy-fighter. Instead, his usual tactic has been to buy up stock quietly until he holds enough to arrive at a directors' meeting with a fat briefcase and the announcement that a major holding of stock strongly implies a major voice in management. He has often been called ruthless, and with reason. When, in 1950, Simon's nominee was refused a seat on the board of a Boston closed-end investment trust, Simon bought up outright control of the trust, filled four of the seven directors' seats with his own men, and moved the company to Los Angeles. The story is an almost exact parallel to the classic and probably apocryphal account of the very rich man who, having been denied accommodations at a hotel, buys the hotel on the spot and fires the manager.

As with Hunt Foods, Simon's usual strategy has been to discover a company whose stock appears to him to be undervalued and whose management appears to be somnolent, to buy up enough stock to give him effective control, to streamline operations and to spend large amounts on promotion. It has, with one notable exception, been a successful formula, and has worked in Simon's acquisition of Ohio Match, Wesson Oil, the McCall Corporation (which includes the *Saturday Review*), Knox Glass, Canada Dry, Swift & Co., and Crucible Steel. Although executives of moribund corporations have developed permanent squints from peering westward as they look out for Simon with all the anticipation of wounded antelopes awaiting a buzzard, the fact is that Simon is not a raider. The corporations he has taken over have (with the same notable exception) done better under his management than they had been doing before.

> What does a pickle and peach man know about running a steel company?
>
> — A steel man

When Simon took over Wheeling Steel in 1963, seven lamplighters were still engaged in trimming the wicks of the kerosene lamps on its railroad switches. The lamplighters were symbolic of what was wrong with Wheeling in a more general way. Located in the bleak industrial ghetto of West Virginia, it manufactured about a sixteenth as much steel as U.S. Steel, and did that by methods thoroughly sanctified in the tradition-ridden business of making steel. The company's management was not visibly inspired to do any better than to keep Wheeling afloat.

Simon opened the proceedings with a blast of dynamite, throwing out four of the five directors and firing the president with the public and undiplomatic observation that he would not even make a good vice-president. He imported a new chief executive, Robert Morris, whom he found not within the clublike confines of the steel industry but at Monsanto Chemical. He also initiated an ambitious advertising campaign, picturing Wheeling as a company whose watchword was "Hustle."

(The ads won a prize for industrial advertising, but won Simon no friends among steel men.)

It is hard to untangle what Simon did wrong at Wheeling and what was so inherently wrong with Wheeling that nobody else could have done any better. Right or wrong, he outraged the steel community by disregarding ways of doing things that are precious to that industry. He changed Wheeling's pricing policy, withdrew from the industry group that negotiates with the United Steelworkers, kept reminding the public that Wheeling was a maverick, and filed lawsuits against U.S. Steel and three other prestigious companies. All of this would have been immaterial if Wheeling had prospered, but, plagued with problems both of production and of skilled and experienced management, it did not. In two years under Simon, Wheeling lost $12,400,000, lost some key executives, and lost customers. The bitterness against Simon in the industry reached a point at which, when other steel men meeting in New York found a bottle of Hunt's catsup on the table, they cried "Get that stuff out of here!"

Reportedly under pressure from the financial community, Simon retired as chairman in the fall of 1966, sold more than half of Hunt's holdings in the company at a loss of $700,000, took four of his five directors off the six-man board, and encouraged Morris to resign as president. Simon declared that Wheeling's needs were "areas in which the necessary vigor and directness of my past actions in cleaning up at Wheeling Steel might be an impediment to further accomplishment." Somewhat more directly, he described his experience at Wheeling as his first black eye.

Whether or not it was a delayed reaction to his rebuff at Wheeling, in May 1968 Simon removed himself from the active management of his firms and became the elder statesman of a conglomerate corporation created by merging Hunt Foods and Industries, Canada Dry, and the McCall Corporation. William McKenna, late of Litton Industries, became chairman and chief executive officer of the new corporation, which bore the simple title of Norton Simon, Incorporated.*

> It is only inner growth, rather than competition, that can possibly lead the individual to realize his maximum capacity.
>
> — *Norton Simon*

In 1933 Simon married Lucille Ellis, who was at that time a social worker not long out of Wellesley. As Mrs. Simon recalls their courtship, "We danced a lot. While he isn't that winning a dancer, his dialogue is great." Their honeymoon was a cruise through the Panama Canal; on the East Coast they toured steel mills, where Simon learned about tin-plating. They have two sons.

The Hancock Park section of Los Angeles is an exceedingly comfortable neighborhood, but not noticeably distinguishable from Upper Suburbia. The Simons live modestly except for their collection of art. Unlike Howard Ahmanson, who lived

---

* One of Norton Simon, Inc.'s first ventures was to begin negotiations to acquire David Susskind's Talent Associates Limited, which Susskind and Alfred L. Levy had founded in 1952 and whose productions had included *Requiem for a Heavyweight* and *Raisin in the Sun.* Under the proposed agreement, Talent Associates would function as an "autonomous operating subsidiary of Norton Simon." Said the executive vice-president: "We took an oath in blood not to discuss any of the monetary considerations."

down the street, Simon is not particularly moved by the pleasures of the table. When he is on the road, he is reported to
walk the streets sometimes, looking for a restaurant where he
can get a decent meal for five dollars. At home, the *cuisine* is
not *haute*. A guest at the Simons' house, Mrs. Edward Fowles,
reported, "They have all of the various Hunt products in
different silver containers, and Norton said to Edward, 'Won't
you have some catsup?' Edward said, 'Indeed not. I wouldn't
spoil good food with that stuff.' Simon's wife laughed and said,
'That's why I've never learned to cook. Norton always pours
catsup over everything.' "

For pleasure, the Simons escape from the city to their place
at Newport Beach. Simon sails, but he doesn't race, nor does he
fish or play golf. As we have already noted, he likes to ride a
bicycle, play the organ, and go to the movies.

Simon rises at six or seven, and like other West Coast
moneymen with nationwide interests, begins his phone calls
early, over his breakfast of tea, toast, and fruit. (The available
evidence suggests that a light breakfast seems to be almost a
prerequisite for great financial success.) He has two offices, one
at Hunt's headquarters in Fullerton and the other on Wilshire
Boulevard in Los Angeles. Once a week he flies east to tend to
his affairs there. He is also in attendance at meetings of the
board of regents of the University of California and of the
trustees of Reed College in Oregon.

When I asked Simon why he continued to operate out of
California when so many of his business interests were in the
East, he mentioned not only the obvious things — the weather
and the sense of expandability — but also the westward shifting

of the national center of gravity. "People do cross here and it's much more of a crossroads than Chicago used to be," he said. "People say, the next time you're in Los Angeles, drop in. New York is the only other city you can say that about." When I mentioned his city's urban problems, he went on, "I have a feeling right now California is being split apart. This moving forward is part real, part pseudo, and part social. It's always in parts, and a struggle is going on which one predominates. It's hard when you're on two sides of the fence."

And here, almost inadvertently, we are offered a useful key to some of the puzzling aspects of Norton Simon. He is often found on both sides of the fence. Notably, he has retained to a high degree the outlook of the classical entrepreneur, while at the same time he has operated successfully within a manager-oriented industrial structure. Of this he has said, "I've had to be a professional manager, and I haven't liked it particularly. It's been very rewarding and quite a lesson, but I'm damned glad to be rid of it. I like to work with things in a creative fashion, and that role is different from the professional manager's."

In an echo of Tex Thornton, Simon explained to me his view of the function of the modern entrepreneur: "If corporations can free themselves up, the entrepreneurial spirit can operate *within* the corporation. Textron, Litton, and Ling are constantly fighting for the entrepreneurial spirit. The answer is not to run an authoritarian establishment, but to organize power so that it works from the bottom up." Clearly, however, Simon is talking about other people and not about himself as an entrepreneur.

Simon is also found on the opposite side of the fence from

most of the other Great Big New Rich, who as we have seen tend toward uncritical acceptance of the Horatian gospel. Simon is an intellectual. This is not to say that he has a profound knowledge of any area of scholarship, but that he is much possessed by original thought. If at times his statements are ambiguous or positively obscure, it is characteristic of his tortuous and subtle mental processes. Among the Simonisms that have appeared in print are:

"I am in the process of becoming."

"I have a rigidity of flexibility."

"I believe in a paradoxical form of life. I don't believe anything is wholly right, but both right and wrong. There is a thin line between. There is a Chinese proverb that 'Life is a search for truth and there is no truth.' It is important to know that truth carried too far becomes destructive."

Creation and destruction appear to be much on Simon's mind, a phenomenon that should not surprise his critics in the industrial world. As Simon himself has put it, "Something destructive goes in before the constructive comes out. The question is, how much destruction can be tolerated?"

You think it doesn't take brains to collect art?
— *Joseph H. Hirshhorn*

The impulse to amass a personal collection of works of art is buried somewhere in the mists of prehistory and the equally mysterious depths of individual psychology. In this country, our admiration for the collector has often been evoked less by our admiration for his taste (which, indeed, may be the taste of his

263

salaried curator or favored dealer) than for the dollar-value of the collection. Norton Simon's $2-million-plus for *Titus* makes a deep impression on our collective consciousness; it is a symbol we can all understand, whereas the question of whether or not Simon's collections are distinguished by taste and integrity is a matter we are more than pleased to leave to the effete editors of the art magazines.

So let us stick to money. At its height, William Randolph Hearst's collection was appraised at about $50 million. The Mellon and Widener collections were each said to be worth about $20 million. Although, thanks to the inexorable progress of inflation, it is hard to make direct comparisons, it is a fact not without interest that the collections of Norton Simon and of Joseph H. Hirshhorn have been reported to be valued in the neighborhood of $50 million apiece.

As representative types of the subspecies *collector* of the Great Big New Rich, Simon and Hirshhorn make an interesting study. Simon is a born Westerner who has never lived east of the Sierra Nevada; Hirshhorn was an immigrant boy from Eastern Europe. Simon is an idiosyncratic industrialist; Hirshhorn is an idiosyncratic speculator. Simon was born in comfortable circumstances; Hirshhorn was born poor. Simon is tall; Hirshhorn is short. Simon is an introvert; Hirshhorn is an extrovert. Simon is dour; Hirshhorn is ebullient. Simon has been married once; Hirshhorn has had four wives.

I'm only a little Hebe who was brought up in the gutters of Brooklyn.

— *Joseph H. Hirshhorn*

Born in Latvia in 1900, the penultimate of a family of thirteen children, Hirshhorn was brought to the United States at the age of five. His widowed mother went to work in a sweatshop that manufactured pocketbooks. As Hirshhorn recalls that era of his life, "Poverty has a bitter taste. We ate garbage."

At the age of fourteen, Hirshhorn went to work on Wall Street. His driving myth was not that of the Horatio Alger books but of B. C. Forbes's *Fifty Men Who Made America*, a love letter to the Robber Barons. Hirshhorn, fifteen years old, dropped into Forbes's office, where he evidently made an impression on the author, for Forbes sold him a copy of the $10 book at half price.

By the time he was seventeen, Hirshhorn had put together a working capital of $255, with which he went into operation as a broker on the curb market. He prospered, and by the end of the year had made $168,000. Something went wrong at the end of World War I and he lost all but $4000. He did not make another mistake ten years later, and like Joe Kennedy and Howard Ahmanson, he sold out just before the crash, realizing some $4 million.

> I'm not an investor. I'm a speculator. I'm not interested in blue chips and their dividends. They are okay for grandma and the kiddies, but I've always wanted the proposition that costs a dime and pays $10,000.
> — *Joseph H. Hirshhorn*

The greater part of Hirshhorn's fortune, which is said to be something in excess of $100 million, was made in uranium.

After World War II, he bought 470 square miles of land in Canada, and moved to Toronto, where the brash five-foot-four-inch American-Jewish speculator was not universally admired by the starchy Canadian business community. His greatest stroke came in 1953, when he managed by heroic organization to stake 1400 claims on 56,000 acres in the Algoma Basin, north of Lake Huron, which contained more uranium than anybody else had ever discovered.*

Hirshhorn's career as a collector began when, as a boy, he decorated his room with Christmas calendar art. Since then he has amassed a collection of 4000 paintings and some 1500 sculptures. Heavy on such American painters as de Kooning, Ben Shahn, Eakins, Winslow Homer, Edward Hopper and Morris Graves, the collection also includes 14 Daumiers, 17 Rodins, 22 Degas, 23 Giacomettis, 53 Henry Moores, and 21 Matisses. Nobody has actually ever seen the Hirshhorn collection, for a good part of it is always in a warehouse.

It is, consequently, something of a pig in a poke that the American people have acquired to be displayed in the Joseph H. Hirshhorn Museum and Sculpture Gallery that will open on the Mall opposite the Smithsonian in Washington sometime in 1969 or 1970.

---

* The first American uranium millionaire, Charles Steen, became rich overnight when in 1952 he located uranium ore on the desolate plateau of eastern Utah. In the fall of 1968 he was declared bankrupt by a Federal referee in spite of listed assets of $12 million. Steen's troubles were back income taxes ($2.3 million) and $6 million of debts that were maturing faster than he could raise ready cash. In 1966, at the height of his career, the forty-six-year-old Steen was living in an eccentric house near Reno which was said to be worth $2 million, and running for the Nevada state senate.

Joseph H. Hirshhorn, who made most of his fortune in Canadian
uranium. MARTHA HOLMES.

Washington was not the only supplicant for the honor of making public the $50-million collection. A new museum in Regent's Park, London, was offered by the Tate Gallery. Israel's cause was promoted by Billy Rose. Los Angeles wanted it for the new Los Angeles County Museum of Art. Nelson Rockefeller wanted it for New York State. Baltimore made its bid. Hirshhorn himself was reported as thinking either of turning his estate at Round Hill in Greenwich, Connecticut, into a museum, or of taking it to a new town he was going to build in Canada and christen Hirshhorn.

Securing the collection for the United States was accomplished by those two accomplished horse traders Lyndon B. Johnson and Mrs. Johnson. The President invited Hirshhorn to lunch in May 1966. Lady Bird and Lynda Bird followed up with a visit to Round Hill. In October Congress voted $15 million to build the new museum on the Mall. As Hirshhorn said with satisfaction, "I am an American. What I did, I accomplished here, in the United States. The collection belongs here."

As we have just noted, nobody has actually seen the Hirshhorn collection nor had the opportunity to go through a catalogue. Its quality is due partly to Hirshhorn's drive to amass works of art and then more and still more, and partly to his curator, Abram Lerner, whose relation to Hirshhorn has been described as a "gentle, protective presence." (Hirshhorn met Lerner in 1946, when a very small man walked into the gallery where Lerner was working and began ordering paintings. Disturbed by this eccentric behavior, Lerner phoned the gallery's owner, who recognized an important customer and vouched for Hirshhorn's bona fides.) A sophisticated appraisal of the collection has come from the painter Vivien Raynor, who after visiting Round Hill wrote in the *New York Times Magazine* that "as an entirely subjective assessment, half the pictures and sculptures I have seen are excellent; the rest are mediocre, including a sprinkling of choices I would call unfortunate."

Hirshhorn is currently living at his 24-room, 24-acre Tudor estate at Round Hill with his fourth wife, a young and pretty woman. (He has other houses at Cap d'Antibes and in California. In the late 1930's he tried life in the Poconos, but as "the only Jew in captivity," he never made much contact with his WASP neighbors.)

Outside the house stands a collection of heroic sculptures, notably Rodin's *Balzac* and *The Burghers of Calais*. Inside, every wall is covered with paintings, but the presence of Hirshhorn himself is inescapable. One visitor came away with an impression of a man who was "brash, bragging, arrogant, lover of art and of mankind." Another, Vivien Raynor, was more astringent: "A chance remark about his luck in mining can cause him to turn from a warm lover of life to a bird of prey. 'Luck! There's no luck in it. Mining takes money, brains, guts, and ingenuity.' "

FOURTEEN

Rich Men's Taxes

$$\$\$\$\$\$\$\$$$

The tax collector is never esteemed as a lovable man. His methods are too blunt and his power too obnoxious.

— *Woodrow Wilson*

Over —	But not over —		of excess over —
$180,000 —	$200,000	$97,180 plus 69% —	$180,000
$200,000	. . . .	$110,980 plus 70% —	$200,000

— *1968 Tax Rate Schedule*

Once a year those of us who form the great body of honest taxpayers pause for a moment in the midst of our lonely travail to thank God that we are not taxed like the rich. If 70 percent were deducted from a taxable income of, say, $12,000, there would be precious little left to keep a roof over one's head and shoes on the children's feet. Alas, poor Simon! Poor Mecom! Poor Ludwig!

Rich Men's Taxes

Our sympathy is of course misdirected and our understanding of the workings of the income tax and its ultimate effects is seriously mistaken. We are *not* taxed like the rich — but if we were we would all stand to gain substantially. Philip M. Stern has calculated that if the loopholes in the income tax were closed (oddly in a democracy, loopholes exist only for the rich and never for the poor), all tax rates could be cut by 45 percent.

In the affairs of the very rich, the tax rate table performs a poetic rather than a literal function. The mythic nature of the rate schedule for the rich was made quite clear when during the Kennedy administration the maximum rate was reduced from 91 percent to 70 percent. There was at that time neither a deafening outcry from the Left nor a chorus of hosannas from the Right, for, politicians being practical men, it was recognized that nobody was actually obliged to pungle up all but 9 percent of his income. Nobody (speaking, perhaps, poetically) even pays the current maximum of 70 percent, although the maximum rate is frequently invoked for rhetorical purposes.

The inventor J. J. Mascuch, for example, once said, "I'm in the ninety percent tax bracket. I have to make three hundred thousand dollars a year just to put the key in the front door of my house and that is very conservative in the way of an estimate." Perhaps so, but one may be forgiven for the thought that Mascuch has stretched things a little in order to make his point. If not, he needs a new tax adviser.

Like the rest of us, very rich men are not given to advertising their tax affairs, yet a certain amount of information is in the public domain. John Mecom, for instance, has let it be known that he keeps about $10 million a year out of an income of about $15 million. If the difference of $5 million were all

Federal income tax, it would represent a rate of 33⅓ percent, or less than half the maximum rate. In 1959, when rates were higher than they are now but his income was lower, James J. Ling kept $100,000 of an income of $150,000, preserving the same ratio as Mecom. Samuel G. Routbord of Apeco grossed a personal income of $325,000, on which he paid $125,000 income tax. This works out to 38.5 percent. In the same year, Ralph E. Schneider, chairman of the board of the Diners Club, had an income of about $600,000, of which only $60,000 was salary, the bulk of the rest being in the form of capital gains. His total tax came to about $175,000, or about 29 percent.

It is, of course, possible for the tax to go much lower. The reform-minded tax lawyer Jerome R. Hellerstein has cited the case of an unnamed oil operator whose total net income over five years was $14 million, but who paid a total of only $80,000 income tax — or a little more than one-half of one percent. It is also possible to pay much more, though it is hard to understand why anybody having competent professional advice should feel obliged to do so. Nevertheless there are such people. One is James W. Walter, who as the Jim Walter Company merchandises shell houses, and who has said, "I don't fool around with income taxes. I just grit my teeth and pay." And he does. In 1960, Walter estimated that he would have a personal income of $226,000, of which $146,000 would be paid the Internal Revenue Service. This comes to about 65 percent, or almost twice what John Mecom is presumed to pay.

> An income tax must always have within it elements of gross inequality and must always be to a certain extent a tax on honesty.
>
> — *Theodore Roosevelt*

Rich Men's Taxes

Mebbe 'tis as bad to take champagne out iv wan man's mouth
as round steak out iv another's.

— Finley Peter Dunne

Two phenomena are sure to catch the attention of every
traveler through the jungle of our income tax policy. The first is
that the highest rates are paid by salaried and professional men
whose income, though respectable, is considerably below the
threshold of great wealth. In 1967 a man reporting taxable income of $50,000 would have paid $17,060, or 34 percent, in
income tax; a man whose taxable income was $75,000 would
have paid $30,470, or about 41 percent; a man whose taxable
income was $100,000 would have paid $45,180, or 45 percent.
Few of the Great Big New Rich pay at such a rate.

The second phenomenon is that the great bulk of tax
revenue comes not from the rich at all but from the middle
classes, including notably those whose taxable income puts
them in the lowest bracket. Whereas thirty years ago, two-
thirds of the income tax revenue was contributed by citizens
reporting incomes of $100,000 or more, ten years ago the greater
part of the tax was squeezed out of those earning $10,000 or
less.

During World War I, when the income tax was young, and
for many years thereafter, government taxing policy could not
unfairly be described as Soaking the Rich. Since World War II,
however, our motto appears to have become Soak the Poor.

Present laws are also notably favorable to the person who has
wealth as opposed to the individual who is only earning it.

— John Kenneth Galbraith

273

> Probably the best functional way of viewing our patchwork
> taxing disorder is as a system of subsidies.
>
> — *David T. Bazelon*

Among the various devices available to protect a prosperous taxpayer from the full horrors of our monster system are the astute use of expense accounts; the establishment of a personal corporation here or a letter-drop corporation abroad; the deferment of immediate income in favor of stock options; the shelter offered by trusts and family partnerships; investment in tax-free bonds; the acquisition and subsequent donation of expensive works of art; a canny policy of charitable contributions; the taking of income in capital gains; the option of not taking income at all; the making of money in oil and other minerals favored by the depletion allowance; and, finally, the strategy of simply not declaring one's income. (It is estimated that in 1957 $28 billion of personal income never appeared on tax returns.)

All of these devices offer little relief to the wage earner and the salaried man. The history of the development of our taxing policy has been the history of opening up escape routes for the rich and powerful while closing the garrote ever more snugly about the necks of the relatively poor and meek. Even such a benevolent-seeming provision as that which allows husbands and wives to split their income has a strong bias built into it. As Stern has pointed out in regard to the joint return, "Married Couple A, with 20 times the income of Married Couple B, can enjoy 319 times as much tax benefits." (It is not, incidentally, generally appreciated that the idea of the split income is not to encourage the married condition but comes from the western states, where under the influence of Spanish law the husband and wife are treated as a community, with half of a man's earnings belonging to his wife. It was not until 1948 that Congress made this a matter of general application.

The motivation behind the peculiarities of the tax code is not always what it appears to be. Income from state and municipal bonds, for instance, is tax-free, a provision which, one might suppose, had been created as a matter of public policy in order to encourage support for the necessary and laudable projects of the local governments. That is not the case. The fact is that in 1913, when the income tax law was devised, the Congress exempted income from local bonds only because of a fear that to tax such income might be an infringement on the holiness of states' rights.

Tax-free bonds, which yield a relatively low return (currently a maximum of 5 percent), are an attractive investment only for the affluent, and are consequently held largely by rich people. The classic case was that of Mrs. Horace Dodge, Sr., who invested her entire legacy of $56 million from the automobile business in tax-exempt bonds, which at 3 percent yielded an income of about $1,680,000 a year. Not only did Mrs. Dodge not pay any tax, she did not even have to file a return.

The tax policy of the Great Big New Rich is to avoid taxable income with the religious horror of devout Moslems avoiding even the smell of pork. The two principal means of holding the purity of their faith are offered by the capital gains tax and the oil depletion allowance, which operates almost entirely for the benefit of prosperous residents of Texas and Oklahoma. The depletion allowance relieves the producers of oil of paying any taxes on the first 27.5 percent of their oil income, the argument being that by taking oil out of the ground they are reducing the value of their property. An operator who at the end of the year has a gross income from producing oil of a million dollars can deduct $275,000 on his tax return, a sum which may exceed the cost of producing the oil. Thanks to this clause, oil producers have been known to pay as little as 5 or 6 percent in income tax.

Although the word *depletion* appeared in the 1913 income-tax law, it was not until 1926 that the Congress enacted the loophole in its present form, complete with the mystical figure of 27.5 percent, which was originally merely a compromise between the 25 percent suggested by the House and the 30 percent suggested by the Senate. As Stern puts it, "The more zealous defenders of the oil depletion allowance sometimes behave as if that 27½ percent was arrived at by heavenly decree, and that to reduce it to, say, 27¼ or (perish the thought) 27 percent, would cause the earth to tremble."

The religious status of the depletion allowance should not be underestimated. Some years ago John Mecom and ten other independents took a full page in the Houston *Post* in order to inform the public of their determination to "stand united against the common and undivided forces which seek to destroy us and the system of competitive free enterprise our industry so clearly typifies." They were, of course, talking about the depletion allowance. (While chairman of the American Petroleum Institute, Jake Hamon put the matter in somewhat more earthy terms: "What you don't realize is that most people in the United States think we are a bunch of overbearing braggarts with a tax gimmick. Unless we change that unfair attitude about us, we're going to lose our depletion allowance and generally go down the drain.")

When in the 1960 campaign John F. Kennedy suggested that it might not be a bad notion to take another look at the depletion allowance, the old Christian patriot H. L. Hunt saw to it that 200,000 reprints of an anti-Catholic sermon delivered by his spiritual adviser, the Rev. Dr. Wallie Amos Criswell, were distributed to the voters. ("If Senator John Kennedy is elected, it will sound the death knell of religious liberty in America.")

The oil depletion allowance has notoriously had a baleful influence on the politics of the oil-rich states. Whereas Senator Robert A. Taft once said, "Percentage depletion is to a large extent a gift . . . a special privilege beyond what anyone else can get," Senator Lyndon B. Johnson opined of the tax plank of his party's platform, "The platform pertains only to loopholes, and I see none in oil." It was thanks to service such as this that for many years "Lyndon and Mr. Sam" were regarded in Texas as the twin defenders of Freedom and God. The ultimate accolade came from H. L. Hunt, who takes unto himself credit for the amendment restricting a President to two terms, but who has also said, "Johnson is the kind of President who can lead Congress around by its nose. I wouldn't mind seeing *him* in there for three terms."

It is not generally recognized that depletion allowances apply to other mineral industries, though at different rates. Some eighty-five other minerals, including the shells of oysters and clams, are judged worthy of depletion allowances. The argument in each case is that an irreplaceable resource is being used up — an argument that might equally be applied to the depletion of talent suffered by athletes, young actresses and even the writers of books. Occasional forays have been made by such special-interest groups, including the Jockeys' Guild of America, which urged a depletion allowance on the grounds that their average riding life was less than four years. Senator Eugene McCarthy suggested with his characteristic turn of wit that a similar allowance might in all justice be extended to U.S. senators.

In spite of the theoretical cogency of such arguments, minerals, and oil in particular, remain singularly blessed.

> There is nothing sinister in so arranging one's affairs as to keep taxes as low as possible. Everybody does so, rich or poor, and all do right, for nobody owes any public duty to pay more than the law demands.
>
> — *Learned Hand*

For the very rich man, the arrangement of his affairs to keep his taxes as low as possible usually involves organizing his income so that it is taxed as capital gains rather than as ordinary income. The maximum rate on a capital gain is 25 percent; the maximum rate on ordinary income is 70 percent. The principle should need no further explication.

Although every taxpayer who enjoys a long-term capital gain benefits from the special rules that apply to this form of income, only those persons in the top bracket of over 50 percent receive any benefit from the alternative tax option. It is a feature of our tax code which is of particular benefit to the wealthy man who makes money buying and selling pieces of property and whose tax consultant belongs to that earnest band of Talmudic scholars whose object of devotion is the definition of a capital gain.

On first acquaintance, the definition of a capital gain appears to be a simple thing. The capital gains tax is levied against profits made on the sale or exchange of property that has been held for six months or more. Straightforward as this may seem, the interpretation of what is and what is not property in the eyes of the law has turned into a major branch of legal sub-literature. A novel sold to the movies does not create a capital gain; an invention sold to a manufacturer does. A harvest of wheat does not create a capital gain; a harvest of Christmas trees does. The profits made from subdividing a piece of land are not capital gains; the profit made from simply holding and selling a piece of land is a capital gain. And so it goes, with the capital gains tax providing the single broadest avenue down which the Great Big New Rich and the Lesser Rich can march in happy brotherhood, safe from the slings and arrows of the tax rate table.

In 1965, *U.S. News & World Report* made a survey of the investment practices of millionaires and produced the following table of their average holdings:

Corporation stocks	65.1 percent
Tax-exempt bonds	8.5
Real estate	6.7
Checking accounts and cash	4.3
U.S. Government Bonds	4.2
Mortgages and notes	1.8
Insurance	1.8
Other	7.4

The point to be observed is that of these holdings, only the 1.8 percent in mortgages and notes produces ordinary taxable income. (Dividends from stocks are treated differently than the dividends from savings-and-loan associations, mutual savings banks, cooperative banks and credit unions, which, in a graceful gesture toward the middle class, are considered as simple earnings.)

The Great Big New Rich who have made large sums of money in the real estate game have an advantage over the rest of us by working within a tax structure that permits a citizen to make a profit at the same time he is declaring a tax loss. The arithmetic that accomplishes this trick, however fascinating, need not concern us in detail. In essence, what the fortunate real-estate operator is allowed to do is to write off the depreciation on his property faster than the profits accumulate. The profits are real — they are money — but the depreciation is a figure that exists on paper only. In theory, a balance between profit and loss will eventually be struck when the property has depreciated to some fraction of its original value and is finally disposed of at a real loss. In an inflationary economy, however, real estate is seldom sold at an actual loss, while the capital gains provision remains close at hand to anesthetize the pain if the outcome should turn out to be a profit.

It is for reasons such as this that we would not be far wrong if we rechristened the subjects of this book the Income Tax Rich.

> Governments, like corporations, are considered without souls, and according to the code of some people's morality, should be swindled and cheated on every occasion.
>
> — *Benjamin F. Linton, 1835*

Rich Men's Taxes

If the government cannot collect its taxes, a man is a fool to pay them.

— *J. P. Morgan*

The Great Big New Rich are of course honest and honorable men whose lawyers and tax accountants would not permit them to be anything else. Like the rest of us, they take whatever advantage they can of the tax code in order to minimize their payments into the common treasury. In this matter the principal difference between them and us is that many more advantages lie ready to their hands than to ours.

It has not always been so innocent. Prosperous and presumably upright citizens have been incarcerated in Federal bastilles for willful evasion, although the enforcement of this feature of the law often seems to be reserved for men who have made themselves public nuisances on other accounts. Yet it was only in 1953 that a former commissioner of internal revenue, an assistant attorney general, and two collectors of internal revenue were sent to jail, and seven other collectors forced to resign. These unfortunate officials were not entirely responsible for their own corruption, any more than is a seduced girl.

The willful evasion of taxes has an ancient and well-provided history in every land, including our own. Before the income tax became a permanent and prominent feature of our life (the Civil War income tax expired in 1870), the particular bane of the very rich was the personal property and real estate taxes that they endeavored to avoid by all means, legal and illegal. That such evasion was of wide scale can be judged from two notes: In 1846, a report on the property tax in New York City revealed that $30 million of assessable property escaped the collector each year, causing the author of the report to lament that "Our rich merchants and heavy capitalists . . . find excuses to remove their families to nearby points and thus escape all taxation whatever, except for the premises they occupy." In 1891 the Boston Executive Business Association estimated that $2 billion of property in their city escaped taxation, cheating the municipal treasury of $17 million a year.

Some of the most prominent of the very rich of the nineteenth century were revealed to be among those most expert in practicing such evasion. William H. (Billy) Vanderbilt, for instance, annually swore that he was worth no more than $500,000. After his death, $200 million was divided among his sorrowful heirs. Stimulated into action by this prima facie case of evasion, the city tax commissioners tried to force the Vanderbilt family to make good on their deficits of past years. Chauncey Depew, acting for the Vanderbilts, blandly informed the commissioners that if they pushed his clients too hard, the Vanderbilts would convert their holdings to nontaxable securities, cutting off this source of future income to the city. The matter was settled by compromise. Similarly, the Astor real estate holdings in New York, which were vast, were assessed at less than half their true value.

John D. Rockefeller, in Lundberg's words, was the "biggest tax dodger ever seen." Marshall Field, who was generally considered a tycoon of unusual personal honesty, paid taxes on personal property declared to be worth $2.5 million, and threatened to move out of Chicago if this appraisal were raised. It turned out after his death that he had actually owned $17.5

million of taxable personal property, or seven times the maximum he declared. The Chicago corporation counsel sued for $1.73 million back taxes. Again there was a compromise, and Field's trustees delivered a check for one million dollars to the city treasurer.

If income taxes were 99 percent, we'd figure a way.

— *W. Clement Stone*

It is a prime article of our conventional wisdom that high taxes stifle initiative. That nothing can be found in our history to verify the authenticity of this jewel of our folklore has nothing to do with the case. We are still exposed at regular intervals to this old war cry, a sort of college cheer of the conservative rooting section that has about as much to do with the realities of business life as *Boola, Boola* has to do with whether Yale beats Harvard.

This is not to say that the Great Big New Rich do not gripe and bellyache about taxes much as the rest of the human race does. The champion complainer is probably John D. MacArthur, who once unburdened himself to Stewart Alsop of some characteristically pungent comments. There was the occasion, he recalled, when after having attended an all-too-well-provided party, he found himself at a horse auction with a handsome woman of some wealth. Under the pleasant impression that he was bidding on behalf of his companion, he raised a finger at a critical moment and found himself the owner of a $25,000 thoroughbred. As MacArthur described the outcome, "So I race him a couple of times, and then he breaks a leg. So I write him off as a loss, and pretty soon the Infernal Internal Revenue Service come nosing around. They ask me, for what purpose did you buy this horse? I tell them, it's none of your goddamn business what I bought the horse for, but if you want to know, I got stiff as a billy goat is why I bought the horse."

Confrontations like this provide their own delicious rewards, particularly when, as MacArthur did, one wins.

When I asked Howard Ahmanson what effect taxes had on the making of money, he laughed and told me the story of the viewers-with-alarm at the Omaha Commercial Club who thought that young Ahmanson would never have the chance to amount to much. The tax structure, I gathered, was simply another given condition, such as competition, with which one coped as skillfully as one could.

In his richly pontifical way, Clement Stone put the matter well. "The tax structure, together with PMA, or positive mental attitude, *helps* the individual. It's better to pay higher taxes on millions of dollars rather than paying taxes on money that was needed earlier. The government says *Make all the money you can under this structure.*" Stone tapped the ash from the end of his cigar and looked unruffled.

To a family man earning $5000 a year, a 50 percent tax *would* be a catastrophe. To the man earning $50,000 the same tax is burdensome but it would hardly oblige him to put off buying shoes for his children. To the man earning (if in this case *earning* is the right word) $5 million a year, a 50 percent tax may be an outrageous communist plot, but it has very little measurable effect on his general style of living. Indeed, if the personal income tax were 99 percent, H. L. Hunt would still be

John D. MacArthur, who made his millions owning and running insurance companies.

netting $2000 a day, which will buy a good many of his bread-and-cheese sandwiches.

In regard to the putatively dampening effect that high tax rates have on initiative, Jerome Hellerstein has cited some suggestive studies. After World War II a Harvard Business School professor interviewed 160 business executives on the effect of high income-tax rates. He reported, "The cases in which the evidence showed executives to be working harder were at least equal in number to those indicating less effort, and the former were more definitely recognizable as a tax influence."

The economist Walter Heller once asked members of the League of Women Voters to estimate the effect of high income taxes on their spouses. None of the ladies reported that their husbands worked any less. Two-thirds said that they worked about the same, and one third that they worked more.

The influence of taxes on initiative is merely one particular aspect of the broader question of why men work at all. Pacific islanders and other inhabitants of beneficent climates and cultures in which competition is not highly regarded have been reported to work only so hard as they need in order to deliver an adequate supply of fish and yams to their dependents. The American business executive, whose motives have attracted the attention of a large corps of scholarly investigators, appears to be driven by a constellation of pressures that have less to do with money than with maintaining status within his group, with loyalty and obligation to his immediate colleagues and perhaps even with a consuming interest in what he is doing. The motivations of the Great Big New Rich, however, are almost as simple as those of the Pacific islanders, although at quite the opposite end of the scale. They are the arch-competitors of our world and the measure of their success is not fish and yams but money.

To suggest that the initiative either of the executive or of the Great Big New Rich is significantly affected by changes in the rates at which they are taxed is to mistake the cries of the rooting section for the real business of the game.

> The purse of the people is the real seat of sensibility. Let it be drawn upon largely, and they will then listen to truths which could not excite them through any other organ.
>
> — *Thomas Jefferson*

> A deduction for one taxpayer means that every other taxpayer has to pony up that much more, since the revenues to run the Government must be met.
>
> — *J. S. Seidman*

It would be extremely foolish to maintain that the rate of the income tax and the method of its application are matters of indifference to either the very rich or the merely affluent. The power to tax *is* the power to destroy, and the oil barons of East Texas are right in instinct when they invoke the most moth-eaten rhetoric of free enterprise in order to protect the fountains of their wealth. That men who have a choice to do otherwise will not suffer an overly irritative or oppressive tax beyond a certain point is a matter of history: the stamp tax of colonial America and the salt tax levied in Gandhi's India suggest themselves as examples of taxing policy so ill-conceived that they came to be regretted even by their authors.

The point I have been endeavoring to make is quite a different matter, and is limited to the observation that there appears to be a vast lack of evidence supporting the commonly received opinion that high tax rates of the sort we know have dampened the initiative of our entrepreneurs. Furthermore, we have no firm reason for believing that a thoroughgoing reform of the income tax, such as is demanded by its present inequities, would stop the flow of capital into new enterprises or dampen our collective entrepreneurial ardor.

The central proposition of any attack on the gothic fortress of our income tax code is the proposition that since money must be raised to underwrite the legitimate expenses of government, whenever one economic class manages to shuck off part of the burden, another class is obliged, however unwillingly, to take this burden onto its own shoulders. As we have seen, this burden is increasingly being borne by the taxpayers of the middle brackets.

The Great Big New Rich and their counterparts among the Lesser Rich are in fact the Income Tax Rich, and it is we professional and salaried and wage-earning people who have in effect created their wealth. Each dollar that Getty or Hunt is permitted to keep by grace of the depletion allowance must be paid into the treasury by a machinist or a high-school teacher or an insurance underwriter. Whenever John Mecom or Leo Corrigan gains a dollar by depreciating a piece of real estate, that dollar must be found somewhere else. Whenever Joseph Hirshhorn or Charles Allen or Howard Hughes takes a capital gain on a sale of stock, they are creating a tax liability that must be made up by taxpayers to whom no escape routes are permitted.

In spite of the ground fog laid down by the conventional

rhetoric in tax matters, our income tax laws have been consistently directed toward giving aid to the very rich on the theory that the wealth represented by these great accumulations of money will somehow trickle down to enrich the rest of us — a theory which is comforting to the faithful but which has no other visible merits.

> . . . that barely believable document, the Internal Revenue Code . . . now constitutes one of the most closely worked abstractions yet created by Western man.
>
> — *David T. Bazelon*

> . . . all the earmarks of a conspiracy in restraint of understanding . . .
>
> — *Louis Eisenstein*

> . . . a crazy quilt of exemptions, loopholes, counterexemptions and plugs for loopholes to take care of taxes paid on nonsalaried income . . .
>
> — *Frank Gibney*

To anybody except the battalions of tax agents and tax lawyers who play out their unending war games on the shifting dunes of our tax code, it should be manifest that the fine sport of plugging loopholes can only lead our tax policy into further demonstrations of insane inequality. The legitimate interests of the great majority of citizens in paying their own share of the common burden can be met only by burning the ramshackle structure in which we are presently all obliged to live, and putting up in its place a new structure built on a somewhat more solid foundation.

Such a radical solution to such a grievous ill has recommended itself neither to our Presidents nor to Congress. The most recent attempt at reform, that of the Kennedy administration, had the net effect of lowering maximum rates, tightening up some loopholes, and opening up some others. A few more patches were added to the crazy quilt, but virtually nothing else was accomplished.

Merely because the present tax code is such a splendidly Laputan exercise in intricacy, we citizens who have no expert knowledge in such mysteries have always tended to plead our own ignorance and turn the matter over to the experts — who, being experts, are quick to prescribe solutions to the monkey puzzle that direct us to eliminate some old twists and bends here and substitute some new twists and bends there. But just as war is too important to be left to the generals, the income tax is too important to be left to the experts.

In *The Great Treasury Raid*, Philip M. Stern, who though a onetime Deputy Assistant Secretary of State is essentially a journalist, has suggested a scheme of such sanity that one looks for evidence of simplemindedness. Stern's proposal is to wipe the board clean and to start over again with a system having three main principles:

First, all income from whatever sources would be subject to the income tax.

Second, family exemptions would still be permitted to create a minimum level below which the tax would not apply, and the costs of getting one's income would be deductible, as they are now.

Third, the tax would then be computed according to a

graduated scale, as it is now, with a maximum rate of 50 percent.

It is difficult to find an argument against a proposal of such awesome simplicity unless one is prepared to back off into the quicksands of special pleading. It is even more difficult to oppose it if Stern is right in his argument that it would annually recover $60 billion that currently slips through the grasping fingers of our common treasury.

Given the *olla podrida* of pressure groups that makes up the Congress, it is surely easier to close all the loopholes at one time instead of trying to seal them off one by one. The consequent broadening of the tax base would permit the tax rates to be lowered, and make unnecessary such ameliorative devices as medical deductions, earned income credits, income averaging, and the capital gains provisions. The important thing is to accept the principle of a tax code with no loopholes at all and then to proceed from there. If we decline to do so, we will continue, literally, to pay a bitter price.*

So far as the effect of such a logical and inescapable system on the Great Big New Rich goes, it would clearly make certain areas of their activities less attractive than they are now. It would surely compel the very rich to contribute considerably more to our common expenses than they do now. It would

---

* Relief may possibly be on its way. In the summer of 1968 the Treasury was working on a plan for reform that would close off the escape routes offered by capital gains, the depletion allowance, investments in state and municipal bonds, and some types of charitable deductions. Although the Treasury's proposal was not as simple as Stern's, the basic idea was the same — to tax all income, without special deductions or preferred treatment, but at lower rates.

stimulate the Reverend Wallie Criswell and others of their camp followers into magnificent flights of oratory in which we would be assured that the pillars had been knocked out from under all good things and that God Himself was in tears. But it is exceedingly hard to believe that it would have the slightest effect in discouraging the enthusiasm with which these money-driven men have applied themselves to the pursuit of money.

As Clement Stone has put it, "If income taxes were 99 percent, we'd figure a way."

FIFTEEN

The Future of the Rich

> Great personal wealth is a vestigial form in American community life. It is probably the least necessary of all other social forms, yet it persists and is supported by great armies and navies.
>
> — *Floyd Hunter*

Unlike more gifted writers, I confess to a serious disability when I try to perform as a prophet. I am not absolutely sure in which direction the United States is heading. At times, when contemplating our homicidal and self-destructive conduct during the past several years, I can see ahead only a grand catastrophe that will destroy us all. The trained bear is turning up the throttle of his motorcycle and it is only a matter of time before he spins out on a curve or smashes himself against an unyielding wall. In more euphoric moods it seems possible to me that we will

293

evolve into a well-ordered and peaceful beehive; being strongly prejudiced in favor of survival, this prospect does not terrify me as much as it does citizens who yearn to sacrifice themselves for free enterprise and the profit motive. In any case, my purpose in this final chapter is neither to advertise the destruction of the Great Big New Rich along with the rest of us in a thermonuclear holocaust nor to predict a glorious sunrise as the human race becomes more rational, gentle, and humane, but instead to consider the Great Big New Rich as a phenomenon of the United States today and to make some well-qualified guesses as to their future. To put it briefly, I am inclined to think that the Great Big New Rich are not men of our own time, but survivals of an earlier epoch, and furthermore that they are not the men of the future.

Before taking a last look at the Great Big New Rich and their prospects, it will be a useful exercise to remind ourselves of the ways in which they resemble or differ from their predecessors.

Like the Robber Barons, a significant number of the Great Big New Rich were born to parents in modest circumstances.

Like the Robber Barons, most of the Great Big New Rich were born to families of old American stock.

Like the Robber Barons, during the childhood of several of the Great Big New Rich, at least one parent died or left the household.

Like the Robber Barons, the future Great Big New Rich were seized early by a passion for making money and by a corresponding impatience with conventional education.

Like the Robber Barons, the Great Big New Rich began

their careers by plunging directly into a personal enterprise rather than by setting their feet on the bottom rungs of corporate ladders.

Like the Robber Barons, the Great Big New Rich managed to avoid military service.

Like the Robber Barons, many of the Great Big New Rich have made fortunes in times of general disaster.

But unlike the Robber Barons, the Great Big New Rich are virtually unknown, live privately, and most important, have virtually no political power.

> There are never wanting some persons of violent and under-
> taking natures, who, so they may have power and business,
> will take it at any cost.
>
> — *Francis Bacon*

There was never any question that the Robber Barons had to run the country out of simple self-defense. They were not only men who lusted after the titles of power as they lusted after great houses and splendid yachts, but they were also acutely conscious that the good health of their railroad networks, oil empires, and mining ventures depended on the willingness of friendly men in Washington to protect them from the twin horrors of bureaucratic meddling and the growing power of their restive workers.

Among the very rich men who assumed the mantle of states-man were Senator Leland Stanford (who represented the rail-road interests of California), Senator Harry B. Payne (oil, Ohio), Senator William A. Clark (copper, Montana), Senator George Hearst (mining, California), Senator Chauncey Depew (railroads, New York), and Senator Stephen B. Elkins (mining, West Virginia). Even greater than the direct political influence of the Robber Barons was the indirect influence they exerted through "loans" to congressmen, outright bribery, expense-paid junkets and the darker means of persuasion. The Robber Barons were cheats and scoundrels but they were not invisible. Rather, their giant shadows lay over the land. They were tycoons, moguls, nabobs, magnates, and even emperors.

The bribery and corruption of public officials has, of course, passed into the history of the bad old days, and the Senate is no longer a millionaires' club. (The only Great Big New Rich in public office are J. Erik Jonsson, the mayor of Dallas; and David Packard, the deputy secretary of defense, who owns $300 million of stock in his firm, the Hewlett-Packard Company.

This is not to say that the Great Big New Rich are totally without political ideas, although neither the incidence of such ideas nor their quality is particularly remarkable. Their political thinking is on the whole conventional, with the only clear case of class-interest being the oilmen's devotion to any legislator who has demonstrated his loyalty to the sacredness of the depletion allowance.

The most eminent political philosopher among the Great Big New Rich is H. L. Hunt, who for many years has been conspicuous in a not entirely lonely battle to save these United States from atheistic communism. Among the others who have publicly announced their stands on social and political affairs is W. Clement Stone, the profundity of whose ideas we have already had occasion to admire. Another who has not been unwilling to stand up and be counted is Getty, the quality of whose thought can be judged from this sample: "Four million American soldiers should have taken charge after World War I. Then Woodrow Wilson was talked into things. We should have established a just and rational peace. If we had been refused, we should have fought for it. We could then have beaten the whole world. That was the way to talk — in realities. And when we get a President with courage, that is how we shall talk."

It seems not unlikely that there is some Great Big New Rich money behind the five hundred or more right-wing organizations that enjoy a special IRS dispensation as educational, charitable, or religious. Writing in 1964, Arnold Forster and Benjamin Epstein estimated that $14 million a year was going to radical right organizations, their benefactors including 70 foundations, 113 corporations, 25 public utilities, and 250 individuals. But if there is Great Big New Rich money here, it is quiet money, with Hunt remaining the only member of the group who has made a second career of saving the American people from themselves.

> If an old slouch like Hunt really wants to educate the people, he's got lots of money to do it, without putting $27.5 million which is tax-exempt aside for the Life Line Foundation.
>
> — *Wright Patman*

Hunt has been described as looking like "the kindly judge in an early Shirley Temple movie" and as a "shy homebody of a farmer-turned-oilman-turned-financier, devoted to goat milk, clip-on bow ties, Deaf Smith County wheat bread, and some of the farthest right-wing causes of his time." It has been rumored that he started his career in a gambling house in El Dorado, Arkansas. Hunt, however, has denied that he won leases to an East Texas oil field at poker or craps, and has said that he bought them fair and square. His own capsule account of his career is that "I ran a fifty-dollar bankroll, beginning in 1921, up to — well, what I'm supposed to have today." As we have seen, he is supposed to have today about a billion dollars. His oil reserves have been reported as including a billion barrels under Montana; like Getty and Mecom he has extensive leases in the Middle East, as well as a vast field in Libya. Others of his enterprises include ranch and timber lands, canneries, citrus groves, pecan farms, and the laboratory that manufactures a nostrum called Gastro-Majic.

Although Hunt describes himself in *Who's Who in America* as a Democrat, when he has surfaced in national political affairs it has been in such instances as the 1952 Republican convention, where he claims to have come within two hours of making Douglas MacArthur the nominee. (In the 1968 Presidential election, Hunt came out for George Wallace, and was rumored to have given a great sum of money to Wallace. At a rally in California, I heard one of Wallace's campaign assistants deny any financial support. All Hunt had given them, he said, was four cartons of his books.)

Hunt's main impact on our political consciousness, however, has been through the medium of two radio programs, Facts Forum, now defunct (because, Hunt has said, it tried to present both sides), and Life Line, which at last report, reached about five million people a day over 541 radio stations. The general tenor of Life Line can be judged from Hunt's observation that "the battle for Freedom is a battle between Communism and the Profit Motive System."

As Robert Sherrill has reported, in the fall of 1963, Life Line was telling its five million listeners of the tyranny of the Kennedy administration, its affinity for communism, and its suppression of true Americanism. As the tragedy in Dallas approached, Life Line was urging "extreme patriotism." Although Lee Oswald's act sprang out of a different variety of madness, there is a massive irony in Hunt's apparatus of mischief and poison enjoying until 1965 a tax exemption as a "nonpartisan, nonprofit organization for adult education."* Contributors to Life Line have included Hunt, the Hunt Oil Company, Sears, Roebuck & Co., Standard Oil of Indiana, and the great American taxpayer.

Hunt's stature as a philospher is also based on his novel *Alpaca* (H. L. Hunt Publishing Company). *Alpaca*, which has recently been translated into Vietnamese for the guidance of that distressed nation, carries a simple political message: A man's votes should be based on the amount of taxes he pays. Citizens on welfare or drawing sick pay get no votes at all.

(It is surely not surprising that very rich men chafe at being allowed to cast only the single vote that is also permitted a sharecropper or a professor of literature. The late Ernest Henderson, who despite the handicap of being a Harvard graduate

---

* Life Line has managed to keep going as a sponsored program, even though it lost its tax exemption in 1965. The loss of the tax exemption was brought about by Senator Maureen Neuberger of Oregon, who was convinced that the fanaticism of Hunt's program was partly responsible for John F. Kennedy's assassination.

of genteel family ran a single decrepit hotel into the half-billion-dollar Sheraton chain, was also an author and was also much concerned with the vote. It was Henderson's notion that corporations should be given one vote for every five or ten jobs they maintain, and that integrity in both public and private affairs should be enforced through a massive system of lie detectors and truth drugs.)

> In the world of minor lunacy the behavior of both the utterly rational and the totally insane seems equally odd.
> — *John Kenneth Galbraith*

It is probably only in Texas and California that rich men still hold substantial political power. In California it is not the Great Big New Rich but rich men of the second rank who have emerged as kingmakers — if, indeed, that is the proper word to describe men who are responsible for the current eminence of Ronald Reagan, George Murphy, and Max Rafferty.

The kingmakers of Southern California include such conservative Republicans as A. C. Rubel, a retired oilman; Henry Salvatori, another oilman; Walter Knott, who runs Knott's Berry Farm; and Patrick James Frawley, Jr., who controls the Eversharp-Schick and Technicolor enterprises. (A late member of this camorra of the Right was D. B. Lewis, who manufactured dog food and left a million dollars to the John Birch Society.) The interests of these men have ranged from Richard Nixon and Barry Goldwater on the left to Dr. Fred Schwarz's Christian Anti-Communist Crusade on the right, with their practical influence being demonstrated in such elections as those which sent Ronald Reagan to Sacramento and which saw the ineffable Max Rafferty defeat the widely respected Senator Thomas Kuchel for the Republican senatorial nomination.

The most interesting of these men is Frawley, a furtive and eccentric ex-alcoholic who has been identified as an intimate of Ronald Reagan's. "From a distance he often looks like some sort of messianic crackpot, a gray eminence of the far right," a writer for *Fortune* once reported. "Close up, he seems naïve and almost maudlin about politics."

Born a British subject in Managua, Nicaragua, in 1923, Frawley was sent to a Catholic school near San Francisco at the age of five. Some years later he dropped out of the military academy he was attending and went back to Nicaragua to his father's import-export business. During World War II he served in Canada in the RCAF. After his discharge he married a Canadian girl in Vancouver. When the young Frawleys started back to Managua, they discovered that Mrs. Frawley was pregnant and decided to cut short their voyage at San Francisco, where Frawley went into the import-export business for himself. His second year in business Frawley made $200,000. He was twenty-four.

Frawley emerged on the national business scene when he turned a moribund ballpoint pen company, which he had acquired in settlement of a bad debt, into Paper-Mate. In the 1950's he acquired Technicolor, Eversharp, and Schick. In business circles he is thought to be gearing himself up for a billion-dollar empire via the merger route, and if this book were to be rewritten ten years from now it is not unlikely that Frawley would be one of its principal subjects.

A sort of junior Howard Hughes, evasive and eccentric, Frawley keeps odd hours, has been known to work until he drops from fatigue, and is apparently innocent of the fact that other people are not organized as he is. In spite of his evident success as a tycoon, in person he appears highly disorganized. As one observer noted, "A 'conference' with Frawley typically involves the conferee in a strained effort to find the sequiturs in the boss's abrupt transitions."

An alcoholic for twenty years, Frawley's principal enthusiasm outside of right-wing politics is establishing alcoholism clinics whose mode of therapy is conservative rather than left-wing. (The "left wing" approach to alcoholism is that it is a disorder of the personality, while the "conservative" view is that it is a physiological disorder. "The fact is that the Irish shouldn't drink as much as anyone else, but no one told me that," Frawley has said of himself.)

Besides alcoholism, Frawley has shown an interest in the Moral Rearmament movement, and was a prominent financial supporter of an anti-pornography proposition that reached the 1966 California ballot but failed at the polling places. His support of Reagan and Rafferty helped substantially with the bills of their campaigns. When California liberals speak darkly of the faceless men who are responsible for the current ascendancy of the Republican Right in their state, it is often Frawley whom they have in mind.

With the center of political activity among the very rich falling into the hands of cranks like Hunt and Frawley, it is clear that there has been a great change, and a change for the better, since the days when the Robber Barons could deliver messages to Capitol Hill or even to the White House with the certain knowledge that their instruction would be obeyed. The relative political innocuousness of the Great Big New Rich, however, is less a proof of their benignness than it is a function of their relative isolation from the forces that are really at work in this country.

> We have seen that the function of entrepreneurs is to reform or revolutionize the pattern of production by exploiting an invention or, more generally, an untried technological possibility. . . .
>
> — *Joseph A. Schumpeter*

Whatever else was said about the Robber Barons by men who had cause to fear and hate them, they could not be called useless or irrelevant. Steam and steel, the railroads, electrical power, the automobile — all of these provided opportunities for men unburdened by excessive personal honesty and moral scruples but possessed of ability and ambition to amass immense fortunes at the same time that they revolutionized the quality of American life. As we have seen, these revolutions were carried out at great expense both of public funds and of individual suffering. In a more utopian world they might have been carried out quite differently, but as John Dewey once remarked, while the saints engage in introspection, burly sinners run the world. However things should have been done, this is the way they were done.

By contrast, the Great Big New Rich, even though they are richer than their predecessors, seem curiously powerless. The great enterprises of our time are carried out either by the monster "private" bureaucracies such as General Motors or Boeing or a coalition of governmental and private resources. The money that sends men into space or under the sea is public money and the ultimate control of these ventures rests in the hands of the public officials. No great entrepreneur is associated with the computer revolution. Instead the computer is almost synonymous with IBM, a mandarin bureaucracy of awesome magnitude. Although one of our Great Big New Rich, Hirshhorn, found a fortune in uranium, the development of nuclear energy has from the beginning been carried out by the familiar technostructure. Thornton and Ling have become rich through innovations in company organization and management, but again, the enterprises they have put together are essentially servants of the government.

In spite of the earnest rhetoric that men like Thornton and Simon have delivered themselves of on behalf of the entrepreneurial spirit, their calls for renewed dedication are little more than funeral elegies, for the plain fact is that the entrepreneur as a dominant economic force disappeared before World War I.

> It may not be saying too much to assert also that the new thinking about collective enterprise, or managerialism, is about to be recognized as constituting a great theological crisis. . . .
> — David T. Bazelon

And so in the end it seems clear that the Great Big New Rich are not innovators and pioneers, as the Robber Barons were, but are survivals of a world that is no longer with us. Their meaning for us is less in the economic realm than in the ethical. They are the symptoms of our own confusion about where we have come from and where we are going. It is hard for us not to admire them because in all of us there lurks a lingering attachment to the Horatian gospel. They are the visible representations of the national folklore of the poor boy who rises to great wealth in the land of opportunity where the greatest prizes fall into the hands of the young man who has dedicated himself to hard work, thrift, and piety.

The Great Big New Rich are not evil men but they are irrelevant men, as much out of the mainstream of history as an American loyalist in 1776, a rich Southern landowner in 1861, or a Russian social democrat in 1917. While the world moves on to new forms of social and economic organization, they are in theological terms the Old Believers.

The great issues of our immediate time are clearly spread out before us. They include the choice between risking the destruction of our species or coming to an accommodation with the communist half of the world. They include the necessity of coping both at home and abroad with the suffering that comes from hunger and the bitterness that comes from racial differences. They include the resolution of the outright conflict that exists between those of us of the middle generation and the generation that includes the best of our young people and that has raised the flag of rebellion. They include the control of the impulses toward violence that are our national shame. They include our collective sense of purposelessness.

As C. P. Snow argued in his lecture at Westminster College in November 1968, we are living in a time of mounting desperation in which we face the real possibility that the human species can be preserved only if the rich peoples of the world become convinced of the virtues of a deliberate policy of altruism, practiced both nationally and personally. The Great Big New Rich are important to us in this context because they represent the living embodiment of the traditional American dream of success — or, to put it differently, of our collective commitment to the virtues of selfishness. Selfishness, however, may well be synonymous with suicide.

Even in their best aspects, the Great Big New Rich offer little in the way of useful human models in our present distress, for their collective message is that if the Negro, the Asiatic peasant, and the university rebel will only pull up his socks, believe in God, and turn himself to honest work, he too can be successful. It is rather like prescribing aspirin in the midst of a great seismic disturbance.

The Great Big New Rich have raised some magnificent sand castles on the beach on which we all live, but they are sand castles that stand against an incoming tide.

Bibliography

When, after a lunch during which Harry Sions of Little, Brown had suggested that nobody really knew very much about the men who hold the largest accumulations of new money in America today, I began to look into the subject, I found only one source which considered the Great Big New Rich as a class. This was an excellent as well as diverting article by Stewart Alsop in the *Saturday Evening Post* ("America's New Big Rich," July 17, 1965). I remain in debt to Mr. Alsop's pioneering work.

The other magazine literature on the new rich consists of many biographical accounts in such journals as *Time, Newsweek, Fortune,* and *Business Week.* I have attempted to give credit to the authors of signed articles at the appropriate places in the text and will not repeat a listing of magazine articles here. The principal newspapers consulted were the New York *Times,* the *Wall Street Journal,* and the San Francisco *Chronicle.*

The following books were of particular value:

Allen, Frederick Lewis. *The Big Change.* New York: Harper, 1952.
Arnold, Thurman W. *The Folklore of Capitalism.* New Haven: Yale, 1937.
Bainbridge, John. *The Super-Americans.* Garden City, N.Y.: Doubleday, 1961.

Baltzell, E. Digby. *The Protestant Establishment*. New York: Random House, 1964.

Barlow, Robin, Harvey E. Brazer, and James N. Morgan. *Economic Behavior of the Affluent*. Washington, D.C.: Brookings Institution, 1966.

Bazelon, David T. *The Paper Economy*. New York: Vintage, 1965.

Beard, Charles A. and Mary R. *The Rise of American Civilization*. New York: Macmillan, 1934.

Beebe, Lucius. *The Big Spenders*. Garden City, N.Y.: Doubleday, 1966.

Birmingham, Stephen. *"Our Crowd": The Great Jewish Families of New York*. New York: Harper & Row, 1967.

Chamberlain, John. *The Enterprising Americans*. New York: Harper & Row, 1962.

Cooperman, David, and E. V. Walter. *Power and Civilization*. New York: Crowell, 1962.

Davis, Jerome. *Capitalism and Its Culture*. New York: Farrar & Rinehart, 1935.

Dunne, Finley Peter. *Mr. Dooley on Ivrything and Ivrybody*. New York: Dover, 1963.

Forster, Arnold, and Benjamin Epstein. *Danger on the Right*. New York: Random House, 1964.

Fortune, Editors of. *The Art of Success*. Philadelphia: Lippincott, 1956.

Frazier, E. Franklin. *The Black Bourgeoisie*. New York: The Free Press, 1957.

Galbraith, John Kenneth. *The Affluent Society*. Boston: Houghton Mifflin, 1958.

―――. *The New Industrial State*. Boston: Houghton Mifflin, 1967.

Gerber, Albert B. *Bashful Billionaire: The Story of Howard Hughes*. New York: Lyle Stuart, 1967.

Gibney, Frank. *The Operators*. New York: Harper, 1960.

Grund, Francis J. *Aristocracy in America*. New York: Harper Torchbooks, 1959.

Heilbroner, Robert L. *The Quest for Wealth*. New York: Simon & Schuster, 1956.

Hellerstein, Jerome R. *Taxes, Loopholes and Morals*. New York: McGraw-Hill, 1963.

Henderson, Ernest. *The World of Mr. Sheraton*. New York: McKay, 1960.

Bibliography

Hewins, Ralph. *The Richest American: J. Paul Getty.* New York: Dutton, 1960.

Holbrook, Stewart. *The Age of the Moguls.* Garden City, N.Y.: Doubleday, 1954.

Hunt, Haroldson Lafayette. *Alpaca.* Dallas: Hunt Publishing Co., 1960.

Hunter, Floyd. *The Big Rich and the Little Rich.* Garden City, N.Y.: Doubleday, 1965.

Josephson, Matthew. *The Robber Barons.* New York: Harvest Books, 1962.

Kazin, Alfred. *On Native Grounds.* New York: Reynal & Hitchcock, 1942.

Keats, John. *Howard Hughes.* New York: Random House, 1966.

Kolko, Gabriel. *Wealth and Power in America.* New York: Praeger, 1962.

Lampman, Robert J. *The Share of Top Wealth-Holders in National Wealth 1922–1956.* Princeton, N.J.: Princeton University Press, 1962.

Lauterbach, Albert. *Man, Motives, and Money.* Ithaca, N.Y.: Cornell University Press, 1954.

Lundberg, Ferdinand. *America's 60 Families.* New York: Vanguard, 1937.

————. *The Rich and the Super-Rich.* New York: Lyle Stuart, 1968.

Mills, C. Wright. *Power, Politics, and People.* New York: Ballantine, 1963.

Mumford, Lewis. *The Myth of the Machine.* New York: Harcourt, Brace & World, 1967.

Myers, Gustavus. *History of the Great American Fortunes.* New York: Modern Library, 1937.

Rees, Goronwy. *The Multimillionaires.* New York: Macmillan, 1961.

Seldes, Gilbert. *The Years of the Locust.* Boston: Little, Brown, 1933.

Shaw, George Bernard. *The Intelligent Woman's Guide to Socialism, Capitalism, Sovietism, and Fascism.* London: Constable, 1928.

Sopkin, Charles. *Money Talks!* New York: Random House, 1964.

Sorokin, Pitirim A. *Man and Society in Calamity.* New York: Dutton, 1942.

Stern, Philip M. *The Great Treasury Raid.* New York: Random House, 1964.

Stone, W. Clement. *The Success System That Never Fails.* Englewood Cliffs, N.J.: Prentice-Hall, 1962.

Stone, W. Clement, and Napoleon Hill. *Success Through a Positive Mental Attitude.* Englewood Cliffs, N.J.: Prentice-Hall, 1960.

Tawney, R. H. *Religion and the Rise of Capitalism.* London: J. Murray, 1936.

————. *The Acquisitive Society.* New York: Harcourt, Brace, 1922.

Tebbel, John. *The Inheritors.* New York: Putnam, 1962.

Tocqueville, Alexis de. *Democracy in America.* New York: Vintage Books, 1954.

Turner, Frederick Jackson. *The Frontier in American History.* New York: Henry Holt, 1920.

U.S. Bureau of the Census. *Trends in the Income of Families and Persons in the United States, 1947 to 1960.* Washington, D.C.: Government Printing Office, 1963.

Veblen, Thorstein. *The Theory of the Leisure Class.* New York: Modern Library, 1934.

Wall Street Journal, Editors of. *The New Millionaires and How They Made Their Fortunes.* New York: Bernard Geis, 1961.

Warner, W. Lloyd, and James Abegglen. *Big Business Leaders in America.* New York: Harper, 1955.

Whalen, Richard J. *The Founding Father; The Story of Joseph P. Kennedy.* New York: New American Library, 1965.

White, William H., Jr. *The Organization Man.* New York: Simon & Schuster, 1956.

Wilson, Edmund. *The Cold War and the Income Tax.* New York: Farrar, Straus, 1963.

Index